MIGRATION AND REFUGEES
Politics and Policies in the United States and Germany
General Editor: Myron Weiner

Volume 1
Migration Past, Migration Future
Germany and the United States
Edited by Klaus J. Bade and Myron Weiner

Volume 2
Migrants, Refugees, and Foreign Policy
U.S. and German Policies Toward Countries of Origin
Edited by Rainer Münz and Myron Weiner

Volume 3
Immigration Admissions
*The Search for Workable Policies in Germany and the
    United States*
Edited by Kay Hailbronner, David A. Martin and Hiroshi Motomura

Volume 4
Immigration Controls
*The Search for Workable Policies in Germany and the
    United States*
Edited by Kay Hailbronner, David A. Martin and Hiroshi Motomura

Volume 5
Paths to Inclusion
The Integration of Migrants in the United States and Germany
Edited by Peter Schuck and Rainer Münz

Immigration Admissions

The Search for Workable Policies in Germany and the United States

Edited by Kay Hailbronner, David A. Martin, and Hiroshi Motomura

Published in association with the American Academy of Arts and Sciences

Berghahn Books
Providence • Oxford

First published in 1997 by

Berghahn Books

© 1997 American Academy of Arts and Sciences

Library of Congress Cataloging-in-Publication Data

```
Immigration admissions : the search for workable policies in Germany
and the United States / edited by Kay Hailbronner, David Martin, and
Hiroshi Motomura.
      p.   cm. -- (Migration and refugees ; v. 3)
   Includes bibliographical references (p. ).
   ISBN 1-57181-126-5 (alk. paper)
   1. United States--Emigration and immigration--Government policy.
2. Germany--Emigration and immigration--Government policy.
I. Hailbronner, Kay. II. Martin, David A., 1948-   .
III. Motomura, Hiroshi, 1935-   . IV. Series.
JV6483.M54  1997 vol. 3
325.43 s--dc21
[325'.01]                                                    97-27789
                                                                CIP
```

British Library Cataloguing in Publication Data

A catalogue record for this book is available from the British Library.

Printed in the United States on acid-free paper.

Contents

Introduction

Kay Hailbronner and *Hiroshi Motomura*

In recent years, immigration has emerged as one of the most heavily debated social and political issues in the industrialized West. Much of the concern stems from the seemingly endless stream of migrants, many of them spurred to leave their native countries by economic misery, political instability, and civil war. These migrant flows have put the major receiving countries of the West under growing pressure to revise existing immigration law and policy, as well as to formulate new law and policy where none has existed. As a result, immigration law and policy throughout the industrialized West have undergone substantial changes of late. The United States and Germany are two countries that have felt these immigration-related pressures with particular force. For this reason, their experiences—including their responses in the form of immigration law and policy—are particularly instructive, not just for each other but for other receiving countries as well.

The problems that the United States and Germany face have much in common, in spite of differences in their traditional attitudes to immigration and their approaches to administrative law and government regulation generally. In Germany, the traditional notion governing immigration law and policy has been that Germany is not an immigration country and therefore that non-Germans (unless they are citizens of a member country of the European Union) may not enter Germany to take up permanent residence. In fact, however, these traditional principles have not kept Germany from becoming a country of immigration. Its noncitizen population increased by 2.3 million from 1988 to 1993, a historically unprecedented flow of immigrants. In sheer numbers, this increase is comparable only to that in the United States, which has a population almost four times as large. The presence of this immigrant population in Germany is the result of several external factors. Migrant workers originally recruited for temporary employment ended up staying on as immigrants. Reunification of these workers with their family members, who came to join them in Germany, added to the noncitizen population. A growing number of asylum seekers also swelled the numbers, as did a substantial influx of "ethnic Germans" from Eastern Europe and the former Soviet Union. Taken together, these factors have made for a sizable de facto immigrant influx into Germany.

In contrast, the United States historically has viewed itself as a nation of immigrants. But it has also faced substantial problems of immigration control, which in turn have attracted a variety of government responses. Illegal border crossings— mainly across the border from Mexico—and the public reaction to the perceived impact of undocumented aliens have prompted the adoption of border control measures much more stringent than in the past. Concerns about the number of undocumented aliens—not just illegal border crossers but also those who overstay valid nonimmigrant visas—have led the federal government and some states to restrict undocumented aliens' access to public benefits, including public education. Uneasiness about the growing number of asylum seekers has led to the adoption of measures to deter and detect frivolous applications and to adjudicate all applications more expeditiously. Legal immigration to the United States has also become the target of immigration control efforts. The traditional system of immigration quotas based on family ties and employment-related qualifications has come under criticism, especially by those who believe that it pays insufficient attention to the economic interests of the United States.

In short, admission policies, political asylum, and control measures have become the focus of serious public discussion in both Germany and the United States. In both countries, the view is widespread that the current immigration laws do not perform their basic tasks of regulating immigration and providing a clear framework to determine who shall be admitted as immigrants, who shall be admitted temporarily, and who shall not be admitted at all.

In an effort to study and analyze these problems in the United States and Germany from a comparative standpoint, the American Academy of Arts and Sciences convened the German-American Project on Migration and Refugee Policies with the financial support of the German-American Academic Council Foundation. The two-year project brought together thirty leading immigration law and policy experts from both countries, among them lawyers, political scientists, demographers, historians, political philosophers, sociologists, economists, and government officials. A joint German-American steering committee initially structured the agendas and determined the membership of the working groups. One working group examined policies toward countries of origin. A second working group, some of whose papers appear in this volume, addressed admission policies, political asylum, and the crisis of immigration controls. A third working group looked at the character of migration flows and the absorption and integration of migrants in the two countries.

Each working group sought to synthesize the best available academic studies and practical experience on the relevant issues, to examine critically the traditional—but partly outdated—paradigms and norms in the field, and to suggest new policy approaches. Toward this end, each group began by developing draft research papers, which were initially presented at meetings of the separate working groups in March 1995 at the House of the American Academy in Cambridge, Massachusetts. Berghahn Books, in association with the American Academy of Arts and Sciences, is publishing the findings of the working groups in five volumes in a series entitled Migration and Refugees: Politics and Policies in the United States and Germany, of which this is the third.

This volume includes the seven of the revised papers of the working group on admission policies, political asylum, and the crisis of controls. Its unifying theme derives largely from the general agreement that traditional approaches to immigration control admissions in the major receiving countries of the West have serious shortcomings either in concept or in implementation, or at times in both. Volume 4 includes this working group's four other papers, which generally concern the topic of immigration controls. The volume begins with Joseph Carens's paper, "The Philosopher and the Policymaker: Two Perspectives on the Ethics of Immigration with Special Attention to the Problem of Restricting Asylum." Carens addresses key philosophical and moral constraints on the making and implementation of immigration law and policy. In particular, he focuses on the ways in which liberal democratic principles and institutions create obstacles for the project of immigration control. Building on the premise that every normative political theory or moral analysis must satisfy two requirements—criticality and feasibility—Carens poses and suggests answers to a number of difficult but important questions, among them: What forms of control are morally permissible from a liberal democratic perspective? Among the strategies of control that seem problematic, should we distinguish between the more and the less morally objectionable?

The next two papers address immigrant admissions policies. Jörg Monar's paper, "Comprehensive Migration Policy: The Main Elements and Options," analyzes the constituent elements of a comprehensive migration policy, which he defines as a single policy framework that addresses all migration-related issues, including those covered traditionally by immigration policy, refugee policy, and asylum policy. Based on a survey of immigration legislation in the major receiving countries, Monar writes that a comprehensive migration policy must address prevention, admission, control, and integration. He next identifies the main political choices—ranging from active encouragement of immigration at one end of the spectrum to exclusion at the other end—in the formulation of a comprehensive migration policy. Monar then turns to a discussion of the institutions to be involved in the formulation of that policy and concludes with an analysis of the available implementation mechanisms.

Hiroshi Motomura's paper, "The Family and Immigration: A Roadmap for the Ruritanian Lawmaker," turns to one major aspect of admission policy, family reunification, which accounts for much of the legal migration to Germany and the United States. Looking comparatively at German and U.S. practices, Motomura identifies and analyzes the policy questions that legislators must answer in deciding how to consider family ties in the making of immigration policy. These questions include: (1) which family relationships count; (2) whether the number of family-based immigrants should be limited; (3) what delays in family-based immigration are unacceptable; (4) whether citizens should be preferred over resident aliens in sponsoring relatives; (5) whether to accommodate different perspectives as to what constitutes the family; (6) what procedures should decide eligibility; (7) whether family ties should affect exclusion or expulsion; (8) what share of immigration should be family-based; (9) how family-based immigration affects the ethnic composition of the receiving society; and (10) how family-based immigration affects the integration of immigrants into the receiving society.

The next paper is by Olaf Reermann, who is ministry director in charge of matters pertaining to asylum and immigration with the Ministry of the Interior in the German Government. Reermann's paper, "Readmission Agreements," starts with the premise that national immigration and asylum policies no longer suffice to deal effectively with migration patterns. He then discusses efforts to harmonize and coordinate the admission and removal policies of various member countries of the European Union, with the goal of finding a common answer to the problem of illegal immigration. Reermann devotes the bulk of this discussion to agreements under which countries obligate themselves to readmit to their territory their own nationals and perhaps stateless persons and third-country nationals as well.

Rosemarie Rogers's paper, "Migration Return Policies and Countries of Origin," addresses the strategies available to host countries to encourage, facilitate, or force the return of migrants whose entry was earlier welcomed or tolerated with the expectation that their stays would be temporary. The strategies that Rogers examines include return incentive programs, return assistance, and development projects, although, as she points out, the lines between the various types of strategies are not always clear. Rogers studies the roles played by host countries, home countries, third countries, and international organizations, and she focuses primarily on five groups of migrants. The first is "temporary" or "guest" workers; here the focus is primarily on Western Europe. Rogers then turns to persons granted temporary asylum, first discussing this group in developing countries and then discussing their counterparts in industrialized countries. She next analyzes return policies for rejected asylum seekers, first in developing countries and then in industrialized countries.

The two final papers in this volume focus on asylum and humanitarian admissions, which raise very similar issues of legal control in Germany and the United States. The refugee definition of the 1951 Geneva Convention on Refugees has been under discussion ever since large migration movements started to occupy policymakers in Western countries. Joan Fitzpatrick's paper, "Is the 1951 Convention Relating to the Status of Refugees Obsolete?" examines the Refugee Convention in light of changes since World War II in refugee flows and the broader geopolitical context. According to Fitzpatrick, the current challenge is to identify and cure those flaws in the Refugee Convention framework that impede effective protection for today's vast number and variety of forced migrants. To this end, she examines the Refugee Convention from several perspectives: (1) the continued vitality of the nonrefoulement obligation; (2) the vagueness and manipulability of the definition of *refugee;* (3) the lack of an agreed framework for refugee determinations and the risks involved in harmonization; (4) crucial substantive uncertainties in refugee and asylum law; and (5) key gaps in interstate obligations.

Continuing the focus on the concept and definition of *refugee,* the next contribution, Rainer Hofmann's "Refugee Definition," analyzes the problems associated with an extended definition of *refugee.* Hofmann presents the various refugee definitions in contemporary international treaty law, including the 1951 Geneva Convention and various regionally based definitions in Africa and Latin America. He also discusses the absence of regional refugee law in Asia, Europe, and Oceania. Hofmann then analyzes the major problems connected with the interpretation of these definitions, particularly the apparent vagueness of the Geneva Convention's definition of *refugee.* He goes on to address new developments, among them the concepts of safe countries of origin and safe countries of asylum, as well as emerging substantive issues. Hofmann concludes with an analysis of temporary protection.

The concluding chapter of this volume presents the recommendations of the working group with regard to admission policies, political asylum, and immigration controls. To develop these recommendations, the cochairs of the working group drew on the draft papers by the members of the working group and from the working group discussions in March 1995 in Cambridge, Massachusetts. The working group then discussed the resulting draft policy document in July 1995 at a meeting in Ladenburg, Germany. The draft document was further revised in accordance with the suggestions of the working group members. However, none of the working group members was asked to sign the finished document, and it should be understood that not every member agrees with all of the recommendations.

In sum, the purpose of this volume is to review traditional approaches to several key facets of immigration law and policy—the ethics of immigration, immigration admissions, and asylum and humanitarian admissions—to describe and analyze possibilities for new approaches and solutions, and to provoke discussion of future policy initiatives in these areas. While we do not expect one single approach to emerge as a panacea, we do hope that some of the ideas laid down here will find their way to policymakers and others interested in the search for workable approaches to one of the most significant issues of our time.

We are grateful to the German-American Academic Council Foundation for its financial support for the project and to its director, Dr. Joseph Rembser; the Gottlieb Daimler- and Karl Benz-Foundation for its support for a meeting of the participants in Ladenburg, Germany; our editor Sarah St. Onge; Lois Malone, who prepared the index; and Corrine Schelling of the American Academy of Arts and Sciences, who has had principal responsibility for the management of the project since its inception.

Part I

THE ETHICS OF IMMIGRATION

Chapter 1

The Philosopher and the Policymaker

Two Perspectives on the Ethics of Immigration
with Special Attention to the Problem of
Restricting Asylum

*Joseph H. Carens**

How should liberal democrats think about the issues of immigration from a normative perspective? Every normative political theory or moral analysis has to satisfy two requirements: criticality and feasibility. On the one hand, moral language loses all its meaning if it does not provide some perspective from which to criticize prevailing practice. On the other hand, moral inquiry loses its point if it cannot guide practice. As the old dictum has it, "ought implies can."

But different people interpret and combine these two constraints in very different ways. Let me present an ideal typical description of two moral perspectives that might be brought to bear on questions about immigration or other policy issues. The first is that of the moral philosophers. They are primarily concerned with principles and ideals. They accept the feasibility requirement in some sense but do not find it very constraining (Kant 1970). If we adopt this approach in the current context, we will ask what we are obliged to do and what we are obliged

Notes for this chapter begin on page 45.

not to do with respect to immigration, given a fundamental commitment to liberal democratic principles.

The other moral perspective is that of the policymakers. They accept the criticality requirement but regard it as sharply constrained by the requirement of feasibility. They have turned their minds to moral inquiry because they want guidance about how to act responsibly in the world. They accept the existing configuration of power, interests, and institutions as largely given, because it is beyond their control. They want to consider the moral merits and demerits of policies that they regard as politically and administratively feasible. If we adopt this perspective, we will restrict our moral evaluation to immigration policies that have a reasonable chance of being adopted. Furthermore, we will regard the likely consequences of alternative policies as much more relevant to their moral status than the principles and ideals that motivate them.

I do not want to overstate the differences between these two perspectives. First, the degree of tension between them will depend on both the content of one's ideal theory and the range of the policies one regards as feasible. Purely at the level of principle, there are many different philosophical views about the nature and extent of our obligations to others, the legitimate scope of individual and collective self-interest, and so on. Some moral theories are much more at odds with current practice than others. At the level of policy, too, there are different views, with some regarding the range of feasible policies as much more limited than others. Second, most moral theorists concerned with public policies do regard consequences as central to, if not always dispositive of, the evaluation of policies. Similarly, policymakers have to consider the ways in which policies that seem problematic from a principled perspective might undermine the underlying norms of a liberal democratic regime (Zolberg 1993). Finally, it is essential to recall that both perspectives are ideals, identifying extremes on a continuum. Most actual positions fall somewhere between the two.

I have identified these perspectives not to advocate one over the other but because I think each draws our attention to considerations that must be taken into account in a fully satisfactory normative analysis. The question of how we ought to act in a given situation, all things considered, is ultimately inescapable.

Hence the policymaker's perspective, with its emphasis on feasibility, is of vital moral importance. Yet one of the crucial functions of moral discourse is legitimation. If we find ourselves forced to choose between the lesser of two evils, it is essential not to delude ourselves into thinking that the lesser evil is really a good or at least an entitlement. That requires the emphasis on criticality of the philosopher's perspective.

In this paper I will illustrate the usefulness of keeping both of these perspectives in mind by discussing a single issue in depth: the problem of restricting asylum in liberal democratic states. While I focus only on the asylum problem here, I think that the approach I follow will generally be helpful in thinking about other issues in the ethics of immigration.

The Asylum Problem

In recent years Germany and the United States, like other Western states, have seen dramatic increases in the number of people arriving at their borders claiming to be refugees and asking for asylum. Claimants for asylum are not subject to the usual state mechanisms of immigration control. If they meet the criteria for refugee status, they are legally entitled not to be returned to their countries of origin. The administrative and legal processes for determining whether claims are justified are long and costly, especially legal appeals after initial decisions. In the meantime, claimants must either be supported at public expense or given an opportunity to find jobs. Even those who are found not to qualify for asylum are rarely deported.

Many people, officials and ordinary citizens alike, see these developments as threatening the capacity of Western states to control their borders.[1] They conclude that it is essential for Western states to find ways to regulate the asylum process more effectively, specifically to reduce the numbers of people making unwarranted claims to refugee status, to determine the merits of claims more quickly, and to deport expeditiously those found not to qualify.

In this paper I want to explore the ways in which liberal democratic principles and institutions create obstacles for this project of control. The inquiry has both normative and empirical dimensions. My primary competence is in normative political theory, and so I will focus on questions such as the following: What may and should liberal democratic states like Germany and the United States do to control asylum seekers? What forms of control are morally permissible from a liberal democratic perspective? Among the strategies of control that seem problematic, should we distinguish between the more and the less morally objectionable? I should perhaps add that in exploring these normative questions, I will not try to provide an analysis of the legal obligations imposed on states by international law or by treaties or other agreements to which they are signatories but rather an examination of the moral obligations entailed by liberal democratic principles in the circumstances in which Western states find themselves today. These moral obligations may be wider or narrower than legal obligations (Walzer 1977).[2]

The question of how liberal democratic principles ought to constrain restrictions on asylum seekers is not the same as the question of what factors in liberal democratic states actually create obstacles to the project of control. Some of the obstacles to particular strategies of control may have nothing to do with normative considerations. For example, technological limitations or personnel costs may create obstacles to control. Indeed, one can ask whether liberal democratic principles actually play any effective role in this area. Some people have argued, for example, that the whole modern refugee regime was intimately tied to the strategic geopolitical interests of Western states and that the current "crisis" simply reflects a change in those interests (Hassner 1994; Hathaway 1990).

I suspect that this skeptical view is overstated but has some merit. In any event, it is an important empirical challenge to try to identify what role liberal democratic commitments actually do play in constraining efforts to restrict entry by asylum seekers and how they play such a role. I think that liberal democratic values act as effective constraints on some strategies of control and are relatively ineffective with respect to others and that the relative effectiveness or ineffectiveness is only partially correlated to what we would judge to be the relative moral legitimacy of the strategy in question. I will not be able to provide any definitive evidence about these issues, but, as the paper proceeds, I will present some hypotheses about the conditions under which normative considerations are more and less influential in shaping policy.

Conceptualizing the Problem

Why do we have so many asylum seekers? One answer is that it is just too attractive to claim asylum in a country like the United States or Germany. This view holds that many and perhaps most of the asylum claimants have no legitimate moral basis for their demands for entry. They face no real dangers at home, merely the economic disadvantage that comes from living in a poor society. They are not genuine refugees but merely economic migrants seeking to better their material circumstances.

Unquestionably, some asylum applicants fall into this category. One well-publicized example was the arrival in Toronto a few years ago of dozens of Portuguese citizens claiming to be Jehovah's Witnesses fleeing persecution in their native land. (Many of the applicants carried rosaries, crucifixes, and other indicators of their actual faith with them.) They were rightly rejected quickly by the refugee determination process.

However one judges such individuals—in the example above, the applicants appear in part to have been dupes of operators offering to gain them access to Canada for a price—no one supposes that they are genuine refugees, regardless of how liberal a definition one adopts, or that they have any moral claim to use the asylum process. Even people (like me) who have advocated open borders as an ideal recognize that such a principle cannot be immediately implemented and that in the meantime refugees have moral priority over people who are merely seeking better lives (Carens 1987, 1992a). From this perspective, the asylum process is one vehicle for recognizing that priority, and claiming refugee status without warrant is an unjustifiable attempt to jump ahead in the line. A fortiori, those who accept the conventional moral view of the state's general right to admit or exclude nonrefugee migrants at its own discretion would see this as an abuse of the asylum process (Walzer 1983). Denying asylum to people who are merely economic migrants and deporting them thus poses no moral problem in principle. The only difficulty comes in identifying them, specifically in distinguishing them from people with some genuine moral claim, and in carrying out the determination and deportation processes expeditiously.

A second answer to the question of why we have so many asylum applicants is that there are simply too many people in desperate need in the world and more and more of them (though still only a tiny fraction of the total) are seeking entry to Western states as a solution to their problems.[3] People in desperate need who show up at our door have at least some sort of prima facie moral claim to entry (if only temporary) and assistance. Walzer (who, as is well known, is generally a defender of the state's moral right to exclude) calls this the principle of mutual aid: we have an obligation to help others when it is urgently needed and the cost to us is low (Walzer 1983, 33). Now, of course, when the number of supplicants is large, the costs are no longer low, so the principle of mutual aid does not constrain us in the same way. That is why the moral claim to entry is only prima facie.

Perhaps we are morally entitled to exclude some or even most of these new arrivals despite their desperate need. Perhaps not. Leaving that aside for the moment, we can see how recognition of their prima facie moral claim makes a difference as to how we characterize the problem we face. Suppose we say to ourselves, "If there were only a few of you in such desperate straits who were asking for admission, we would be morally obliged to let you in. It would not merely be ungenerous, it would be wrong and unjust to turn you away." Then we cannot (or should not) any longer characterize the problem as one of distinguishing between legitimate and illegitimate claimants, between genuine and false refugees; that characterization is possible only with purely economic migrants, who have no moral claim to asylum, regardless of how many or how few of them there are.

Let me put the point another way. Our obligation to admit others in desperate need changes as their numbers increase. How much it changes depends on one's underlying theory of how extensive our obligations are, but virtually everyone acknowledges, say, a public order limit to the obligation to admit.[4] But while a change in numbers may affect our obligations to respond positively to a given applicant, it does not alter the moral legitimacy of the applicant's request. If she would have been morally entitled to admission when numbers were low, the fact that she may not be so entitled now that numbers are high does not make her claim an abuse of the asylum process.

Both answers to the question of why we have so many asylum applicants have some merit, but they lead to somewhat different strategies of control and raise different problems for the evaluation of these strategies from a normative perspective. Take four aspects of the asylum process, each of which offers possible strategies of control: definition, determination, deportation, and deterrence. Using a narrow definition of refugee does not help to reduce the number of economic migrants claiming asylum (except insofar as it may be easier to pretend to meet a broader definition), but it is an important strategy of control with respect to people in real need. If we think of the determination process as needing only to separate genuine refugees from economic migrants, we will face one set of problems; if we think of it as a way of establishing priorities among applicants with genuine moral claims, we will face another. Deportation of economic migrants does not seem troubling; deportation of people in desperate need does. Deterring economic migrants from making asylum claims is clearly a legitimate goal; deterring those with some plausible claim to refugee status is much more deeply problematic. In sum, how we think about controlling the influx of asylum seekers ought to depend heavily on whether we conceptualize the problem as primarily one of preventing abuse by economic migrants or one of restricting the number of successful claimants among people with potentially strong claims.

In the rest of this paper I will focus on these four closely related aspects of the asylum process: definition, determination, deportation, and deterrence. Under each of these headings I will identify alternative approaches and evaluate them in light of the quest for control and liberal democratic commitments.

Definition

To be eligible for asylum, one must be a refugee. But who should be considered a refugee for purposes of asylum? Under the current regime, the most widely recognized formal definition of refugee is determined by the 1951 Convention and the 1967 Protocol as these are interpreted by the domestic legislation of the signatories to these agreements and their court systems.[5] Many people have criticized the convention definition as unduly narrow, conceptually incoherent, and morally illegitimate (Shacknove 1985; Zolberg, Suhrke, and Aguayo 1989; Hathaway 1991; Singer and Singer 1988). What should we make of such criticisms? How should the definition of refugee be related to the issue of control? Is it justifiable to have two or more categories of refugees, and, if so, on what grounds?

From one philosophical perspective, the first task should be to develop a definition of refugee that is conceptually coherent and morally defensible; questions about numbers and control can be dealt with separately (Shacknove 1985). One reason for this perspective's importance should be obvious from what I have already said about the two different answers to the question of why there are so many asylum claimants. It is the issue of legitimation. To say that someone is a refugee is to say that she has a legitimate moral claim regardless of whether we will be able or willing or even obliged to meet that claim.

On the other hand, the term *refugee* also implies a legal status in the context of the asylum process. Someone who meets the requirements is to be granted asylum. Yet because those of us in the receiving states have morally legitimate interests of our own that may outweigh the legitimate claims of those seeking asylum, especially when their numbers and the corresponding costs to us are high, it is important even from a principled and philosophical perspective to pay attention to moral priorities among those with legitimate claims. For that reason, it is appropriate even at the level of moral principle to recognize that a definition of a refugee as someone entitled to asylum entails a threshold that could legitimately be significantly higher and more variable than one established by a definition of a refugee as someone with a legitimate moral claim.

From a moral perspective, the focus on definitions is itself misleading. It encourages us to think about continuous social and moral realities in terms of dichotomies, categories, and thresholds. We establish a definition and judge that people do or do not meet it. They are or are not refugees. Yet however we frame the definition, there will inevitably be some people who barely meet it and others who barely fail it. To think of the former as genuine refugees and the latter as false refugees is not true to the moral realities. The problem persists even if we establish more than one category of refugee.

At one end of the continuum of refugee claimants are the pure economic migrants; at the other end are people personally targeted for torture and death by an oppressive government. In between are most of the claimants, facing various kinds of threats with varying degrees of severity and risk. It is an illusion to suppose that there are any sharp moral lines separating one claimant from the next closest along the continuum.

I am not arguing that we should resist definitions. The allocation of refugee status, like the allocation of any legal status or entitlement, requires definitions, categories, and thresholds. In the language of economists, refugee status is a lumpy good. We might be able to establish two or three distinct refugee statuses, but it is not something (like money) that can be handed out in fine gradations. (Nor would it be morally appropriate to do so, for reasons that I will clarify below, when I discuss the merits of having multiple categories.) The point here is that it is important to be conscious of the discrepancies between legal categories and moral continua. Such recognition is difficult to achieve in practice, especially in public discussions of refugee issues, in part because there are strong political incentives to emphasize legal categories. Yet it is essential to a correct understanding of the issues at the level of principle.

Since we need definitions, we should try to have good ones. To be satisfactory from a philosophical perspective, the definition of refugee must not draw distinctions among claimants that are arbitrary or otherwise morally indefensible. That is precisely what critics of the convention definition say it does.

Recently, David Martin has mounted an interesting and subtle defense of the convention definition, arguing that, properly interpreted, it is not too narrow for purposes of the asylum system because the number of successful applicants must be strictly limited to maintain political support for the system and, given this need, it establishes morally appropriate priorities among asylum applicants (Martin 1991). Martin's argument is simultaneously principled and pragmatic, combining arguments from both of the perspectives—philosophical and policy-making—that I identified above. It provides an excellent vehicle for considering some of the objections to the convention definition.

I will begin with Martin's defense of the priorities established by the convention definition and turn later to the question of numbers and control. Everyone agrees that to warrant refugee status a person must be facing a serious threat to her fundamental interests. Critics argue, however, that the convention places undue weight on a narrowly defined set of political threats to the victim's personal well-being and only those targeted at the victim. These restrictions, they say, make no sense morally. We should focus instead on the severity of the threat and the degree of risk, as well as on the kind of assistance that is relevant to the problem (Shacknove 1985; Zolberg, Suhrke, and Aguayo 1989).

Martin's concern to limit numbers does not preclude him from making principled arguments against certain ways of narrowly construing the meaning of *refugee*. He criticizes a number of decisions made by U.S. courts and agencies that denied asylum to applicants who had personally been targeted with real and severe threats to their physical security. The decisions held that the threats were not clearly causally linked to the five categories listed in the convention definition as reasons for persecution: race, religion, nationality, membership in a particular social group, or political opinion. In Martin's view, this is a technical reading of the law that makes no sense in the context of the fundamental objectives of the asylum system and, moreover, has no foundation in the intent of those who drafted the legislation, so far as that can be determined (see also Aleinikoff 1991, which Martin cites). Martin sees these cases as motivated by the concern to limit the number of successful asylum applicants that he shares but says that in them legal doctrine has gone "radically astray," that some of the cases go to "dishonourable lengths," and that one is "shocking."

On the other hand, in the context of the asylum system, Martin defends the convention's restriction of refugee status to politically generated threats. Because asylum is a scarce resource, he says, the crucial question is not the severity of the need but whether relocation to a foreign country is the only way to meet it. Like others (Walzer 1983; Zolberg, Suhrke, and Aguayo 1989), he observes that basic needs for food and shelter generated by famine or natural and environmental disasters can, in principle, be met in situ. He argues therefore that it is appropriate to reserve asylum for those who cannot be helped at home.

Martin acknowledges that civilians caught in a civil war need relocation and yet are not covered by the convention definition because they are not targeted for persecution. Indeed, he regards this as the least well justified element in the convention definition. Suggesting that this provision may reflect the rough judgment that the needs of such victims may often be met by temporary relocation rather than permanent asylum (unlike the needs of targeted victims of persecution), he nevertheless admits that this may often not be true. In a note, he seems to lean toward an expansive interpretation of the convention definition that would, in effect, count civilian populations in war zones as targeted victims when the risk was sufficiently great.

Having defended the convention's emphasis on political threats to human rights, Martin goes on to argue that the other morally relevant factors are the severity of the threat and the degree of risk and that the terms *persecution*, for the former, and *well-founded fear*, for the latter, provide good threshold criteria.

In contrast to Martin, Aristide Zolberg, Astri Suhrke, and Sergio Aguayo have argued that the convention establishes the wrong priorities because it offers protection to people suffering certain forms of political abuse that may be severe enough to qualify as persecution (such as restrictions on religious freedom) but are much less morally significant than threats to life from civil wars or other forms of violence. Like Martin, they recognize refugee status as a scarce resource (or "a privileged form of migration") and hence the need to limit the numbers who receive it. They argue, however, that in allocating this scarce resource, the morally appropriate criteria for setting priorities are "the immediacy and degree of life-threatening violence" (Zolberg, Suhrke, and Aguayo 1989, 270). The emphasis on violence rather than other forms of threats to life reflects their view that the status of refugee should be reserved for those who cannot be helped in situ. Unlike Martin, however, they would include famine and starvation as forms of life-threatening violence. Like others, they reject the assumption (implicit in both the convention definition and Martin's analysis) that there is a sharp distinction between political and other threats to well-being, since the threats to life posed by famine or the aftermath of natural disasters are usually intimately connected to the political system.

Zolberg, Suhrke, and Aguayo reject the principle that being targeted, whether individually (activists) or collectively (targets), establishes a stronger moral claim to refugee status than merely being a victim.[6] For that reason they criticize as inadequate the contemporary practice of providing only a second, lesser form of refugee status to mere victims of violence. Ideally, in their view, we would revise the convention definition to give moral priority to those in the greatest danger from life-threatening violence.

I think that Zolberg et al. are right to argue that threats to life carry more moral weight than most threats to freedom and that being targeted is not intrinsically a crucial moral variable. For these reasons, the convention definition is deficient at the level of principle. I will consider below the implication of this view for questions about numbers and control and ultimately for the question of whether the definition should be revised. (My answer is probably not.) First, however, I want to take up two other issues at the level of principle: the reservation of refugee status to those whose needs cannot be met in situ and the legitimacy of two or more categories of refugees.

Both Martin and Zolberg et al. would restrict asylum to those who cannot be helped in any other way. Zolberg et al. use the term *violence* to distinguish threats to life that require asylum from threats to life that do not. At a purely conceptual level, the restriction seems to make perfectly good sense because it matches the remedy to the problem. But the argument depends on a degree of abstraction from reality that may not be appropriate even at the level of principle.

Why should the hypothetical possibility of available assistance carry any moral weight, if the assistance is not actually available?[7] After all, every refugee claimant could in principle be helped at home if either the state officials (or other human agents) responsible for the threats altered their behavior or the international community intervened. These may not be realistic options, but alternative solutions to nonviolent threats to life may not be realistic either. The crucial question at the level of principle is not whether adequate assistance could be made available in principle but whether it is actually available. It is one thing to deny refugee status to someone who has been protected, if only minimally, from a threat to life, another to deny status to someone who enjoys no such protection, whose life is at risk when we say no.

Now someone may object that the formula "threat to life" is too expansive. For example, it might seem to justify refugee status for someone with a life-threatening medical condition that could be addressed by the medical resources of an affluent society but not by those of a poor one. That is a reasonable concern, and it points to the fact that an adequate theory of asylum necessarily presupposes some background understanding of entitlements and responsibilities, both individual and collective, including some consideration of the limits to entitlements and responsibilities both within a political community and outside it. Perhaps one could distinguish between the broad category of threats to life and the narrower category of threats to life from a failure to protect and provide for basic human rights and argue that it is only the latter that are morally relevant to our responsibilities toward people seeking asylum (Shue 1980). Basic human rights would presumably not include expensive medical care, but they might include protection from forms of state failure that could not reasonably be encompassed by the term *violence.* The relevant question then would be not whether the basic human rights essential to the survival of the person seeking asylum could be met at home but whether they were actually being met and would continue to be met if she went back. If not, the person has (in principle) a strong moral claim to be regarded as a refugee and granted asylum.

The second issue of principle concerns the possibility of establishing two or more categories of refugees. So far, I have focused only on the convention definition and alternatives, as though only one legitimate definition of refugee were possible, at least for purposes of asylum. In practice, many Western states provide some form of refugee status (humanitarian, de facto, B-class) and asylum to at least some people who do not meet the convention definition but are recognized to be fleeing from some genuine threat, thus implicitly or explicitly establishing a second, legally relevant definition of refugee. Thus we find both a narrow definition, carefully applied to claimants on an individual basis and carrying with it an entitlement to permanent asylum and a broad panoply of other rights, and a broader definition, sometimes applied on a less rigorous and less individualistic basis and sometimes carrying with it only revocable permission to remain and/or a less extensive bundle of rights.[8] Many of those whom Zolberg et al. classify as victims of violence are granted asylum under this second definition. Is this morally defensible, either in the way it is carried out now or in some alternative version?

The two-tier arrangement has obvious attractions as a strategy of control because it gives the receiving state more flexibility. From the perspective of the goal of limiting the number of asylum entrants to some reasonable number, the convention-based system has severe drawbacks. Because the right to asylum is an individual legal entitlement for anyone who meets the requirements of the system, it is impossible to establish an upper limit on admissions in principle. Moreover, because the determination process is almost always institutionalized in a highly formalized, highly legalized manner and carried out by agents who are normally deeply immersed in a liberal legal culture with its norms of individualized adjudication and due process, it is much more difficult for policymakers to control the process so as to produce no more than the desired number of successful applicants.

I do not mean to overstate the insularity of the convention refugee-determination process from politics but rather to draw attention to its relative insularity compared with the administration of many policies and especially with the policy flexibility provided by the second kind of definition of refugees. In some states, like the United States, the convention determination process has a history of being very porous indeed, and in every state political and policy considerations have a significant overall effect on it. But the highly politicized nature of the U.S. system has been widely noted and widely criticized (Anker 1991; Zucker and Zucker 1992), and even in the United States the process requires a degree of public rationalization in relation to explicit norms that creates obstacles to discretion not present in other areas.

In contrast to the convention system, classification of people as refugees under the second definition tends to be more directly under the control of policymakers and less subject to legal review. Most importantly, this definition is presented from the outset in the context of a discretionary policy rather than a system of legal entitlements. The state assumes no formal obligation to admit people who meet the definition or to permit them to stay once admitted. Thus, if the number of successful asylum claimants under either category appeared to be growing too large, the state theoretically would be able to contract admissions under this heading. Whether such a contraction would be justifiable would depend again on one's overall theory of asylum entitlements and state responsibilities, as well as on the details of the situation. Here I want only to address the question of whether establishing such a system is morally legitimate, both in principle and in practice, and whether it actually provides such a useful strategy of control that states should resist expansion of the convention definition and instead use this vehicle to meet morally persuasive asylum claims beyond those recognized under the convention.

In principle, it seems to me, it could be justifiable to have two or more legally relevant definitions. Recall that the moral claims of asylum seekers are best conceived as positioned along a continuum. From a moral perspective, the proper function of a definition of refugee is to draw a line across the continuum, to separate those with stronger moral claims to asylum from those with weaker moral claims. Of course, there is no reason why we cannot draw two (or more) such lines. In short, multiple definitions are permissible so long as the definitions correspond to the moral priorities. And although different people will have different views of the extent of our moral obligations toward asylum seekers, most would agree both that we are not morally obliged to admit everyone on the continuum and that we are morally obliged to admit those with the strongest claims. It would seem appropriate then to construct one definition—the narrower— linked to an entitlement to asylum for those with the strongest claims as a way of institutionalizing our fixed and strongest moral obligations, and a second, wider definition, linked to a more discretionary system, for those with good but weaker claims whom we will accommodate according to the number of those entering under the first definition, the extent of our generosity, and so on. The definitions should perform this way regardless of how extensive or limited our obligations are and regardless of how many refugees we ought to admit.

The current practices of liberal democratic states fit this model in a formal sense, but they are deeply flawed because of the way in which they construct the different definitions. As I have just argued, the convention definition does not establish the proper moral priorities because it includes some people who need the safety provided by asylum less urgently than do some of those it excludes. Some of those admitted under the second definition as humanitarian refugees (and perhaps some of those turned away altogether) face greater threats to their most fundamental human rights and hence have stronger moral claims to asylum than do those admitted as convention refugees.

Would the construction of two different definitions warrant differential treatment of refugees once admitted? Specifically, would it be morally permissible to make entry granted under the discretionary system more conditional or the bundle of other rights provided less substantial?

Take the issue of conditional entry first. Why might we want to have the option of deporting someone whom we have acknowledged to be a legitimate refugee? (Recall that the broader definition is still intended only to include those who are legitimate refugees, not economic migrants.) Two answers occur to me: a change in the circumstances in the receiving country that makes the presence of the refugees more burdensome and a change in the circumstances of the country of origin that makes return there less dangerous.

Even if its economy worsened significantly or something else happened to make the refugees' presence more burdensome, the receiving country would need a much stronger justification for deporting a legitimate refugee than for refusing admittance in the first place. It is a familiar (though admittedly disputed) point in moral theory that depriving someone of a good she already enjoys is more harmful than failing to provide the good in the first place. More concretely, it would seem especially cruel to create hope by granting admission only to snatch it away later.

While a change in circumstances in the country of origin can, in principle, justify repatriating people who were once but are no longer in danger, this principle applies equally to refugees admitted under both definitions. There is no reason to suppose that the likelihood of such a transformation corresponds to the strength of the initial claim to refugee status. At the least, any such correlation is far from perfect. So, if we are actually prepared to send refugees back once circumstances have changed, why not apply that principle to all refugees regardless of the category under which they were initially admitted? Indeed the Geneva Convention already formally permits the termination of refugee status and repatriation when circumstances in the country of origin change sufficiently, although it is a provision that is rarely used in practice.

Why do liberal democratic states so rarely send people back once circumstances have changed? Part of the answer surely lies in the fact that over time the refugee's claim to stay becomes less tied to the initial reasons for granting entry. The longer people stay in a country (assuming that they have not been kept in isolated safe havens but have been integrated to a significant degree into the general population), the more they acquire the social ties that make them members of the society with a moral right to remain for that reason (Carens 1989). Empirically, it is certainly true that the longer refugees stay, especially in Western countries, the less likely it is that they will return to their countries of origin (Stein 1990).

To turn now to the second issue, it is far from clear why it would be appropriate to grant different rights to people admitted under different definitions. The question of what rights refugees deserve or need to live decent lives in the receiving country would appear to be independent of the relative strength of their eligibility for refugee status. Suppose someone argues that we can afford to take in more refugees if we grant them fewer rights (Weiner 1995). That may or may not be true empirically; after all, many of the rights and programs provided for refugees are simply wise economic investments that pay off in reduced social costs and higher social benefits down the road. But even if we assume that there is a trade-off between the numbers of refugees we admit and the benefits we provide, it is not clear why that trade-off is affected by the strength of the original claim to entry.

One implication of this line of argument may be to call into question Martin's assumption that it is a great humanitarian achievement that the nonrefoulement provisions of the convention have actually created a full-fledged asylum system with secure status and a full panoply of rights for those who meet the convention definition. Martin argues that such a generous status must necessarily be a scarce resource. But if it must be so scarce because it is so generous, one has to ask whether a less generous entitlement would also be less scarce. At least in principle, his argument seems to suggest that a system more closely tied to the simple principle of nonrefoulement would be able to provide safety and hence protect the most basic rights of more people. If that were indeed the trade-off, it seems to me that a more limited form of asylum would be preferable.

Let me turn now from questions about the principles that should inform the definition of refugee to the question of whether we ought to try to expand or otherwise change the convention definition. In the final analysis, I do not think we should try to change the definition, at least not in any radical way. That may seem a puzzling position, given my criticisms of it at the level of principle. But when we turn to the question of what definition we ought to adopt in practice, we ought to follow a highly consequentialist approach. What is the point of adopting a definition that is better in principle but leaves refugees worse off? Nevertheless, I will insist that the answer to the question "What is to be done?" is not the only bottom line in our normative reflections on practice. It is also important to ask, "What are we doing?" Here I will argue that what we are doing in keeping the convention definition is deeply flawed from the perspective of moral principle even though it is the best we can do under the circumstances.

David Martin argues against expanding the convention definition on the grounds that we need a narrow definition of refugee in order to limit the number who qualify, which in turn is a prerequisite for maintaining political support for the asylum process in Western states. This is a common argument. Indeed the need to adopt a narrow definition as one element in an overall strategy of control is often advanced even by those who criticize the convention definition and want to change it (Zolberg, Suhrke, and Aguayo 1989). Such critics often insist that their proposed reforms are realistic in that they will not increase the overall number of those seeking asylum and so will not undermine the political support essential to the asylum system. I think that arguments such as these, which focus on the need for political support for the asylum system, are drawing attention to an important practical consideration. But such arguments are often presented without sufficient attention to the problem of legitimation.

Let me grant for the sake of this argument that it is empirically correct that if we do not limit the number of refugees granted asylum we run a serious risk of creating a political backlash that will ultimately reduce our openness to refugees.[9] What should we do? We should certainly not adopt a broader definition of refugee if that will have the consequence that fewer refugees actually are admitted. But it is essential that all of us—scholars, policymakers, citizens—inquire into the moral character of the political constraint that we face. Is the limit on the numbers of refugees that the public is willing to accept (and the potential backlash if we exceed it) the product of a morally defensible concern for our own legitimate interests or a morally reprehensible failure to take seriously our moral obligations and responsibilities?

In considering this question, we cannot retreat to a democratic positivism that says whatever the democratic majority decides must be just. That sort of view either confuses the moral legitimacy of the allocation of power with the moral legitimacy of the exercise of power or else confuses moral legitimacy with legality. It is easy to find policies supported by democratic majorities in the recent past that no one today would pretend were just even at the time, despite their popularity.

The fundamental question in this context is whether we would be morally justified in denying asylum to all those people who do not fit the convention definition. (The fact that we may admit some people under a broader definition is irrelevant here because the whole premise of using a narrow definition as a control mechanism is that we are thereby marking out the boundaries of our strict obligations and that the admission of other refugees is an act of discretionary generosity.) If the answer to the question is yes, it shows that we regard the underlying political constraint as no more than a morally permissible concern for our own interests. If the answer is no, it shows that we regard the constraint as a collective moral failure.

My own answer to the question is no, though I will not try to justify that position in this paper. My concern here is to insist on the importance of asking and answering the question in a way that is not circular. We cannot say that we are entitled to exclude people who do not fit the convention definition because they are not "genuine refugees" if we have engineered that definition in the first place so as to limit the number who fit it.

What is Martin's answer to the question? I am not quite sure, and that is what concerns me. On the one hand, he might be read as providing a positive answer to the question, namely that the convention definition strikes an appropriate balance between two competing and legitimate moral concerns: our obligations to refugees and our right to control our borders. Yet his analysis says little about the nature and extent of our right to control our borders, emphasizing instead the political reality that we will do so. The normative defense of the convention definition mainly attempts to show that it establishes the right priorities among potential claimants for a scarce resource. The fundamental question remains: is that degree of scarcity, which is so clearly a product of our political choices, something we are morally entitled to impose?

Determination

Assuming that we have established a definition of a refugee (whether the convention definition or some alternative), we have to determine how that definition applies to particular cases. In other words, we have to establish procedures for evaluating the claims of asylum applicants in order to distinguish those who meet the criteria of the definition from those who do not.

John Rawls has drawn a useful distinction between perfect and imperfect procedures (Rawls 1971). A perfect procedure is one whose outcome is correct or just simply because it is the outcome of the procedure (assuming that the procedure itself has been properly constructed); there is no independent standard of what the outcome ought to be. A lottery is a good example. An imperfect procedure is one in which there is an independent standard of the appropriate outcome. A criminal trial is a good example. The desired outcome is to convict the guilty and acquit the innocent, but any given trial may or may not actually succeed in producing that outcome.

Like a trial, a refugee determination process is an imperfect procedure.[10] The purpose is to distinguish those who fit the definition from those who do not, but the process may or may not succeed in achieving that outcome in any given case. Just as two types of error can occur in a trial (acquitting the guilty and convicting the innocent), so two types of error can result from the refugee determination process (admitting the unqualified, rejecting the qualified). Both processes involve established procedures for gathering and evaluating information. Each requires a system of adjudication, rules of evidence, burdens of proof, and so on. The fundamental challenge is to construct these procedures so as to balance appropriately the two types of risks.

What is an appropriate balance? That depends on the moral weight one places on the harm done by each type of error. The U.S. system of criminal justice, for example, places entirely on the state the burden of proof to prove the guilt of the accused, presumably because the harm of convicting an innocent person is seen as much greater than the harm of acquitting a guilty one. The analogous weighting in the refugee context would be to place the burden of proof on the state to disprove the legitimacy of an applicant's claim. That seems reasonable, given the risk of dire harm to someone who is mistakenly denied refugee status and returned to the country from which she has fled. It is irrelevant here that so few of those turned down are actually deported: that is one of the things that many people are trying to change. Besides, if we say that, because of this risk, it would be wrong to deport someone who has been denied status, we are admitting that we have set the formal balance of risks inappropriately and are trying to rectify that under the table.

While I would personally support the presumptive legitimacy of an applicant's refugee claim as a way of allocating the burden of proof, I am not sure that I could prove that this is strictly required by liberal democratic principles. Many liberal democratic states differ from the U.S. model in the ways they allocate the burden of proof in criminal trials. It is not obvious that the strong presumption of innocence is the only morally legitimate approach. Furthermore, a wrongly convicted criminal faces a certain harm whereas a wrongly deported refugee faces only a risk of harm. This might affect one's judgment about the appropriate allocation of the burden of proof. Even after taking such considerations into account, however, I do not see how one could possibly justify putting all or even most of the burden of proof on the applicant as is commonly done in most states today.

Apart from the burden of proof question, some minimal standards for fair systems of adjudication are recognized by all liberal democratic states. For example, the adjudicators have to have sufficient independence from the parties before them that they can follow the established procedural rules and reach decisions based on the evidence. Parties to an important legal proceeding should not be denied benefit of counsel. And so on. According to a number of observers, some of these minimal standards were not met by the U.S. system of refugee determination in place during the 1980s (Zucker and Zucker 1991; Anker 1991; Martin 1991).

Consider now the proposals for reforming the determination process in the light of these general remarks. Should we tighten procedures (e.g., shift the burden of proof, modify the rules of evidence) as a way of trying to limit the number of people who successfully claim asylum? Given the limited availability of evidence other than the claimant's own testimony in most refugee cases, these sorts of procedural shifts can have a tremendous impact on the outcome of cases. But it is one thing to call for tightening procedures on the grounds that too many phony claimants are getting through the system and quite another to advocate this simply on the grounds that too many are getting through, genuine or not. Changing procedures to produce a desired outcome in terms of the aggregate pattern of decisions cuts sharply against the strong liberal norm that each case in a legal context should be judged solely on its own merits. The convention refugee system is an open-ended entitlement system. It would clearly be illegitimate to impose a numerical ceiling on the number of those who can qualify as convention refugees. It is at least deeply problematic to modify the procedures so as to produce that effect.

There are ways of responding to these concerns and mounting a defense of the reform proposals. For example, one could argue that the current procedures reflect the circumstances of the period when they were established, when the number of applicants was so small that the harm done by letting in those who were not actually qualified was similarly small. Now that the numbers are so much larger, the harmful consequences of admitting those who do not meet the criteria are greater, and so it is appropriate to redress the balance of risks and tighten the procedures. When the number of claimants was small, most states gave the benefit of the doubt to the applicant. As the number of claimants has increased, most have modified this approach, allocating the risks of uncertainty.

For this approach to be more than a pretext for controlling numbers regardless of merits, it would have to be supported by evidence about the numbers and percentages of unqualified applicants being admitted. Moreover, it would be essential to show that due consideration was given to the harmful consequences of tightening the procedures (in terms of the increase in the number of those wrongly rejected). Finally, in identifying the harmful consequences of the current procedures, one could not simply cite the political backlash that can result if people feel too many claimants are getting through or even if they feel, without good reason, that too many false claimants are getting through. As I argued in the previous section, we cannot avoid some normative evaluation of the moral legitimacy of popular demands. If we think it best to throw some innocent victims to the mob to save the rest, we should at least be conscious of what we are doing. If we think that is not what we are doing, then we should be prepared to say why.

From an empirical perspective, the deep institutionalization of the liberal legal system creates important resources for those who wish to resist this sort of procedural reform. Hathaway argues, for example, that attempts to introduce a more restrictive interpretation of the convention definition and the procedural safeguards that are now part of the refugee determination process in Canada are "likely to be stymied by the compelling jurisprudence developed to date and the dictates of Canada's constitutional culture" (Hathaway 1992, 85). He may be a bit optimistic. Law and politics are inevitably intertwined, as is revealed by calls for judges and other legal actors to tighten procedures in response to public policy concerns about the number of refugees.[11] Still, the conventions of legal practice and the norms of legal discourse may well create serious obstacles to the envisaged procedural reforms, at least in some states.

What about the calls for simplification of the asylum process to increase the speed and reduce the costs of decision making? Martin argues that speed in asylum determination is essential to reduce what he calls the "magnet effect," that is, the incentives for people to put forward refugee claims that they have no hope of winning simply to gain entry to an affluent country with the hope that they can drag out the determination process long enough to gain substantial economic benefits and perhaps even establish themselves sufficiently to find a way to stay when their last appeal is exhausted. It seems both legitimate and important to try to minimize such opportunities.

A related concern focuses on the tremendous financial costs of refugee determination systems (Hathaway 1991): several billion dollars per year in the Western states. This expense seems like a terrible waste since the money provides no positive benefit to the refugees themselves and goes mainly to support the middle-class legal professionals who work in the refugee determination system. It would seem to be a great improvement from a normative perspective if some of this money could be spent instead on helping refugees, whether those admitted for asylum in the Western states or those in safe havens abroad.

I find myself sympathetic to these ambitions to increase speed and reduce costs, but I think the obstacles to procedural simplification run deep at the levels of both principle and practice. Every Western state possesses standard legal procedures for assessing contested claims, procedures that are complex, costly, and time consuming because of the need to permit the parties to gather evidence, construct arguments, and press appeals. If we allow less stringent procedural mechanisms to be employed in the refugee determination process, then we are announcing, in effect, that we care more about modest commercial transactions than cases where a mistake could expose someone to the risk of torture and death. That seems hard to justify. In practice, such simplification seems to ask advocates for refugees to trust authorities who take the task of controlling numbers as one of their primary concerns.

Finally, there is the issue of harmonization, an idea that looks attractive at the level of abstract principle. Letting each state establish its own refugee determination process without coordinating with other states that seem likely targets of destination means that states that adopt the best procedural protections will be likely to attract a disproportionate share of asylum claimants. This penalizes the most generous and creates incentives for a competitive race down toward the lowest common denominator. It also enables asylum claimants who have been turned down in one jurisdiction to apply in another. In contrast to this current arrangement, the advantages from a normative perspective of common procedural standards and mutual recognition of decisions seem obvious, provided that the common standards are themselves morally defensible. In practice, of course, this proviso is the crucial problem, because states with procedural standards that are morally inadequate have few incentives to improve them.

As already noted, asylum claimants have strong incentives to seek out the most welcoming determination systems. This is true not just for those with deeply problematic or even marginal claims but even for those with the strongest moral claims. Because of the inevitable uncertainty and fear genuine refugees experience in entering a determination process whose outcome will determine whether they achieve safety and whose workings are bound to appear somewhat mysterious, it is perfectly reasonable for them to want to find the forum that seems most likely to produce a positive outcome. In this context, if a state improves its procedural protections for refugee claimants, it is likely to attract more claimants. This is unlikely to seem an attractive prospect for policymakers intent on strengthening controls and reducing numbers. After all, if they were willing to pursue that goal by adopting morally inadequate procedures in the first place, why would they be tempted to modify them in such a way as to draw applicants away from their current destinations?

One answer is that they would be subject to criticism of their inadequate procedures from both internal and external sources on the basis of underlying liberal democratic principles. Another answer is that they would be subject to political pressure from the states with higher standards, who will press them to assume their fair share of the overall obligation. These answers are not entirely irrelevant, but from an empirical perspective it is easy to see that the incentives for states with stronger procedural protections to weaken them are likely to be much greater than the incentives for states with weaker procedural protections to strengthen them.

In practice in recent years, harmonization seems to have meant mainly a reduction in procedural protections for refugee claimants.[12] This is achieved both directly, through a weakening of the standards within a given state, and indirectly, through a willingness to recognize as binding other states' decisions on refugee status and an attempt to establish criteria for allocating jurisdictional responsibility for adjudicating particular refugee claims among some set of states, as in the Dublin and Schengen conventions and the recent amendment to section 16 of the German Constitution (Neuman 1993).

In some respects these indirect ways of weakening procedural protections are the most troubling from a moral perspective. Changes in internal procedures may or may not be morally defensible, but at least they have to be done publicly and so can come under critical scrutiny in a context where institutionalized liberal legal norms carry some weight. The indirect ways of weakening protection tend to render the procedural problems much less visible because they occur elsewhere and are sheltered both by the normative presumption that we should not be judging how other states conduct their own affairs (though, of course, every human rights claim and the whole refugee system is a challenge to that presumption) and the empirical obstacles first to producing an informed critical evaluation of procedures in another country and then to disseminating it in a politically effective way.

Consider the issue of mutual recognition first. On the one hand, submission of multiple asylum claims is a real problem in terms of costs, and harmonization would greatly reduce the incentives for people to file a series of claims so as to maximize the likelihood of a successful outcome or even take advantage of being in one Western country after another while the claims are being adjudicated. From a moral perspective, it would seem that a claimant is entitled to a fair hearing (including appropriate appeals), not to a series of fair hearings. It also seems reasonable to acknowledge that another state does not have to adopt exactly the same procedural rules as one's own in order to be just. Different liberal democratic states have different legal traditions and procedural practices. Within some range, these differences are certainly morally acceptable as different ways of institutionalizing just procedures.

On the other hand, there must be some limit to the range of acceptable differences in procedural rules. The mere fact that a state generally has a liberal democratic character cannot mean that all of its procedures and practices must be presumed to be just. For example, in a number of liberal democratic states the death penalty has been abolished not merely because people see it as ineffective but because they regard it, like torture, as a violation of fundamental human rights. Other liberal democratic states, most notably the United States, continue to use the death penalty. Some states, in fact, will not extradite people accused of a crime to states where the accused will be subject to the death penalty in the subsequent proceedings. Clearly, we cannot abandon all responsibility for the quality of the procedures used in another country if we are prepared to use the outcomes of those procedures as a reasonable proxy for the outcome that we ourselves would reach in the case (which is the effect of mutual recognition of refugee determination decisions).

The dangers inherent in multiple recognition are extended further in the practice of assigning responsibility for adjudicating particular claims to particular states, as in the Dublin and Schengen conventions and the amendment to section 16 of the German Constitution. As Neuman observes, the problem of multiple submissions could be solved, in principle, simply by an agreement on mutual recognition. The insistence on having claims heard in a particular country can only be construed as an attempt to prevent forum shopping. But from a moral perspective, to require someone to have her only hearing in a particular state increases our responsibility to ensure that the hearing meets what we regard as fundamental standards of fairness. Neuman's observation seems entirely appropriate: "Without further guarantees of consistent adjudication, mandatory jurisdictional rules of the Dublin and Schengen type have the potential to enlist buffer states in decreasing the quality of refugee processing. Such regimes may permit wealthier countries to disclaim responsibility for decisions they could not justify making themselves. Judge Rothkegel aptly labels this disclaimer as the Pontius Pilate objection" (Neuman 1993, 526).

In sum, while some versions of harmonization are certainly justifiable in theory, the practices adopted so far are deeply problematic from a moral perspective. At the same time, from an empirical perspective, moral objections to these practices are likely to be less effective than objections to other ways of using procedural reform of determination as a strategy of control because it is more difficult to use the institutional resources of liberal legal systems to challenge harmonization policies.

Deportation

Some people argue that one essential element of a control strategy is to make deportation policies much more effective, because as it stands many, perhaps most, of those who are not granted refugee status are still able to remain for extended periods in the countries in which they have made their claims. From a normative perspective, there is clearly no problem in principle in deporting asylum abusers, i.e., economic migrants who have no plausible claim to be refugees. But we need more empirical information about what proportion of those denied refugee status could properly be construed as asylum abusers if we are to understand how much such abuse contributes to the problem and how significant a contribution would be made by improved deportation processes.

The only study that I have seen cited reports that of 57,605 unsuccessful asylum seekers in Germany in 1989, 34 percent were allowed to remain as de facto refugees and another 16 percent were permitted to stay temporarily, with their status to be reconsidered every six months (Marshall 1992, 256). Clearly, even in the eyes of the authorities, these were not people who should have been deported even if it were legal to do so. What about the others? We do not know enough to say.

Some determination systems employ categories such as "manifestly unfounded claim" to simplify the procedural treatment of claims that have no real chance of success. It might be tempting to suppose that we could at least deport all claimants who fell into such categories. That might work in determination systems, such as Canada's, that use it only to reject frivolous and abusive claims, but in others (as, for example, the German system) it is used to reject people who are (only) fleeing armed conflict, presumably on the (not unreasonable) view that this alone will not qualify them as refugees under the convention definition as interpreted in Germany (Kanstroom 1993, 197). But as the discussions above demonstrate, there are good moral grounds for supposing that such victims of violence should not be deported, and in fact Germany generally does not deport them.

I can say this much. Although the various strategies of control that I consider in this paper would all reduce the number of those who enter and remain by means of the asylum process, the strategies stand in some tension with one another from a normative perspective. The narrower the definition and the tighter the procedures, the more likely it is that people who deserve refugee status will not be granted it. At the least, many people whom it would be wrong to deport will fail to qualify as refugees on technical grounds. Some, though perhaps not all, of these will be recognized as de facto refugees and hence partially protected from deportation.[13] Others presumably will not. Hollifield (1994) reports, for example, that in February 1994 Germany canceled expulsion orders for over 100,000 Croatian refugees, but it is not clear whether they were granted formal status as humanitarian refugees.

Deportation of a genuine refugee can quite literally be a death sentence. It is at least possible that the fact that so few failed claimants are actually deported reflects a concern not to make this sort of mistake. In principle, if we struck the right balance of risks in constructing the procedures for the original adjudication system, this concern should not be an obstacle to deportation. But perhaps we cannot be so confident that the right balance has been struck, especially when we are simultaneously using a convention definition that so clearly excludes many people whom we acknowledge in other ways as deserving protection. Many of those denied status have serious moral claims; they are not just asylum abusers. Deportation brings home, in a way that merely denying status does not, the significance of saying to someone, "Your moral claims to enter here are outweighed by our legitimate interests in keeping you out." It forces us to weigh the merits of the competing moral claims more carefully. Stories about people being placed in handcuffs on planes are more gripping than stories about some bureaucratic decision.

The issue of deportation also points up the futility of trying to use a narrow convention definition as a strategy for controlling the number of successful asylum applicants. In effect, the use of such a definition requires us to construct a second definition and second set of procedures for distinguishing those whom we are morally justified in deporting from the rest.

In sum, while a more efficient deportation system may contribute to a reduction in the worst forms of abuse of the asylum system, it will make an important contribution to the overall problem of control only if we see flagrant abusers as a major source of asylum claims.

Deterrence

I deliberately eschew the phrase "humane deterrence," much in vogue these days, because I object to the legitimating function of the word *humane*. Deterrence has two basic variants: making it more difficult for people to enter a country and claim asylum and making it less attractive to seek asylum because of the conditions claimants face. I label the former "external deterrence" and the latter "internal deterrence." Each can take several forms.

In general, I characterize external deterrence as the approach to control that is the most problematic from a principled moral perspective and the least controversial and most attractive— and hence the least likely to be changed—from a political perspective. As with deportation, there can be no objection to trying to deter asylum abusers from arriving. The problem comes when states also try to deter people with legitimate moral claims to refugee status. Whatever the formal obligations of states under international law, it is clearly a violation of the fundamental principles underlying the refugee regime to take steps to make it more difficult for people to leave states where they are in serious danger of or actually suffering from violations of their basic human rights.

Now, it might be said that deterrence policies do not prevent people from leaving their home countries but rather merely make it harder for them to enter the countries of their choice. But as each additional state creates its own barriers to refugees, the rest face stronger incentives to do likewise. Eventually, if all states followed suit, there would be no place to escape to. The affluent states of the West seem to be relying on the good will or administrative limitations of third world states to prevent this competitive dynamic from reaching its logical conclusion. It is hard to imagine what principled justification could be offered for trying to direct the burden of caring for refugees to those least able to afford it. Moreover, in signing an agreement like the Geneva Convention a state has committed itself, not others, to accept refugees if they arrive. To try then to prevent them from arriving so that one does not have to accept them seems a bit underhanded, to put it mildly.

As with mandatory jurisdictional rules that attempt to assign the task of refugee determination to other states (which I discussed above in the section on determination), external deterrence seems to rest on the assumption that we are only morally responsible for what happens to refugees if we actually consider their cases. As with the jurisdictional rules, this is a form of Pontius Pilatism, an unpersuasive attempt to shift moral responsibility. External deterrence is not significantly different, in moral terms, from denying an application for asylum. If we take steps to keep refugees from applying for asylum in our state, we become morally responsible for their fates.[14]

The most widely used mechanisms of deterrence are visa controls and carrier sanctions against companies that transport people without proper documentation. Virtually every Western state has adopted these over the past decade in response to the dramatic rise in asylum applications during the 1980s. These mechanisms do not even attempt to distinguish between genuine refugees and those with no legitimate moral claim. Indeed, the system has a Catch-22 logic to it. If a refugee claimant has managed to obtain proper documentation, that may be taken as an indication that she is not really a refugee. If the claimant has obtained false documentation or lied on the visa application about her reasons for traveling, that is taken as an indication that she is untrustworthy.

What makes these forms of controls attractive from a policymaker's perspective is that they are inexpensive and easy to operate, relatively effective in reducing the numbers of people who might otherwise arrive and claim asylum, and politically uncontroversial. I do not mean that these policies have escaped criticism from academics and refugee advocates. Indeed, nonpolicymakers seem almost unanimous in condemning them. Politically, however, they have met with no serious challenge.

The lack of controversy stems mainly from the fact that the operation of these controls takes place abroad and can be presented as a neutral and normal operation of government. After all, we are all required to get travel documents of one kind or another. Unlike open interdiction (which I will discuss in a moment) the force that lies behind a refusal to grant someone a document or permit someone to board an airplane is so much a part of everyday life that it is largely invisible and difficult to communicate effectively. It is hard to get a dramatic television picture of a bureaucrat failing to stamp a passport or someone

failing to get on an airplane. Indeed, those excluded by these
processes are not easily identified as individuals. Domestic legal
forums do not lend themselves to challenges to this sort of control in the way that they accommodate objections to the tightening of procedures. In sum, the whole process of control and
exclusion occurs largely out of public view through mechanisms
that appear to be routine.

Another form of external deterrence is more old-fashioned:
the open use of armed force to prevent would-be asylum claimants
from landing on one's shore. The most shocking example of this
in Western states in recent years was the U.S. policy of stopping
on the high seas boats filled with Haitians planning to come to
the United States to seek asylum and forcibly returning the passengers to Haiti without any serious pretense of considering
their claims to be refugees.[15] To be sure, Haiti is a very poor
country, and many Haitians would undoubtedly like to come to
the United States purely for economic reasons. But the Haitian
regime that overthrew Aristide (like the ones that preceded him
and perhaps like his) was violent and repressive. Many reports,
including televised ones, provided clear evidence about state-
sponsored or -tolerated violence against Aristide supporters,
including people at the grass roots level. There were well-docu-
mented cases of killings and torture. Former public officials
close to Aristide were shot down in the streets with impunity. In
this context, it was utterly unreasonable to suppose that people
fleeing Haiti had no well-founded fear of persecution but were
instead merely economic migrants. Yet that is precisely what
U.S. public officials established as the cornerstone of a policy
that gave only the most cursory consideration, if that, to the
claims of these people.

Unlike visa controls and carrier sanctions, this policy was
widely discussed and publicly criticized. Yet from another perspective, what is truly disturbing about this episode was the
ineffectiveness of the challenges and the degree of public support that the policy enjoyed. It should be a sobering reminder to
people who claim that one or another aspect of the refugee
regime is so deeply entrenched in liberal democratic states that
it cannot be seriously threatened. A more direct challenge to the
principles of fair hearings and nonrefoulement is hard to imagine. Thus invisibility is not the only reason for the adoption of

policies of external deterrence. The widespread support for "keeping them out" also plays a role.

I have not seen any attempt to defend policies of external deterrence from a principled perspective. (I have heard arguments to the effect that such policies are not illegal under international law, but those arguments tend to have a technical, legalistic cast.) Academic commentary has generally been highly critical, even from people quite sympathetic to the goal of improving control over the asylum process (Martin 1990). Nevertheless, it seems useful to try to imagine what form such a defense might take. I have come up with three arguments that I regard as having some plausibility, though I am not persuaded by any of them. I invite readers to suggest others, not because I am eager to supply legitimation for these policies but because I think that this is a forum in which we should try to explore all sides of difficult questions. It is precisely because I find such policies of external deterrence to be so indefensible that I wonder whether I have really heard the other side.

The first defense is "Everybody's doing it." (I have heard this advanced, at least informally, by public officials in Canada, for example.) At first glance, this defense sounds like an appeal either to equity or to reasonableness. The two are closely related though distinct. The appeal to equity says, in effect, that it is unfair to expect one country to adhere to a moral standard that most others are not respecting. The appeal to reasonableness says that moral standards themselves must be reasonably possible for most people to uphold and, for that reason, must reflect common practice.

The obvious answer, at the same schoolyard level as the first statement, is "The fact that everybody's doing it doesn't make it right." We sometimes have good reasons for asserting principles to be binding even when we know they are not being and probably will not be generally observed. We admire those who do not go along with the crowd in such situations. States, too, can be asked to demonstrate leadership in following principles and can be criticized for failing to do so.

One possible rejoinder to this criticism, in terms less reminiscent of the schoolyard, is that in some cases acting on principle, when most others do not, only entails the cost of forgoing illicit gains, but in cases like this, which have the character of collective action problems, of the prisoner's dilemma variety, any actor who fails to adopt self-protective measures, when many others do, will be exposed to severe penalties.[16] In less technical terms, the argument is that if all other Western states are making use of visa requirements and carrier sanctions, the failure of a few countries to follow suit would expose them to an overwhelming number of asylum claimants. Ultimately, then, the appeal is not primarily to equity and reasonableness but to interest and necessity, which is the second argument.

The simple version of the second argument is "We can't take them all in." Many (though not all) moral theories and legal systems make exceptions to generally binding rules of conduct in cases of extreme necessity. This is perhaps even more true of secular theories of morality, especially those in which self-preservation is taken to be the most fundamental good for both individuals and collectives and moral principles are generally understood as means of advancing long-term interests. Hobbes and Hume are two famous (and quite different) exponents in the Western tradition of this view of morality.[17]

In this view, the crucial term in the argument is the word "can't." The courses of action open to us are inevitably constrained by our fundamental interests. A political community cannot be required or expected to endanger its vital interests for the sake of moral principles (or for the sake of the interests of people outside the community). Here, the Haitians are seen as the advance squad of an armada of potential asylum seekers from the third world whose numbers are simply overwhelming. Given the magnitude of the threat, effective measures of control are urgently necessary, and therefore some forms of external deterrence, especially visa requirements and carrier sanctions, are justifiable.

The problem with this argument is that it unduly expands the concept of necessity, which must be strictly construed for the argument to hold. We cannot slide from the view that a threat to our very self-preservation justifies overriding the conventional restraints of morality to the view that whatever is in our interest is necessary and so morally permissible. In the latter case, we simply abandon the moral perspective altogether. If we really care about moral principles, we are obliged to seek out and actively pursue alternatives that may reconcile our vital interests with the requirements of morality, at least to a large extent.

Suppose we accept the claim that there is a serious danger of an overwhelming tide of asylum seekers coming to the West and that some arrangement that effectively controls and limits the influx is a vital interest. The question ought to be whether we can find a way to protect that interest while still meeting asylum seekers' needs for safety. There might be many possible answers. For example, James Hathaway (1991) has suggested that we modify the asylum system so that the place in which refugees file their claims is no longer automatically the place in which they are granted asylum, if the claim is recognized to be legitimate. As Hathaway points out, the present arrangement privileges those refugees who are able to reach Western states in order to claim asylum, and these claimants tend to be younger, healthier, more educated, better off economically, and more commonly male than refugees generally. From a moral perspective, refugees are entitled to safety and basic provisions for their wellbeing, not a choice of where these needs will be met. If we constructed a system that fairly allocated responsibility for taking in refugees among all states (including the financial assistance necessary for poorer states to perform this function adequately) and if we broke the link between filing a claim in the West and finding a permanent home there, we could eliminate the incentives for refugees to come to the West to file asylum claims while simultaneously meeting their needs for protection.

One big problem with Hathaway's proposal is that it would require money, not infinite amounts but undoubtedly much more than Western states would be willing to spend. But if the problem is money on that scale, then we can no longer speak of the issue as though it were a question of fundamental survival. The necessity defense fails. Of course, there may be other problems with Hathaway's proposal, but the point is that if our priority were to reconcile an effective system of control over the asylum process with the requirements of justice toward refugees, there might be many possibilities to explore. But our real priority is only to have an effective system of control. That is why we settle for external deterrence, and that is why external deterrence ultimately cannot be justified on grounds of necessity.

The third argument on behalf of external deterrence takes a more indirect route and focuses on techniques, such as visa controls and carrier sanctions, that are largely hidden from public sight. This account acknowledges that we do not fully live up to our moral commitments to refugees and that we have no real justification for failing to do so. Yet the moral commitments still matter, because we do meet some of them, with the result that some refugees are better off. Therefore it is important to the maintenance of those limited commitments that we do take seriously and are prepared to respect that we keep our violations of our own principles as much as possible out of sight. Conor Cruise O'Brien writes in a recent book of "hypocrisy and cultivated inattention" as the "traditional built-in antidotes" to the ethical demands we impose upon ourselves (1994, 132). From the perspective advanced here, he might have described them not only as antidotes but also as prerequisites for a viable ethics (and indeed that seems to fit with O'Brien's line of argument). Staring facts in the face will not lead to more moral behavior but rather to greater ruthlessness and to the abandonment of such protections as we now provide to refugees, protections that are an important good, for all their limitations. So the hidden character of visa controls and carrier sanctions is actually a good thing. We will exclude one way or another, as the Haitian interdictions show, but open violations of our principles, as in the Haitian case, do far more damage to our commitments to refugees than those that are obscured from our view.

I am not sure what to think of this line of argument.[18] There is much about it that I do not like. It is antidemocratic, legitimating the insularity and discretion of elites by means of reasons that, by their own logic, can only be shared with other elites rather than the general public. Like the defense of necessity it easily degenerates into a self-serving rationalization of whatever policies one wants to pursue. Like all forms of strong consequentialism (i.e., that justify departures from accepted moral principles), it relies on calculations that are highly contestable and assumes away negative unintended consequences.[19] One of the advantages of sticking to principles in contexts where consequences are difficult to foresee is that one is less tempted to construct hypotheses about consequences that justify a course one has chosen because it serves one's interests. Still, despite all these objections, this third argument might contain a grain of truth.

I turn now to the issue of internal deterrence, the tactic of making it less attractive to seek asylum because of the conditions claimants will face. This approach is based on an economic model that treats asylum seekers (or at least a subset of them) as rational actors. The general theory is that if there is no material advantage to be gained by claiming asylum, then economic migrants and those with marginal claims will be deterred from coming in the first place, while genuine refugees who need safety will not.

Internal deterrence involves placing restrictive conditions on asylum seekers. In one version, the restrictive conditions cover only the period when claims for refugee status are being considered. After that, those denied status are (in principle) sent home while those admitted as refugees are granted residence permits and the normal rights that residents enjoy. In another version, the restrictive conditions persist even after status has been granted, either for an extended period or indefinitely. In its strongest variant, this would involve replacing the form of asylum now practiced in Western states, which aims to integrate acknowledged refugees into the host countries, with something much closer to the form of asylum granted in most third world countries, which provides safe haven for refugees while keeping them socially and physically isolated from the host population (e.g., through the construction of refugee camps).

The normative justification for internal deterrence in both versions is that we only owe refugees safety and security, not access to all the economic advantages of life in a rich country. This argument has some validity, in my view, although liberal democratic principles will place significant constraints on acceptable forms of internal deterrence, as I show below. The practical objections to internal deterrence in liberal democratic states are even stronger and often prove impossible to overcome. In general, in my view, internal deterrence is much less morally objectionable in principle than external deterrence but much more difficult to implement as a practical policy.

Consider first predetermination restrictions on claimants (which includes the assumption that those who are accepted as refugees will then be permitted to join the general population), the form of internal deterrence most commonly practiced in Western states.

There are various ways of restricting asylum claimants so as to make it less attractive to file unwarranted claims. First, one can deny them access to the labor market. This denies those coming for economic opportunity the thing they want most, although it does not entirely eliminate the economic incentive, because even a meager public allowance may furnish them with enough money to be able to send some home. The problem is that if claimants are denied the opportunity to earn money they must be supported at public expense. This is irritating to taxpayers, who see people able and willing to work to support themselves but forbidden to do so by the public authorities. Thus deterrence and financial/political considerations collide under this system. In some states, such as Germany and Canada, the policy has oscillated back and forth.

If one denies claimants access to work but permits them to live with the general population, many may seek work in the underground economy anyway. Again, public response to such behavior is apt to be mixed, especially on the part of those opposed to the prohibition in the first place, and feasible sanctions are limited because one cannot reasonably assume that a real refugee would not want to work (especially given the limited level of public subsistence usually provided).

In view of this problem, if one is intent on maintaining some form of internal deterrence, it may seem necessary to create stronger barriers between claimants and the rest of the population so as to prevent circumvention of the rules against working. Separate housing alone will not be sufficient. It must be accompanied by some sort of security. What is required then is some sort of detention facility for refugee claimants.

This is more effective as a form of deterrence, but it is also much more expensive and much more problematic from a moral perspective. Even if facilities and the accompanying treatment were to meet high standards not only for food, clothing, and shelter but also for such human needs as physical activity, recreation, stimulation, and social interaction, confinement under prisonlike conditions is painful and distressing. In practice, facilities and treatment are often both expensive and well below high standards for reasons familiar to us from other institutional settings.[20] In addition, such arrangements foster and reinforce tendencies in the public to perceive asylum seekers as threats and outcasts (Kanstroom 1993, 195).

Recall, too, that in this model those who are acknowledged to be legitimate refugees will be integrated with the general population—just not before they suffer a long, undeserved period of social isolation and deprivation as the introduction to their new home, at the moment when they have supposedly reached safety. It is at best an ungracious welcome.

This shows again the importance of how we construct the problem of control. If we think that economic migrants constitute a huge proportion of the asylum claimants, then perhaps such expensive yet ungenerous treatment is necessary to control the flow. But if we find only a small proportion to be people whose claims are so spurious that we are willing to deport them (and justified in doing so), then it is hard to see what could warrant imposing such a heavy burden on genuine refugees and such a heavy financial cost on ourselves for such a small increment of control. Moreover, in this context, "genuine refugees" must be construed as including not just those who satisfy the convention definition but anyone whom we are not willing to deport, for reasons that should be clear from the earlier discussion of deportation.

Someone may object that I overstate the burden placed on refugees by temporary detention because it lasts a relatively short time. But even leaving aside questions about the importance of the early experiences of refugees for their successful subsequent integration, the claim that the determination process is conducted expeditiously cuts the other way. Speedy determination constitutes an important disincentive for economic migrants because they will not have enough time to earn money before they are deported (Martin 1990). At best, then, detention prevents people from going underground and staying on as illegals, but there may be ways of preventing this that are both more cost-effective and more humane.

In addition to restrictions on employment, housing, and mobility, receiving states may seek to limit the access of refugee claimants to other social services, such as health care and education. These sorts of restrictions seem even more problematic than those just mentioned. In most Western states (with the United States being an obvious exception), health care is treated as a basic right. Even in the United States, under Proposition 187 in California—the most draconian restrictions proposed so far—provision is still made for emergency medical care for illegal aliens. Moreover, asylum claimants are not illegal aliens, at least not in the sense in which that term is normally used, and restrictions of medical care to emergency services may be irrational from a public policy perspective for any segment of the population. In short, restrictions on most health care services would be hard to justify.

With respect to education, time is again the crucial variable. In the short term, restrictions serve no useful function; in the long term, they are not justified because they impose too great a cost on those affected.

In general, I have seen no serious argument to the effect that the availability of social services independent of economic opportunity creates a significant incentive for economic migrants to pose as asylum seekers. Since the fundamental rationale for policies of internal deterrence of the kind we are now considering is to discourage economic migrants, there is no obvious justification for restricting the provision of social services to asylum applicants.

Let me turn finally to the second version of internal deterrence: the creation of more or less permanent refugee camps within the borders of Western states. From a very abstract perspective, this approach has a significant attraction, in that it removes almost completely the incentive to pretend to be a refugee in order to gain entry to affluent Western states while still providing safety and subsistence to refugees. Indeed, if third world conditions could be reproduced in the camps together with effective measures to prevent escape to the wider society, the incentive for asylum abuse would be virtually nil. No one pretends to be a refugee in order to gain access to a camp in Malawi. Thus we could adopt very broad definitions and use very simple and generous procedures to establish refugee status.

To state the proposal in this way, however, is to reveal its limitations. In the third world, refugee camps make some sense. Conditions in the camps are often not much worse than conditions in the surrounding society, and keeping refugees in camps enables the international community to gain access to them in order to provide crucial material assistance. None of this would apply to camps in Western states. As affluent states, they are generally expected to provide for the refugees they take in.[21] The incentives to escape from the camp and to try to blend into the larger society would be enormous. But the most powerful objection has to do with the disjuncture between such camps and the institutions and values of the liberal democratic society in which we are to imagine them established.

First, there is the fact that settling people within our borders would bring them within the purview of our legal regimes. While this would not necessarily guarantee them all the rights afforded other residents, it would give them and their supporters access to a range of resources to press their claims that were not available when they were outside our jurisdiction or even when their status was as yet undetermined. Since, among other things, this arrangement would entail a dramatic reduction in the rights currently held by acknowledged refugees, refugee advocates would be sure to resist it strenuously in legal and political fora, regardless of promises of greater openness in return, partly out of (anticonsequentialist) principle and partly out of a (reasonable) concern that such promises would not be kept once a new and lower threshold of treatment had been established. We could imagine a two-tier system establishing individual asylum on the current model for those who met the convention definition and safe havens for de facto refugees, but there is no obvious justification for such an arrangement, given what I said above about the relative moral priorities of these two categories. Moreover, such an arrangement would still require the expensive administrative apparatus for determining convention refugee status and so would eliminate one of the attractions of the safe haven alternative.

Second, establishing such camps within our borders would make the people living in them much more visible, and the media would have their usual incentives to dramatize their plight. Since residents of the camps would be, by hypothesis, people whose refugee claims we have accepted, we could not so easily tell ourselves stories about how they were really dangerous threats or economic migrants. It would be harder not to see them simply as victims of violence held in these miserable conditions because we were unwilling to share our privileges with them.

I do not mean to say that Western societies are incapable of tolerating such a situation. We have only to consider how easily those of us who live in North America, and increasingly even those who live in Europe, have become accustomed to the sight of homeless people living in parks and on the streets.[22] But it would not be easy to introduce this sort of arrangement because it would constitute a dramatic departure from current policies regarding postdetermination treatment of refugees, and it would meet with a great deal of resistance.

Ironically, a policy that replaced external deterrence with internal deterrence, even of the postdetermination variety, would be markedly superior from a moral perspective. Internal deterrence does not restrict the basic right to asylum of genuine refugees. That is what makes this policy, for all its problems and limitations, so different from and so superior to external deterrence. Yet there is no political incentive to replace external deterrence with internal deterrence, especially of the postdetermination variety. That is why I see virtually no chance of such a development.

Conclusion

The goal of this paper has been to identify and clarify some of the ways in which moral considerations might be relevant to policies aiming to achieve better control over the influx of asylum seekers. Much of the work of legitimating the exclusion of asylum applicants comes from constructing the problem as one of excess demand caused by economic migrants trying to gain access to affluent societies through an illegitimate back door. This construction is facilitated by the narrowness of the convention definition and the procedures used in the determination process, such that many Western states generate very high nonrecognition rates for those seeking formal refugee status. At the same time, the practices of these states with respect to deportation reveal that we recognize the validity of many of the moral claims that we deny in the formal process. Finally, the ease with which we employ mechanisms of external deterrence, especially of the hidden variety, reveals the limitations of moral norms when they are detached from an institutional and political location that can support principle with power.

Notes

* My thanks to Rainer Bauböck and David A. Martin for comments on an earlier draft of this paper.

1. An important question is whether this concern should be regarded as well founded. Some people argue that politicians have greatly exaggerated the problem for their own political ends and that the public has reacted hysterically, out of all proportion to the reality. For example, the landing of a couple of ships of refugee claimants from India and Sri Lanka in Newfoundland did not in fact presage a flotilla of refugee-laden ships headed for Canada, though that is how it appeared from the treatment in the press and the reactions of public officials. From this perspective, the increase in asylum applications is not really a serious problem, certainly not a crisis of controls. Rather, the real problem lies not with the political response to the asylum seekers. A proponent of this view might object that an inquiry like mine, which proposes to consider the moral legitimacy of various strategies of control, serves to legitimize the overreaction even though it may criticize certain techniques of control, because it implicitly accepts the seriousness of the issue. Such a person might say that the first task of a normative inquiry should be instead to challenge the assumption that there is a crisis of controls. I think there is something to this objection, which is why I mention it here, where it can serve as a kind of warning flag about the inquiry that follows. At the same time, I think the questions I propose to address ought to be considered regardless of whether one believes that there is today a genuine crisis of controls. And, in any case, throughout my discussion I will pay explicit attention to the ways that political considerations interact with moral judgments.

2. In saying that moral obligations may be narrower than legal ones, I do not mean to imply that states are not morally obliged to keep their agreements or fulfill their legal obligations. Normally they are, and, in that sense, moral obligations may be wider but not narrower than legal ones. Rather, I meant to draw attention to the fact that some legal obligations have independent moral sanction and others are morally binding only because the state has agreed to them. An example of the former would be the obligation not to violate basic human rights, which is binding on states regardless of whether they have signed any particular documents, so that the legal obligations of agreements on basic human rights reinforce rather than create the moral obligations (though they also institutionalize and concretize them). By contrast, a free trade agreement might be an example of something that most people (though not some economists) would regard as a morally optional policy, i.e., one that states are free to adopt or not as they judge best. In that sort of case, the moral obligations are narrower than the legal ones in the sense that the moral obligations are entirely derivative of the agreement and disappear if the agreement is (lawfully) terminated.

3. I use the phrase "desperate need" so as to avoid prejudging the question of how we ought to define the term *refugee*, which I will address below.

4. Of course, as with all such categories, "public order" may be construed very broadly or very narrowly. For a discussion, see Carens 1987.

5. Technically, designation as a convention refugee normally entails only a guarantee of nonrefoulement, not asylum. In practice, however, someone

who gains entry to a Western state and subsequently claims and is found to meet the convention criteria will effectively enjoy asylum status (Martin 1991). The German case is further complicated by article 16 of the Basic Law (Neuman 1993, 510).

6. Of course, being targeted is one indicator of the degree of risk, but only one.

7. Both Martin and Zolberg et al. are sensitive to this problem, but I do not think their sensitivity adequately informs their theoretical positions. Martin discusses the question in a footnote and concludes, "Refugee law and moral theory have no answer for this very real problem" (1991, 48 n. 13). Zolberg et al. observe that the Irish and the Jews in the nineteenth century might in theory have been assisted in their home countries but were legitimately regarded as refugees because such assistance was not in fact forthcoming. Yet their subsequent theoretical formulations emphasize the possibility (rather than the actuality) of assistance in place and use that principle to reject, for example, claims to refugee status from people who move as a result of natural disaster (Zolberg, Suhrke, and Aguayo 1989, 32–33)

8. See Hailbronner 1986 for a critique of the view that the distinctions between the two categories of refugees no longer has much legal or practical significance. (There could, of course, be more than two definitions, but I do not think that would change the principles at stake.) In addressing this question, I will touch on some of the issues I discuss later under the heading of determination. But I will defer to the discussion of deterrence consideration of the arguments for making the bundles of rights under the second definition so much less extensive (as in safe haven arrangements) that some potential claimants might be deterred from coming at all. All these topics are so intertwined that this sort of overlap is unavoidable.

9. I add the qualification "for the sake of this argument" because I do not want to suggest that such a development is spontaneous and inevitable. In fact, there are lots of intervening variables. Politicians play a key role in defining "the refugee problem," and they sometimes have considerable room for maneuver, often much more than they pretend. On the other hand, I am not persuaded (even though I wish it were true) that hostility to refugees in Western states is entirely or even primarily attributable to the manipulation of public opinion by politicians.

10. The criminal justice system provides a number of useful comparison points with the refugee determination process, including the fact that, in some jurisdictions, there are public and political claims that too many people are getting away with something under the current system and corresponding demands to tighten, simplify, and speed up procedures. There are dangers in the analogy as well, however. For one thing, it risks reinforcing the tendency to associate refugees (or at least those whose claims are denied) with criminals as threats to society. For another, it may encourage people to think of refugee claimants in dichotomous categories (innocent or guilty, genuine or phony) rather than as occupying varying points along a continuum of people with moral claims of some sort to entry (though to a large degree this risk is inherent in a process that grants status to some and denies it to others). Despite the risks, the analogy is sufficiently illuminating to warrant its use.

11. Martin 1991, for example, says that because of the need to keep asylum as a scarce resource, "courts and agencies must resist the temptation to expand the legal standards" (37). Though this is an argument against

expansion rather than for contraction, the point is still the same. The temptation to expand presumably comes in part from the logic of the law on these issues. Ironically, Martin insists earlier in the article on the importance of the law/politics distinction (30).

12. As Rainer Bauböck has pointed out to me, under some circumstances harmonization may entail a strengthening rather than a weakening of protection for refugees. The 1951 Convention and the 1967 Protocol can be regarded as instruments of harmonization. This fits with my general point that harmonization is not objectionable in principle. It seems hard to imagine today, however, what change in circumstances would make it possible for harmonization not to involve more restrictions and exclusions than the present system.

13. On the legality of deporting humanitarian refugees, see Hailbronner 1986.

14. Peter and Renata Singer (1988) have argued that the whole asylum regime rests on a false distinction between actions and omissions and that we should replace it with a refugee regime based more directly on principles of need. I think their argument is profoundly misguided at the levels of both principle and practice. At the level of principle, I think it makes sense to say that we have a special responsibility not to return to a dangerous situation those who appear at our door asking for safety and a corresponding obligation not to prevent them from coming to the door in the first place. But this is quite different from saying that we are obliged to seek out the most needy and oppressed in the world. In other words, the distinction between actions and omissions can make good sense in certain moral contexts, and external deterrence should be regarded as a form of action for which we are responsible. For a fuller version of this argument, see Carens 1992b.

15. In recent years, the policy was changed so that instead of being returned to Haiti, claimants were transported to a safe haven in Guantánamo Bay where their claims were, in principle, to be given serious consideration. This policy is much more defensible, if still far from satisfactory. I discuss safe havens as a form of deterrence below.

16. Of course, this is the same competitive logic that transforms the ideal of harmonization into a policy of establishing the lowest common denominator as the shared policy.

17. For a contemporary account, see Buchanan 1990.

18. Perhaps I should flip the argument back on itself and say that even if it were true it would be a mistake to articulate it in print.

19. Bernard Williams poses similar objections to what he calls Government House utilitarianism (1985, 108–10).

20. For a chilling description of some of the realities in the United States, see Helton 1991.

21. Of course, one can imagine a more equitable arrangement for burden sharing, but such plans are as unrealistic politically as Hathaway's, and for the same reasons. If one is going to work on a plan for reform that seems unlikely to be realized, then it might as well be one like Hathaway's, which has a more fundamental justification.

22. Perhaps camps for refugees would make it easier to think of camps as a solution to the problem of homeless people. This points again to the grain of truth in the third rationale for external deterrence discussed above: it may be morally dangerous to contemplate the truth about ourselves.

Bibliography

Aleinikoff, T. Alexander. 1991. "The Meaning of 'Persecution' in U.S. Asylum Law." In *Refugee Policy: Canada and the United States*, ed. Howard Adelman, 292–320. Toronto: York Lanes.

Anker, Deborah. 1991. "Determining Asylum Claims in the United States: Executive Summary of an Empirical Study of the Adjudication of Asylum Claims Before the Immigration Court." In*Refugee Policy: Canada and the United States*, ed. Howard Adelman, 268–81. Toronto: York Lanes.

Buchanan, Allen. 1990. "Justice as Reciprocity versus Subject-Centered Justice." *Philosophy and Public Affairs* 19, no. 3: 227–52.

Carens, Joseph. 1992a. "Migration and Morality: A Liberal Egalitarian Perspective." In *Free Movement*, ed. Brian Barry and Robert Goodin, 25–47. London: Harvester Wheatsheaf.

———. 1992b. "Refugees and the Limits of Obligation." *Public Affairs Quarterly* 6, no. 1: 31–44.

———. 1989. "Membership and Morality: Admission to Citizenship in Liberal Democratic States." In *Immigration and the Politics of Citizenship in Europe and North America*, ed. William Rogers Brubaker, 31–49. Lanham, Md.: University Press of America.

———. 1987. "Aliens and Citizens: The Case for Open Borders." *Review of Politics* 49: 251–73.

Hailbronner, Kay. 1986. "Non-Refoulement and 'Humanitarian' Refugees: Customary International Law or Wishful Legal Thinking." *Virginia Journal of International Law* 26, no. 4: 857–96.

Hassner, Pierre. 1994. "La théorie et la pratique des relations internationales devant le probleme des réfugiés." Paper prepared for the Sixteenth World Congress of the International Political Science Association, Berlin, Aug.

Hathaway, James. 1992. "The Conundrum of Refugee Protection in Canada: From Control to Compliance to Collective Deterrence." In *Refugees and the Asylum Dilemma in the West*, ed. Gil Loescher, 71–92. University Park: Pennsylvania State University Press.

———. 1991. "Reconceiving Refugee Law as Human Rights Protection." *Journal of Refugee Studies* 4, no. 2: 113–31.

———. 1990. "A Reconsideration of the Underlying Premise of Refugee Law." *Harvard International Law Journal* 31, no. 1: 129–83.

Helton, Arthur. 1991. "The Detention of Asylum-Seekers in the United States and Canada." In *Refugee Policy: Canada and the United States*, ed. Howard Adelman, 253–67. Toronto: York Lanes.

Hollifield, James. 1994. "The Migration Crisis in Western Europe: The Search for a National Model." Paper prepared for the annual meeting of the American Political Science Association, New York, Sept.

Kanstroom, Daniel. 1993. "Wer Sind Wir Wieder? Laws of Asylum, Immigration, and Citizenship in the Struggle for the Soul of the New Germany." *Yale Journal of International Law* 18: 155–211.

Kant, Immanuel. 1970. "On the Common Saying: This May Be True in Theory, But It Does Not Apply in Practice." In *Kant's Political Writings*, ed. Hans Reiss, ed. 61–92. 1793. Reprint, New York: Cambridge University Press.

Marshall, Barbara. 1992. "German Migration Policies." In *Developments in German Politics*, ed. Gordon Smith, et al. 2d ed., 247–63. Durham, N.C.: Duke University Press.

Martin, David. 1991. "The Refugee Concept: On Definitions, Politics, and the Careful Use of a Scarce Resource." In *Refugee Policy: Canada and the United States*, ed. Howard Adelman, 30–51. Toronto: York Lanes.

_____. 1990. "Reforming Asylum Adjudication: Navigating the Coast of Bohemia." *University of Pennsylvania Law Review* 138, no 5: 1247–1381.

Neuman, Gerald. 1993. "Buffer Zones against Refugees: Dublin, Schengen, and the German Asylum Amendment." *Virginia Journal of International Law* 33: 503–26.

O'Brien, Conor Cruise. 1994. *On the Eve of the Millennium*. Concord, Ontario: Anansi.

Rawls, John. 1971. *A Theory of Justice*. Cambridge: Harvard University Press.

Shacknove, Andrew. 1985. "Who Is a Refugee?" *Ethics* 95: 274–84.

Shue, Henry. 1980. *Basic Rights*. Princeton: Princeton University Press.

Singer, Peter, and Renata Singer. 1988. "The Ethics of Refugee Policy." In *Open Borders? Closed Societies?* ed. Mark Gibney, 111–30. New York: Greenwood.

Stein, Barry. 1990. "Prospects for and Promotion of Voluntary Repatriation." In *Refuge or Asylum*, ed. Howard Adelman and Michael Lanphier, 190–219. Toronto: York Lanes.

Walzer, Michael. 1983. *Spheres of Justice*. New York: Basic.

_____. 1977. *Just and Unjust Wars*. New York: Basic.

Weiner, Myron. 1995. *The Global Migration Crisis*. New York: HarperCollins.

Williams, Bernard. 1985. *Ethics and the Limits of Philosophy*, Cambridge: Harvard University Press.

Zolberg, Aristide. 1993. "Why Not the Whole World? Ethical Dilemmas of Immigration Policy." Paper prepared for the annual meeting of the American Sociological Association, Miami, Aug.

Zolberg, Aristide, Astri Suhrke, and Sergio Aguayo. 1989. *Escape from Violence*. New York: Oxford University Press.

Zucker, Norman, and Naomi Flink Zucker. 1992. "From Immigration to Refugee Redefinition: A History of Refugee and Asylum Policy in the United States." In *Refugees and the Asylum Dilemma in the West*, ed. Gil Loescher, 54–70. University Park: Pennsylvania State University Press.

———. 1991. "The 1980 Refugee Act: A 1990 Perspective." In *Refugee Policy: Canada and the United States*, ed. Howard Adelman, 224–52. Toronto: York Lanes.

Part II

IMMIGRATION ADMISSIONS

Chapter 2

Comprehensive Migration Policy

The Main Elements and Options

Jörg Monar

That governments have policies on all major developments affecting their countries, internal and external, seems to be self-evident. Yet in the area of migration this is far from obvious. If having a policy means pursuing a defined course of action with respect to a set of interrelated public issues, only a few of the industrialized countries can claim to have a policy on migration worthy of the name. Apart from traditional countries of immigration such as Australia, Canada, and the United States, most countries still lack any longer-term strategy for dealing with migration. Instead, they tend to react to the problems arising in this area with ad hoc measures of limited scope that are best described as operations of temporary damage control.

Yet it seems that time is running out for such ad hoc, piece-meal approaches to migration problems. Under the impact of such major factors as increased political instability in many parts of the world, the economic marginalization of many regions in the continuing process of division of labor in the international economic system, population growth, climatic change, and the resulting sharp differences in living and working conditions, international migration has become one of the major political challenges of the end of this century. It is a challenge that not only represents a humanitarian tragedy of unknown dimension

Notes for this chapter begin on page 75.

but also has a growing and potentially destabilizing effect on the economic, political, and social situations of many countries.

Changes are evolving quickly, and even countries used to migration are finding themselves in dramatically changed circumstances. Italy and Spain, for example, have for many decades sent hundreds of thousands of workers to their northern neighbors. Now they have to face increasing immigration pressure, mainly from Africa but also from Eastern Europe. Even countries that have a long tradition of immigration politics must increasingly rethink their policies because the challenge is changing in size or nature. The pressure on the southern border of the United States, the considerable number of asylum seekers entering Canada via the United States, and the considerable number of illegal immigrants in Japan may be mentioned in this respect.

As these examples show, the problems of immigration vary considerably from one country to another. However, the pressure of increasing international migration flows is such that there is a general need for more comprehensive political responses to this major challenge. Any response must take into account such a broad variety of political, economic, social, and cultural aspects that it is impossible to cover them all in the context of this paper. Its aim must be much more modest: focusing on the problems raised by labor-market-based immigration pressure on industrialized countries, it tries to identify the main elements and options of a comprehensive political answer to the challenge of immigration. For systematic reasons, it deals in turn with (1) the main components of a comprehensive migration policy, (2) the main political choices and actors, (3) the institutions to be involved in the formulation of comprehensive migration policy, and (4) the instruments and mechanisms of comprehensive migration policy.

Main Components of a Comprehensive Migration Policy

The term *comprehensive migration policy* needs a clarification. How can a policy be more comprehensive than traditional immigration, refugee, and asylum policies? The answer is that it can and should be more comprehensive in two respects.

First, comprehensive migration policy should address within a single policy framework all the migration issues a country has to face. At this point, many countries still have a tendency to distinguish rather sharply among "immigration policy," "refugee policy," and even "asylum policy." Policy options for each of these areas are frequently developed by different bodies and sets of officials working under different guidelines and priorities. As a result, the obvious links among problems of economic immigration and the admission of various refugee categories are often not sufficiently taken into account, an inflexible categorization is adopted, and measures taken with respect to one category of migrants have undesirable effects in other areas of migration.

Germany provides a well-known example in this respect. Being based on a fairly rigid distinction between (economic) immigrants and political and other refugees, the present German approach to immigration allows working permits to be issued only to foreigners who have lived in Germany for quite a long time and whose conditions of residence are regulated in agreements with their countries of origin. Even those migrants seeking only temporary residence and work in Germany (with the exception of war refugees) are forced to apply for asylum if they want to enter Germany or cease being illegal immigrants. A question of economic immigration is thus transferred to the sphere of asylum policy, where it creates problems that clearly cannot be solved by asylum policy instruments alone. Avoiding these kinds of difficulties would require a single policy that adequately assessed the differences among various categories of migrants but took into account the political, economic, and social links connecting all aspects of migration problems.

The second element of comprehensiveness involves the need not only to try to control and limit the effects of international migration pressure on the receiving country but also to combat its causes in the countries of origin. Traditional immigration policy has consisted almost exclusively of internal measures taken in response to flows of migrants appearing at borders. It is increasingly acknowledged now that at least in a longer-term perspective preventive measures in the international context and in the countries of origin are no less important for a successful answer to the challenge of migration.

Like any efficient policy, migration policy needs to define its objectives in the longer term based on a comprehensive assessment of all major factors and political alternatives. Again, this is not automatic. During recent years, for example, France, Germany, and Italy have often made important decisions on migration policy issues on an ad hoc basis in reaction to strong public feelings, with no consideration of longer-term perspectives.[1] This has led to serious contradictions in policy making, inefficiency, and political irritations. Indeed, the lack of any clear longer-term strategy indicates that none of these countries has an actual migration policy.

Migration policy must result from determined and comprehensive planning that in turn requires a high degree of precise information on migration flows and their causes in the countries of origin. In its communication on immigration and asylum policy to the EC Council and the European Parliament of February 1994, the European Commission rightly emphasized the importance of the availability of comprehensive migration statistics, analyses of migration causes, and prospects for an efficient European migration policy (COM [94] 23 final, III.2.1). It goes without saying that migration policy must also be based on comprehensive information on the economic and social situation of the receiving country (labor market, social structures, culturally motivated and other problems of acceptance, etc.). Integrated use of these various internal and external data seems to be rather well developed in Australia, Canada, and the United States but much less so in many European countries. In Germany, problems of adequate information sometimes result from the federal structure because the level of information on socioeconomic aspects of immigration and their assessment varies from one *Land* to another.

On the basis of sufficient information, migration policy has to establish general political guidelines regarding at least four major components that might be regarded as subpolicies of a comprehensive migration policy.

Prevention Policy

The main task of prevention policy is to influence migration flows outside the territory of the receiving country. It comprises cooperation on migration issues with the countries of origin (including the conclusion of readmission agreements), cooperation with international governmental and nongovernmental organizations, foreign policy measures in favor of international stability, and conflict resolution and economic measures in the areas of development and external trade policy.

Admission Policy

The main tasks of admission policy are to define the various categories of migrants, the principles governing their admission, targets as regards the number of immigrants to be admitted, and criteria for their selection. Here again planning is an essential element. The examples of Australia and Canada show that planning the number of admissions as an essential part of a comprehensive migration policy can be successful. This planning can be either rigid or flexible. Whereas the United States operates with rigid, legally fixed immigration quotas, Australia and Canada revise the number and composition of their immigration admissions on an annual basis (see Wessely 1991, 36–38 and 89–91).

Control Policy

Without effective measures of control even the most sensible admission policy is likely to result in a failure. Although there will normally be a strong restrictive element in control policy, its primary task is not restriction but the management of migration flows in accordance with the guidelines set by the admission policy. This comprises, inter alia, measures to ensure adequate border controls, combat against illegal immigration, and foster the efficient and speedy implementation of the norms and procedures set in the framework of admission policy.

Integration Policy

The main task of integration policy is to create positive economic, social, and cultural conditions for the integration of legally admitted migrants. It involves concrete economic measures such as facilitating access to the labor market as well as wider sociopolitical tasks such as fighting racism and xenophobia.

Main Political Choices and Factors in the Formulation of a Comprehensive Migration Policy

Shaping each of these subpolicies depends on certain basic political choices. Whereas decisions on the admission of economic migrants are normally at the total discretion of governments, decisions on the admission of refugees are not. International norms like those enshrined in the Geneva Convention restrict the margin of choices, and humanitarian considerations can (and should) bear heavily on policy making. Nevertheless, even with respect to the admission of refugees, a receiving country's position regarding immigration in general exerts a strong influence on policy formulation. From a schematic point of view, four basic choices are available: (a) a policy of active encouragement of immigration; (b) a liberal policy; (c) a restrictive policy; and (d) a policy of more or less complete exclusion. Which of these policies or combination thereof a country adopts is determined by at least four major factors.

The Historic Factor: Political and Cultural Traditions

Countries such as Australia, Canada, Israel, New Zealand, and the United States have a historic tradition of immigration. They have grown with and by immigration, immigration has become part of their national identity, and they have acquired considerable experience in dealing with immigration problems. With the exception of Israel, whose immigrants mostly share a Jewish cultural background, traditional immigration countries are used to a high degree of multiculturalism. Some of them have even made multiculturalism a policy, Canada being probably the foremost example.

By contrast, the European nations and Japan have never been countries of immigration; indeed, some of them—Ireland, Italy, and Japan, for instance—have at times been the reverse, i.e., countries of emigration.[3] For all these countries, then, massive immigration is a relatively new challenge that calls into question to a considerable extent their self-identities as monocultural entities with national and ethnic characters developed over centuries in sharp differentiation from those of other nations. They also have comparatively little experience with the admission and integration of migrants, although, thanks to the Common Market, the EU member states are used to a high degree of transborder worker mobility. That mobility, however, only takes place among countries sharing important elements of a common cultural background, and it is to a large extent temporary.

These political and cultural factors strongly influence the general approach to migration problems. Traditional countries of immigration may have changed their migration policies quite considerably over time. Most of them now pursue much more restrictive policies than they did in the last century, having adopted a whole range of restrictive and selective measures. Yet immigration is still regarded as a natural fact of national life, there is an official policy on migration, and certain immigration-linked values of multiculturalism continue to shape cultural self-understanding. Such countries tend to develop longer-term strategies relating to migration and to establish liberal or restrictive rules according to their perceptions of the benefits certain groups of immigrants will bring to the country. This tendency is reflected in the introduction of sophisticated admission criteria and instruments, such as the Canadian "point" system, and the U.S. "preference class" system.

The European countries and Japan, on the other hand, still perceive immigration as a somewhat exceptional phenomenon that they frequently feel is not compatible with their political and cultural identities. Even those countries that, as a result of the large numbers of legal and illegal migrants who have entered their territory (France, Germany, Italy, and the United Kingdom), are already de facto countries of immigration still insist officially that they are not (which, because of a certain deterrent effect, may make sense) and are reluctant to define an official policy on migration problems (which seems much less rational). It is thus much more difficult for them to arrive at clear and consistent positions on central issues of migration policy and to adopt effective measures governing prevention, admission, control, and integration. As a result, the possible benefits of immigration do not yet count very much in their decision-making processes, which remain heavily influenced by an uneasy reluctance to deal with migration problems that leads to half-hearted measures of restriction or exclusion.

The Moral Factor: The Role of Moral Standards and Fundamental Values

In the area of immigration policy, many issues raise central questions of moral standards and fundamental values for policymakers.[4] The most basic of these is probably the question of whether the "national interest" (however it may be defined) should in general prevail over the interests of migrants or whether more fundamental values may justify choices not in line with this interest. But there are also other value questions of major importance, such as whether it is morally acceptable to treat migrants differently on the grounds of skills, nationality, and parentage, as selective admission policies do.

It is true that a whole range of fundamental values is enshrined in constitutions and international conventions. Yet the margins for interpreting the provisions are notoriously broad, their legal consequences are often far from clear, and frequently they easily serve as political instruments rather than absolute standards of policy making. Immigration policymakers have to face their responsibility to make central choices as regards the definition and hierarchy of moral standards. Within the respective democratic context of their particular countries they draw their legitimacy from their fellow citizens and are thus subject to a whole range of values resulting from this democratic mandate. For example, a policymaker's decision to reserve employment possibilities for the unemployed of his or her own country may be such a value. Inevitably some of these so-called democratic values will be in conflict with moral values termed more universal. In the process of finding the necessary compromises, policymakers will always be strongly influenced by their own moral feelings but also by the political culture of their countries, the ideals of its society, and their expectation of finding support (or not) for certain moral positions among their electorates.

The Economic Factor: The Labor Market, Demographic Development, and Financial Aspects

The economic factor is much more tangible than the historic or the moral one. It comprises mainly three criteria of decision making.

The Labor Market

According to classic liberalism one might argue that the labor market by itself will determine the numbers and categories of immigrants by way of employment possibilities and wage levels. Reality is somewhat more complex. Economic immigrants are likely to travel even to countries with high levels of unemployment. Being willing to accept very low wage levels they are likely to distort parts of the existing labor market. As a result, major immigration flows can have a negative impact on natives' wages and employment (Zimmermann 1993, 8–9; Bailey 1986). It has also been argued that in the longer term importing unskilled labor may lead to a loss of competitiveness in the host country because it can slow down the adjustment process of passing from low-quality to high-quality production (Wehrmann 1989). On the other side, immigrants can create new jobs, particularly in the public sector, in small business, and in the services sector (Papademetriou 1994, 676–677; Johnson 1980, 331–41).

Whether the labor market effects are on the whole more positive or more negative is controversial. The answer certainly depends considerably on the structure and flexibility of the market. Yet governments facing considerable migration pressure have in any case to consider the possibility that making legal labor immigration impossible can lead many migrants to seek other ways of entering the country, e.g., by abusing the right of asylum. As economic immigrants they may contribute to the country's welfare; as asylum seekers in the waiting process they normally will not.

Industrialized countries may need to import labor during boom phases. The admission of larger numbers of temporary immigrants seems to be the obvious answer here. Germany made extensive use of this option from the Italo-German agreement of 1955 until the recession following to the first oil crisis of 1973. Yet the German experience has shown that temporarily imported labor tends to become permanent, making it very difficult to export unemployment during recessions (Bhagwati, Schatz, and Wong 1984).

The labor market may make it desirable for a country to attract immigrants with certain skills to compensate for specific labor shortages on the national market. Such a country has the possibility to adopt a highly selective admission policy, combining incentives and restrictions with respect to various categories of migrants (Ritzen and van Dalen 1992). (The Australian "Employer Nomination Scheme," "Tripartite Negotiated Arrangements," and "distinguished talents" category are examples of such a selective approach [Wessely 1991, 98–100.]) The advantages of aiming at importing only certain skills are obvious. Yet the results are likely to be rather limited—high-skilled workers normally have little to gain from migration—and the selective approach can provoke political problems because of its unequal treatment of migrants.

Demographic Development

Most if not all industrialized countries will sooner or later have to face what is commonly called the demographic challenge: the prospect of a dramatically shrinking and aging native population. This process is a particular threat to public budgets and social security systems. It is now frequently argued that a liberal immigration policy could at least partly counterbalance the low birth rates in the native population and produce the income needed to stabilize public budgets and social security systems (Schmid 1994). Yet the demographic challenge is such that full compensation would require a constant and very high number of immigrants. It has been calculated that in the German case 300,000 to 400,000 immigrants would be needed annually (Donges et al. 1994, 38). There can be no doubt that such a constant flow of immigrants would put national, ethnic, and cultural identities under severe strain and cause considerable problems of acceptance. Nevertheless, demographic development may lead more and more governments to more liberal migration policies. Even if full compensation for low birth rates by immigration appears politically impossible, immigration—if perhaps at much lower annual rates—remains one of the most powerful tools for meeting the demographic challenge. Here again traditional immigration countries are likely to be less reluctant to adapt migration policies to their needs than, for example, Japan and most of the European countries will be.

Financial Aspects

Immigration entails important financial consequences. Many immigrants need at least temporary financial help, and public authorities must provide additional services for them, as well as investing in public infrastructure such as schools, roads, and temporary accommodation. On the other hand, most immigrants are likely sooner or later to contribute their part to the national budgets and social security systems. Whether in the longer term the financial balance will be positive or negative is, again, difficult to predict because this depends on many economic and political factors.[5] Yet it seems evident, for instance, that countries with high structural unemployment will certainly take a higher financial risk by adopted a liberal migration policy than will those with more favorable labor market situations.

In addition, any kind of more comprehensive prevention policy entails additional financial consequences. Trying to ameliorate living and working conditions in countries of origin requires considerable public funds. Even if some measures may be financed out of normal development aid budgets, the specific aim of combating the causes of emigration requires measures going beyond the scope of classic development policy. These measures will need supplemental funding, even if they are limited to information campaigns on the real situations in the receiving countries. Contributions to international governmental and nongovernmental organizations working in the field of international migration also have a financial dimension, in terms not only of direct financial contributions but also of national administrative support, national officials' participation in meetings, etc. If one thinks about the controversies on the contribution to the UN budget that have arisen in a number of countries, it becomes clear that in this respect, too, governments will consider their options carefully before committing themselves.

The Social Factor: Acceptance and Integration Capacity

In formulating their policies on migration, governments have to take into account the problems of migrants' social acceptability. What are sometimes euphemistically called "reservations" about foreigners may not only cause occasional attacks against immigrants but strengthen support for political parties and groups demanding extreme anti-immigrant policies. The spectacular growth of support for the racist and nationalist Vlaams Block in Belgian Flanders during the early 1990s was motivated to a considerable extent by its radically negative attitude toward immigration and multicultural influences. Deeply rooted problems of social acceptance can undermine any policy of integration—for instance, by making the housing and schooling of migrants very difficult enterprises.

Because of this, governments need to take into account the factors determining social acceptance. Three of these are of particular importance.

Tensions in the Receiving Society

Tensions in the receiving society resulting from important social and economic changes tend to reduce acceptance of foreigners. The loss of traditional values and group identities creates feelings of insecurity, and reactions to these feelings easily turn against migrants, whose different cultural backgrounds are perceived as a threat.[6] High levels of unemployment resulting from economic adjustment are always likely to foster the threatening perception that migrants take away jobs from the native population. Difficulties in the housing market also frequently lead to hostile reactions against migrants, who are—rightly or wrongly—seen as dangerous competitors for cheap accommodation. Temporary adjustment problems are always likely to result in ideological debates on migration that can bear heavily on policy making (Zimmermann 1993, 35–36).

The Territorial Distribution of Immigrants

The overall numbers of migrants entering a country certainly have a powerful impact on public opinion. The "the boat is full" argument that has been widely used by parts of the press in Germany and the United Kingdom owes a lot of its demagogic potential to the sheer numbers with which it is connected. Yet social acceptance depends much more on the distribution of the overall numbers of migrants within the receiving countries. Segregated concentrations of migrants in certain urban areas almost everywhere cause severe problems of acceptance. The enormous tensions resulting from concentrations of North African migrants in certain quarters of Paris and Marseilles are a prominent example in this arena. Governments have to start from the assumption—and certainly not without reason—that larger numbers of immigrants become socially acceptable only when dispersed. Yet unresolved problems of ethnic grouping and ghettos and previous failures of governmental efforts to prevent migrants from gathering together inevitably influence a government's general policy on migration.[7]

The Integration Capacity of Immigrants

Experience has taught governments that some immigrants are more difficult to integrate into their societies than others. The ethnic-racial origins of migrants frequently determine social acceptance. The Mexican immigrants to the U.S. Southwest and the Puerto Rican immigrants in New York City, for example, are perceived as being different in a way that European or Near Eastern immigrant groups are not (Glazer 1992, 274). Whatever the reasons for reduced social acceptance in a given case—cultural, racial, and/or religious—decision making on migration policy will be influenced by experiences with the integration or assimilation capacities of migrants from different countries of origin.

Institutions to Be Involved in the Formulation of Comprehensive Migration Policy

The involvement of institutions in the formulation of migration policy varies considerably from one country to the next depending on the constitutional framework, political culture, administrative structure, existing laws on migration, and so on. This is not the place to describe the various existing procedures, but I will consider which institutions should be involved in order to secure the coherence and efficiency of comprehensive migration policy.

A first consideration concerns the role of the legislative branch. In most countries, involvement of the legislative is limited to the establishment of framework laws on migration and to debates on general principles when a migration issue has become topical; otherwise, migration policy is largely left to government regulations. This low degree of involvement seems to be less and less adequate. The challenge of migration is such that it is likely not only to cause heated debates in the populations of receiving countries but also to entail long-lasting consequences on their economic, social, cultural, and political development. Any comprehensive migration policy therefore needs a constant democratic legitimation, which can only be ensured by regular and close cooperation of the government with the legislative. Canada provides a positive example in this respect: there, sixty days before the start of each new calendar year, the government is obliged to submit to parliament a report on the number of immigrants it plans to admit, and the government cannot carry out its planning without parliamentary approval (Wessely 1991, 36–38).

It is no less important that there be sufficient possibilities for parliamentary committees to control policy formulation and implementation. A hearing organized by the European Parliament in 1993 revealed that there is a serious lack of parliamentary scrutiny in the fields of immigration and asylum, in particular in Belgium, Ireland, Portugal, and Spain ("European Parliament" 1993).

A second consideration is related to the organization of government authorities. By their very nature, migration issues normally fall within the sphere of competence of several ministries, such as the interior, justice, labor, foreign affairs, and development. This increases inevitably problems of competence and coordination. Because of this, but also in view of the increased public visibility of migration policy, it would make sense for the formulation and implementation of a comprehensive migration policy to be directed and coordinated by a special ministry responsible for migration affairs. The Australian Department of Immigration, established in 1945, which is in charge of planning Australian immigration policy as well as supervising the implementation of most parts of integration policy, is a good example of this (Wessely 1991, 91).

Problems of organization are not limited to the national level. The European Union faces a particular problem in that not only must it struggle with the different immigration laws, policies, and objectives of the fifteen member states but also the competences on migration-related matters are split between the union and the national level. Competence for immigration as such still rests with the member states, who have only undertaken to regard this area as a "matter of common interest" within intergovernmental cooperation under the so-called Third Pillar of the Union Treaty (Art. K.1 TEU). Yet legislation on matters relating to migrant workers within the internal market is a matter of community competence, as is the determination of the third countries whose nationals must be in possession of visas when crossing the external borders of the member states (EC Treaty, Art. 100c). Together with the cumbersome mechanisms of intergovernmental cooperation—requiring the consensus of all fifteen member states for every step taken and favoring the adoption of nonbinding resolutions rather than legally binding texts—this division of competences makes the development of a comprehensive approach to migration problems extremely difficult. Not surprisingly, the results achieved so far have been very meager. As a result, in the report of the Reflection Group preparing the EU intergovernmental conference of 1996, many member states emphasized the need to bring immigration policy, asylum policy, arrangements for aliens, and rules for external border crossings fully under community competence (Council of the European Union, SN 520/95 [Reflex 21], point 49).

A third consideration concerns the involvement of regional and local authorities in the formulation and implementation of migration policy. Migration problems have the most direct impact on local and regional authorities, administratively, socially, and in many cases financially as well. It is on this local level that migration policy with and for the migrants is mainly implemented (Statz 1992, 52–53). In some countries—France, for instance—local authorities have taken important initiatives in the sphere of integration and have become focal points for public debate on migration problems.[8] In Canada, in practice, the provinces play a much greater role in the formulation of national migration policy than could be expected based on the constitutional norms (Wessely 1991, 40–41). In various respects, close involvement of local and regional authorities seems to be a major advantage: they can provide the expertise of direct experience; they can function as early warning agents with respect to particular economic, social, and cultural problems; and they are in any case responsible for ensuring the implementation of important parts of the national migration policy.

The involvement of international governmental and nongovernmental institutions must also be taken into consideration. International institutions like the UN bodies (not only UNHCR), the institutions of the European Union, and the Council of Europe not only provide essential fora for cooperation but also serve both to increase the level of information and to develop long-term prospects. Nongovernmental organizations and their institutions can provide precious help with humanitarian aid and the integration of immigrants but also with assessing migration problems in a longer-term perspective.

A final consideration concerns the role of the courts. In order to secure efficient judicial control in the area of migration policy, the courts' spheres of responsibility must be clearly established. The Australian example of a special independent court (the Immigration Review Tribunal) responsible for administering immigration law is very interesting. Satisfying solutions are far from obvious, however. In the European Union, for instance, there is a continuing debate over judicial control in the area of cooperation in the fields of justice and home affairs that also covers cooperation in the areas of immigration and asylum policy. The central question is whether the European Court of Justice (ECJ) should obtain jurisdiction here or whether judicial control should remain fully within the responsibility of the member states' courts. In the report of the Reflection Group preparing the EU intergovernmental conference of 1996, a majority of the member states have advocated stepping up the role of the ECJ in justice and home affairs in order to ensure the protection of individual rights (Council of the European Union, SN 520/95 [Reflex 21], point 120). There can be no doubt that such a move would considerably improve legal uniformity and certainty in the interpretation of immigrants' rights under community law.

Instruments and Mechanisms of Comprehensive Migration Policy

Looking at the instruments and mechanisms of comprehensive migration policy, it seems useful to return to the four major components of comprehensive migration policy that were described in the first section.

Prevention

The best strategy for preventing labor-market based immigration would obviously be to improve significantly the living and working conditions in countries of origin. Development policy seems to pursue precisely this aim, yet it normally focuses on the development of countries' productivity, competitiveness, educational systems, and general infrastructures, and not precisely on preventing emigration. This last aim requires aid measures targeting those parts of the population most likely to leave the country in search of better living conditions. Approaches might include, for example, creating jobs and fighting poverty, particularly in certain regions or working sectors. Comprehensive migration policy therefore requires more specific targeting of at least some of the funds used for development.

The German program for the "training and short-term employment of workers originating from developing countries or countries of Central and Eastern Europe" is an example of a better-targeted measure, in that it aims at improving the labor market chances of workers in areas already generating growing numbers of actual and potential immigrants (Collinson 1993, 135–36). Yet even such measures will have little success if no new job opportunities are created in countries of origin, something that will require substantial funds.

Trade policy certainly furnishes opportunities to improve economic situations in developing countries (a category that can be extended—for our purposes—to the countries of Central and Eastern Europe). Yet it can do so only if trade liberalization is not offered only on a reciprocal basis, that is, if industrialized countries open their markets widely while developing countries are allowed to maintain protective measures. Yet both the Lomé Convention and the Europe agreements concluded with the countries of Central and Eastern Europe show that industrialized countries are still not prepared to accept the painful adjustments in certain sectors that a rigorous opening of their markets would entail. The Common Agricultural Policy of the European Community is a particularly striking case in point.

In order to reduce the number of refugees, effective contributions to stability and conflict resolution in regions affected by wars or internal unrest are essential. Diplomatic means can be successful, but one must concede that frequently they are almost totally ineffective. The use of military means in the framework of peacekeeping or peace making operations may also be considered, but this is always a costly alternative, in terms of both money and the potential loss of lives. The aim of reducing migration pressure is in any case unlikely to rank very high when it comes to deciding on military action. Sending people to die in foreign countries in order to reduce migration pressure would certainly not be a very convincing political argument for the electorate. The example of the UN intervention in Somalia has also shown that the effects of such operations can be close to zero anyway.[9]

Creating the necessary conditions for returning refugees and economic migrants is an essential part of any prevention strategy. Returning refugees on a larger scale requires a whole set of political, economic, and perhaps even protective military measures. If the right conditions are not created before refugees are returned, new unrest and a new wave of migration will almost certainly follow (Ogata 1993, 121–24).

Return migration of economic migrants may be fostered by financial incentives for potential remigrants. Yet this is an expensive option, and success on a larger scale is far from certain. A French return migration program of 1977 largely failed, and a German program introduced six years later had only limited results, even though the financial incentives offered were three times as high (Körner 1986, 65–72; in general, see Zimmermann 1993, 21–22).

Readmission agreements can commit countries of origin to readmitting certain categories of migrants if this is requested by the receiving country. Yet such agreements are normally limited to illegal immigrants and rejected asylum seekers, their negotiation can be difficult, and they must usually be linked with economic or political concessions to the country of origin.

Another element of a comprehensive prevention policy is cooperation with other receiving countries (most likely those in the immediate neighborhood) regarding the harmonization of immigration and asylum procedures. Progress in this area can prevent migrants from concentrating on the country with the best procedural guarantees, a phenomenon that can eventually lead the country—Germany is a good example in this respect—to reduce its guarantees, thereby causing a de facto harmonization on the lowest level. As the experience of the European Union shows, however, harmonization of procedures is particularly difficult because of the different political priorities, legal systems, and traditions of receiving countries. After almost a decade of efforts in this direction, the member states of the European Union are still far away from effective harmonization (Nanz 1994; Hailbronner 1995).

Admission

All the industrialized countries are by now pursuing restrictive migration policies. Some of the European countries (France, for instance) followed a rather liberal policy in the 1950s and 1960s but adopted an overall restrictive approach in the 1970s after the first oil crisis. Germany followed its active recruitment policy of foreign workers only until the early 1970s. The United Kingdom has maintained a relatively liberal policy only in respect to people from the Commonwealth (Howard 1993).

To pursue a restrictive migration policy means to limit the inflow of people. This can be done by establishing criteria for admission, defining the duration of stay, or imposing overall ceilings (quotas). In most cases, these instruments are used in combination.

Admission Criteria

Admission criteria allow receiving countries to structure the composition of the overall inflow of migrants. There is a broad variety of possible criteria, family links, ethnic or regional differences, specific skills, educational levels, and—in the case of refugees and asylum seekers—humanitarian considerations being among the most important. Traditional immigration countries have developed complex sets of criteria. Australia, for instance, applies a system that combines family criteria ("preferential" or "concessional," i.e., conditional, depending on the category of relatives), skill criteria (business migration, employer nominations, independent qualified workers, and special talents), and humanitarian criteria (refugees and politically persecuted people) (Wessely 1991, 89–107). In both Australia and Canada educational skills (general, specific, and language) play an important role in most selection procedures because they have the double advantage of ensuring a higher degree of productivity among immigrants and reducing the receiving country's educational costs (Steineck 1994, 179). The United States has put greater emphasis on family reunification and humanitarian considerations, although there are also skill criteria for independent migrants (Keely 1993, 60–84); it also grants a limited number of visas by lottery (50,000 in 1995), which also functions as a kind of admission criterion. Criteria in most European countries focus on family reunification and humanitarian considerations, with skill criteria playing only a minor role until now. Switzerland is unique in that it restricts migration generally to people coming from the European Union, the European Free Trade Area (EFTA), and former Yugoslavia (Hoffmann-Nowotny and Killias 1993).

Duration of Stay

The duration of stay is regulated by visas, which may be combined with work and residence permits. Temporary visas allow the temporary import of labor, to meet seasonal or other short-term needs (with "short term" being defined as several months or even years). Through the possibility of renewal temporary visas are a particularly flexible instrument for controlling temporary and selective labor immigration. Switzerland operates a highly efficient although not uncontroversial system of admission on the basis of temporary, rotation-based work and residence permits (Hoffmann-Nowotny and Killias 1993).

Quotas

Quota systems permit the imposition of ceilings on the numbers of overall migrants, as well on the numbers of migrants falling into certain categories, as defined by selection criteria. Migration policy planning in Canada, for example, is based on annual overall quotas that are divided into subquotas for the major categories (family class, refugees, independent immigrants, assisted relatives, business relatives, retirees) (Wessely 1991, 36–39). Comprehensive quota systems are also used in Australia and the United States. In Europe, however, they are rather unusual, although, the Swiss system of temporary work and residence permits is based on fixed annual quotas.

Quota systems are certainly one of the most important instruments for executing admission policies. Yet their effectiveness depends to a high degree on the political will not only to establish them but to implement them effectively. The latter task is often very difficult because political pressure groups tend to disagree more or less strongly on quotas, so governments frequently find themselves under considerable pressure to let in more or fewer migrants belonging to certain categories than was originally established. Quotas for refugees are obviously difficult to maintain in the face of sudden major refugee flows caused by military conflicts or internal disorder.

Control

Any form of restrictive migration policy creates a potential for illegal immigration. If admission criteria, visas, and quotas are not combined with efficient mechanisms of control any restrictive policy is likely to fail more or less completely. More efficient border controls are obviously of central importance, but the high number of illegal entries at the U.S.-Mexican border and across the eastern border of Germany show the extreme difficulties of this task. In addition, the costs for more effective systems of control can become intolerably high. Readmission agreements, transport prohibitions, and the establishment of carrier responsibility seem to be more cost-effective instruments, but they cannot resolve the problem of illegal border crossings (Gusy 1994, 149–52).

Even more difficult to tackle than illegal entry is the problem of people entering legally but staying on illegally. Tighter checks during stays of visitors, employer sanctions, and legislative measures increasing the differentiation between legal entry and immigration appear to be the most promising instruments for combating this problem.[10]

Integration

Without question, integration policy must go beyond initial financial support and housing, linguistic training, and schooling measures for legal immigrants. Ethnic grouping and ghettos must be prevented, better information must be supplied to the native population about immigrants and their social and cultural contexts is necessary, and migration policy must be combined with an active policy against racism and xenophobia. Of particular importance is the removal of the legal uncertainties that can plague immigrants (regarding their work and residence permits or the prospects for family reunification, for instance). Immigrants will always be more willing to integrate themselves fully if the guidelines governing their futures are clear-cut and reliable.[11] Here again, agreements concluded with countries of origin can play an important role. Association and cooperation agreements and the so-called Lomé Conventions ("Fourth ACP-EEC Convention" 1989) concluded between the European Union and third countries contain provisions on migration-related matters that are seen as major steps toward the gradual extension of equal treatment to migrant workers from third countries.

Clearly, however, there are limits to what central government authorities can do. The success of any integration policy also depends on close cooperation between national government authorities and the local authorities and private aid organizations that are in a much better position to assess problems of integration on the spot and to develop adequate instruments and mechanisms for dealing with them. In this sense, integration policy also depends heavily on an adequate application of subsidiarity.

Conclusion

There is certainly no universal design for a successful comprehensive migration policy. The challenge of migration takes too many different forms, and different national priorities, traditions, and economic and social situations inevitably require different policies. Yet when looking at the many elements and options of comprehensive migration policy, one can discern at least six basic conditions for success:

1. A high level of information on migration flows and regular assessments of their consequences
2. The definition of an overall approach and strategy covering all aspects of migration, from prevention over admission and control to integration
3. Longer-term planning
4. Effective coordination, both political and administrative, and a consistent combination of instruments and mechanisms of prevention, admission control, and integration

5. The involvement of a broad set of relevant institutions below and apart from the national government level (regional, communal, NGOs) in policy formulation and implementation

6. Comprehensive international cooperation with third countries (both countries of origin and other receiving countries) and relevant international organizations

To create all these conditions for success is admittedly a huge task for any government, but the consequences of failing to respond effectively to today's challenge of migration will be much greater.

Notes

1. See the critical assessment of French immigration policy in Weil 1994, 719–29. On the Italian case, see Cammarat and Todino 1995, 207–15.

3. The case of the *Aussiedler* (from East European countries) and *Übersiedler* (from the GDR) did not give Germany much additional experience with international migration flows because the migrants were all ethnic Germans.

4. Stephen Legomsky very appropriately calls these the "overarching philosophical issues" of immigration policymaking (1993, 322–23).

5. For the United States, Papademetriou comes to a rather positive assessment (1994, 672–73), whereas Donges et al. think that in Germany the overall financial consequences will be negative (1994, 26–28).

6. For a comprehensive study of this process, see Treibel 1990.

7. For the French case, see de Rudder 1992, 248–50 and 257–60.

8. The important role of local authorities in France is described in Body-Gendrot and Schain 1992, 416–21.

9. On the British case, see Howard 1993.

10. On the many problems immigration control has to face, see Chiswick 1988.

11. This point is underlined—correctly—in European Commission, COM [94] 23 final, III.2.1, points 124 and 126.

References

Bailey, T. 1986. *Immigrant and Native Workers: Contrasts and Competition.* Boulder: Westview.

Bhagwati, J., K. W. Schatz, and K. Wong. 1984. "The West German Gastarbeiter System of Immigration." *European Economic Review* 26: 277–94.

Body-Gendrot, S., and M. A. Schain. 1992. "National and Local Politics and the Development of Immigration Policy in the United States and France: A Comparative Analysis." In *Immigrants in Two Democracies: French and American Experience*, ed. D. L. Horowitz and G. Noiriel, 411–38. New York: New York University Press.

Cammarata, A., and M. Todino. 1995. "The Italian Experience of Immigration Policy: Making Up for Emergency." In *Towards a European Immigration Policy*, ed. G. D. Korella and P. M. Twomey, 207–15. Brussels: European Interuniversity Press.

Chiswick, B. R. 1988. "Illegal Immigration and Immigration Control." *Journal of Economic Perspectives* 3: 101–16.

Collinson, S. 1993. *Europe and International Migration.* London: Pinter.

Donges, J. B., W. Engels, W. Hamm, W. Möschel, M. Neumann, and O. Sievert. 1994. *Einwanderungspolitik—Möglichkeiten und Grenzen.* Frankfurt: Frankfurter Institut.

"European Parliament: Cooperation among Member States in the Fields of Justice and Home Affairs." 1993. Working paper W-4. Luxembourg.

"Fourth ACP-EEC Convention (Concluded for Ten Years)." 1989. *International Legal Materials* 29 (15 Dec.).

Glazer, N. 1992. "The New Immigration in the American City." In *Immigrants in Two Democracies: French and American Experience*, ed. D. L. Horowitz and G. Noiriel, 268–91. New York: New York University Press.

Gusy, C. 1994. "Möglichkeiten und Grenzen eines effektiven und flexiblen europäischen Einwanderungsrechts." In *Das europäische Einwanderungskonzept*, ed. W. Weidenfeld. Gütersloh: Bertelsmann.

Hailbronner, K. 1995. "Migration Law and Policy within the Third Pillar of the Union Treaty." In *Justice and Home Affairs in the European Union*, ed. R. Bieber and J. Monar, 95–126. Brussels: European Interuniversity Press.

Hoffmann-Nowotny, H. J., and M. Killias. 1993. "Switzerland: Remaining Swiss." In *The Politics of Migration Policies*, ed. D. Kubat, 231–46. New York: Center for Migration Studies.

Howard, C. 1993. "United Kingdom II: Immigration and the Law." In *The Politics of Migration Policies*, ed. D. Kubat, 108–24. New York: Center for Migration Studies.

Johnson, G. E. 1980. "The Labour Market Effects of Immigration." *Industrial and Labour Relations Review* (Apr.): 331–41.

Keely, C. B. 1993. "The United States of America: Retaining a Fair Immigration Policy." In *The Politics of Migration Policies*, ed. D. Kubat, 60–84. New York: Center for Migration Studies.

Körner, H. 1986. "Das Gesetz zur Förderung der Rückkehrbereitschaft von Ausländern vom 28. November 1983: Eine kritische Bilanz." In *Die "Neue" Ausländerpolitik in Europa: Erfahrungen in den Aufnahme- und Entsendeländern*, ed. H. Körner and U. Mehrländer, 65–72. Bonn: Neue Gesellschaft.

Legomsky, S. 1993. "Immigration, Equality, and Diversity." *Columbia Journal of Transnational Law* 31, no. 2: 322–23.

Nanz, K.-P. 1994. "The Harmonization of Asylum and Immigration Legislation within the Third Pillar of the Union Treaty." In *The Third Pillar of the European Union*, ed. J. Monar and R. Morgan, 123–33. Brussels: European Interuniversity Press.

Ogata, S. 1993. "Strategie für eine umfassende Flüchtlingspolitik." In *Fluchtziel Europa*, ed. L. Drüke and K. Weigelt. Bonn: Moderne Industrie.

Papademetriou. D. G. 1994. "Les effets des migrations internationales sur les pays d'accueil, les pays d'origine et les immigrants." *Politique étrangère* 4: 676–77.

Ritzen, J. M., and H. P. van Dalen. 1992. "The Economic Consequences of Selective Immigration Policies." In *Migration and Economic Development*, ed. K. F. Zimmermann, pp. 231–64. Berlin: Springer.

de Rudder, V. 1992. "Immigrant Housing and Integration in French Cities." In *Immigrants in Two Democracies: French and American Experience*, ed. D. L. Horowitz and G. Noiriel, 247–67. New York: New York University Press.

Schmid, J. 1994. "Zuwanderung aus Eigennutz? Der demographische Aspekt des Einwanderungsbedarfs in den EU-Mitgliedstaaten." In *Das europäische Einwanderungskonzept*, ed. W. Weidenfeld, 89–124. Gütersloh: Bertelsmann.

Statz, A. 1992. "Migration als Brücke." Institut für Internationale Politik. Arbeitspapier No. 16. Wuppertal.

Steineck, A. 1994. "Soll die Europäische Union Einwanderer aus Drittstaaten nach Bildungsmerkmalen auswählen?" *Zeitschrift für Ausländerrecht und Ausländerpolitik* 4.

Treibel, A. 1990. Migration in modernen Gesellschaften in *Soziale Folgen von Einwanderung und Gastarbeit*. Weinheim: Juventa.

Wehrmann, M. 1989. *Auswirkungen der Ausländerbeschäftigung auf die Volkswirtschaft der Bundesrepublik Deutschland in Vergangenheit und Zukunft.* Baden-Baden: Nomos.

Weil, Patrick. 1994. "La politique de la France." *Politique étrangère* 4: 719–29.

Wessely, T. W. 1991. "Einwanderungsrecht im internationalen Vergleich: Kanada, Australien und die USA." Working paper. Königswinter: Friedrich-Naumann-Stiftung.

Zimmermann, K. F. 1993. "Immigration Policies in Europe." *Münchener Wirtschaftswissenschaftliche Beiträge.*

Chapter 3

The Family and Immigration
A Roadmap for the Ruritanian Lawmaker

*Hiroshi Motomura**

Introduction

In the immigration debate now raging in Congress, one of the most important questions is how family ties should be taken into account. Of course, family reunification principles significantly affect who comes to the United States. But more is at stake. Our treatment of family ties reflects many fundamental assumptions underlying immigration and citizenship laws, especially assumptions about the integration of new immigrants into U.S. society. Difficult problems arise if family-based admissions and these fundamental assumptions are inconsistent.

This essay analyzes the role of the family in immigration law and policy by drawing lessons from recent U.S. American and German experience and applying them to an imaginary, newly formed country, which I call Ruritania.[1]

If Ruritania were to consider whether and how to base its immigration law and policy on family ties, it would need to consider at least ten basic questions: Which family relationships will count? Will the number of family-based immigrants be limited? What delays in family-based immigration will be considered unacceptable, and what remedies will be adopted? In sponsoring immediate relatives, will citizens be preferred over resident

---

Notes for this chapter begin on page 113.

aliens? Will different perspectives on the "family" be accommodated? What will be the procedures for deciding eligibility? Will
family ties affect the application of exclusion or expulsion
grounds? What share of total legal immigration will be family
based? How will family-based immigration affect the ethnic composition of Ruritanian society? How will family-based immigration affect the integration of immigrants into Ruritanian society?

My goal is not to provide an exhaustive treatment of each of
these ten questions.[2] Rather, I hope to fill a significant gap in the
literature by exploring the broader implications of the role of
family in immigration law and policy.

Which Family Relationships Will Count?

In answering this question, Ruritania can look to the United
States and Germany as models.

United States

Under U.S. immigration law, the most favored family members
are "immediate relatives," which the Immigration and Nationality Act (INA)[3] defines as "the children, spouses, and parents of
a citizen of the United States, except that, in the case of parents,
such citizens shall be at least 21 years of age" (INA § 201 [b] [2]
[A]). "Child" means an unmarried person under twenty-one
years of age who qualifies as a legitimate child, stepchild, or
adopted child or, in some cases, as an illegitimate child or an
adopted child qualifying as an "orphan" (see INA § 101 [b] [1]).

The United States also recognizes four categories (known as
"preferences') of family-based immigrants who are not "immediate relatives" (see INA § 203 [a]). The first family preference
includes unmarried sons and daughters of United States citizens. (The "sons and daughters" category includes offspring
who would be "children" but for their age or marital status.)
The second preference includes spouses and unmarried sons and
daughters of permanent resident aliens. The third preference
includes married sons and daughters of citizens. The fourth
preference includes brothers and sisters of citizens, if the citizens are at least twenty-one years of age. Finally, there is a cat-

egory for spouses and children of aliens who became permanent residents under the legalization provisions of the Immigration Reform and Control Act of 1986 (IRCA) (Pub.L. 101-649).

These categories are presently the subject of much debate in Congress. In June 1995 the Commission on Immigration Reform, chaired by former congresswoman Barbara Jordan, released its interim recommendations on "legal immigration reform." The commission proposed, among other things, that the first, third, and fourth family preferences (for the adult sons and daughters and siblings of citizens) be eliminated and that the second preference be limited to spouses and minor children of permanent residents.[4] A major legislative proposal by Congressman Lamar Smith (R-Tex.), chairman of the House Subcommittee on Immigration and Claims, would similarly eliminate the first, third, and fourth family preferences and would also restrict the second preference to minor children of permanent residents (H.R. 2202).

In addition to these family-based immigration categories, a key instrument of family unity is INA § 203 (d), which confers derivative immigration status on the spouse and children of each family preference immigrant. INA § 203 (d) allows a spouse or child to "accompany" or "follow to join" the principal alien; there is no time limit for "following to join."[5] INA § 203 (d) applies not only to the family preferences but also to several other major groups of legal immigrants: the five employment-based preferences for skilled and unskilled workers and investors (see INA § 203 [b]) and the "diversity" category, which allocates additional visas by lottery to natives of countries with low rates of recent immigration to the United States (see INA § 203 [c]). There are similar derivative status provisions for refugees and asylees (see INA § 207 [c] [2], 208 [c]).

Germany

Germany "is neither to be nor to become a country of immigration" *(Einwanderungsland)*, at least according to official government policy (Federal Ministry 1993, 4). In spite of this self-description, there has been a significant amount of immigration into Germany in the past several decades. Much of the flow is authorized by the Aliens Act *(Ausländergesetz)*, which allows certain family members to join relatives already residing in Germany (see AuslG §§ 17–27).

Under AuslG § 23, alien spouses and unmarried minor children of German citizens residing in Germany are entitled to a residence permit *(Aufenthaltserlaubnis)*. The same provision provides residence permits to alien parents who care for an unmarried minor German citizen child residing in Germany.

Other family reunification cases involve resident aliens rather than German citizens. Many of these residents (or their parents) first came to Germany under "guest worker" *(Gastarbeiter)* agreements between their native countries and Germany. Designed to alleviate labor shortages in Germany, these agreements began with a 1955 agreement with Italy that was soon followed by similar agreements with Spain (1960), Greece (1960), Turkey (1961), Morocco (1963), Portugal (1964), Tunisia (1965), and Yugoslavia (1968). By the time this recruitment ended in November 1973, the number of alien workers in Germany had risen from 80,000 in 1955 to approximately 2.6 million, or 11.9 percent of the entire German workforce (Federal Ministry 1993, 8).

While some of these first-generation guest workers brought their families with them, still more sent for their families later. Ironically, the end of recruitment in 1973 spurred a large influx of family-based immigration because alien workers in Germany realized that movement in and out of the country was soon to become more difficult. Once reunited in Germany, these *Gastarbeiter* families settled there and had children who have had little or no contact with their parents' native land (Federal Ministry 1993, 8).

These labor policies resulted in a sizable resident alien population. According to official figures, the percentage of aliens in Germany was 8.0 percent (6.49 million) as of 31 December 1992 (Federal Ministry 1993, 12). Aliens are even more concentrated in urban areas; for example, they constitute over 20 percent of the population in Frankfurt and Offenbach and account for only a slightly lower percentage in Munich and Stuttgart. It is official German policy to integrate these "aliens living legally in our country, particularly recruited foreign workers and their families," even while the government restricts further immigration from outside the European community (Federal Ministry 1993, 4; Bade 1994, 38–52).

German citizenship law generally relies on jus sanguinis principles, which confer citizenship based on descent regardless of the
place of birth. Children born in Germany to resident aliens do not
acquire German citizenship at birth because their parents are not
German. They can become German citizens only through naturalization (see Citizenship Act [Reichs- und Staatsangehörig-
keitsgesetz] §§ 4, 8). Relatively few have done so. An alien child
born in Germany can acquire legal resident status under a predominantly matrilineal system: If the child's mother has a residence permit *(Aufenthaltserlaubnis)* or right of unlimited
residence *(Aufenthaltsberechtigung),* the child automatically
receives a residence permit *(Aufenthaltserlaubnis)* (see AuslG § 21
[1]). If the child's mother has a temporary residence permit
(Aufenthaltsbewilligung, or "residence title for specific purposes";
see AuslG § 28), the child receives the same permit (see AuslG §
29 [2]). Likewise, if his or her mother has an *Aufenthaltsbefugnis*
("residence title for exceptional circumstances")—for aliens
allowed to stay in Germany for pressing humanitarian reasons
related to international law or for political reasons (see AuslG §
30)—he or she receives the same permit (see AuslG § 31 [2]).

Many family reunification cases in Germany involve people
who wish to travel to Germany to join "first-generation" aliens.
Other cases involve "second-generation" aliens in Germany, a
group that includes both those born in Germany and those who
immigrated to Germany as minors. (Note that U.S. citizenship
law relies primarily on jus soli principles, which confer citizenship based on birth within the national territory. As a result,
those born in the United States to immigrant parents are U.S.
citizens by birth, while those who immigrate to the United
States as minors are not; see U.S. Const., Am. XIV, § 1).

All resident aliens who wish to have family members join
them in Germany must usually satisfy three general requirements: (1) a residence permit *(Aufenthaltserlaubnis)* or right of
unlimited residence *(Aufenthaltsberechtigung),* (2) sufficient living space, and (3) means of financial support (AuslG § 17 [2]).[6]
Once these basic requirements are fulfilled, residency is by right
in some cases. For example, the spouse of a first-generation alien
is guaranteed entry if the first-generation alien has a right of
unlimited residence *(Aufenthaltsberechtigung).* In addition, the
spouse of a first-generation alien who has a residence permit

(Aufenthaltserlaubnis) is guaranteed entry, but only if the marriage predates the first-generation alien's arrival in Germany. Residency is also by right for the spouse of a second-generation alien who has legally resided in Germany for eight years and has an indefinite residence permit *(Aufenthaltserlaubnis)* or a right of unlimited residence *(Aufenthaltsberechtigung)* (see, e.g., AuslG § 18 [1]).[7] A third group with a right to residency comprises unmarried children under sixteen who are joining both parents (see AuslG § 20 [2]). Administrative discretion rules in other cases, including those of children under sixteen who are joining only one parent (see AuslG § 20 [3]), unmarried minor children who are sixteen or older (see AuslG § 20 [4]), and any other relatives where admission is necessary to avoid extraordinary hardship (see AuslG § 22).

How Are Qualifying Relatives Defined?

In both U.S. and German law, eligibility to immigrate based on family ties depends not only on the relationship between the parties but also on the alien's age and marital status. Younger and unmarried children are given preference because they more clearly belong to the same family unit as their parents. In Germany, there has been serious discussion of reducing the maximum age of a child recognized for family reunification purposes; some have proposed lowering it to six.

In the United States, age plays an additional role: citizens must be twenty-one years old before they may petition for a parent to be allowed to join them. This age requirement is attributable to jus soli citizenship law. Without a minimum age, an undocumented alien could cross the border, give birth in the United States, and immediately have the newborn citizen child file a petition for his or her parents to immigrate.

Are Family-based Criteria Constitutionally Limited?

The lawmaker's rules for family-based immigration may be constrained by constitutional or other superlegislative norms. For example, would the lawmaker violate the Ruritanian Constitution by adopting family reunification categories that favor women over men or legitimate over illegitimate children?

Some U.S. Supreme Court decisions outside the immigration law context suggest that there is a constitutional interest in family reunification. Prominent in this respect is *Moore v. City of East Cleveland* (431 U.S. 494 [1977]), which struck down a zoning ordinance that prohibited a homeowner and one of her grandsons from living in her house at the same time. According the Court, this ordinance was unconstitutional because it interfered excessively with the integrity of the family unit. Another important case is *Stanley v. Illinois* (405 U.S. 645 [1972]), which struck down an Illinois statute under which the children of unwed fathers became wards of the state on the death of the mother. In so holding, the Supreme Court recognized a father's constitutional interest in the custody of his illegitimate child.

The next question is whether any such constitutional interest constrains the government's power to limit family-based immigration. The answer may be no. In the United States, courts are likely to rule that *Moore* and similar precedents are trumped by the plenary power doctrine, which generally precludes constitutional judicial review in immigration cases, especially those that challenge substantive admission rules.[8] A leading example of the plenary power doctrine in a family reunification context is the Court's 1977 decision in *Fiallo v. Bell* (430 U.S. 787 [1977]). *Fiallo* summarily rejected a constitutional challenge to the INA's definition of "child," which at that time recognized an illegitimate child's mother but not his or her father for immigration purposes.[9] Whatever the basis for family unity in U.S. constitutional law generally, the concept has lent only weak support to constitutional challenges to the admission categories and numerical limits established by Congress.[10] The underlying assumption in the United States seems to be that constitutional rights apply only after anterior questions of membership (i.e., of immigration) are resolved.

Germany provides a different model for constitutional limits on family reunification rules. The express purpose of reunification under AuslG § 17 is to foster protection of the family under sections 1 and 2 of Basic Law, Article 6, which provide that "(1) Marriage and family shall enjoy the special protection of the state. (2) The care and upbringing of children are a natural right of, and a duty primarily incumbent on, the parents. ..."

The German Federal Constitutional Court has applied these general constitutional provisions in immigration cases. It has not excluded immigration cases from its general constitutional analysis, and in fact it appears to pay serious attention when immigration decisions come under constitutional challenge. In 1987, for example, the court found that Article 6 applies to family relationships between aliens already residing in Germany and aliens seeking to reside in Germany (judgment of 12 May 1987, 76 *BVerfGE* 1 [2d Sen. 1987], discussed in Neuman 1990, 57–63).[11] While the court declined to find an absolute right to enter the country to join relatives, it held that any government regulation of entry must meet the general constitutional requirement of "proportionality," i.e., the need for regulation must be balanced against the impairment of family unity as protected by Article 6.

The provisions in question—which have since been repealed—allowed a second-generation resident alien to bring in a spouse only if the resident alien met three requirements: being at least eighteen years old, having resided continuously in Germany for at least eight years, and having been married for a certain length of time. The court struck down the version of the rule that was then in effect in the state *(Land)* of Baden-Württemberg, which required the marriage to have been in existence for at least three years before the spouse could immigrate. In the same decision, the court once again applied the same proportionality analysis and upheld the one-year spousal waiting periods that were required in the rest of Germany.

Beyond the realm of domestic constitutional constraints, the Ruritanian lawmaker also must consider the possibility of transnational or supranational constraints. A number of laws specific to the European Community and some bilateral and multilateral treaties also address family unity issues. For example, Article 8 of the European Convention for the Protection of Human Rights and Fundamental Freedoms provides:

1. Everyone has the right to respect for his private and family life, his home, and his correspondence.
2. There shall be no interference by a public authority with the exercise of this right except such as is in accordance with the law and is necessary in a democratic society in the interests of national security, public safety, or the economic well-being of the country, for the prevention of

disorder or crime, for the protection of health or morals, or for the protection of the rights and freedoms of others.

This language does not establish an absolute right to family reunification. For example, the European Court of Human Rights has held that the United Kingdom did not violate Article 8 by barring foreign husbands from joining spouses who were permanently settled in its territory.[12]

Article 16 of the Universal Declaration of Human Rights of 1948 recognizes a right to "found a family" and further provides that "the family is the natural and fundamental group unit of society and is entitled to protection by society and the State" (10 Dec. 1948, art. 16, G.A. Res. 217A [III], at 71, U.N. Doc. A/810 [1948]). The same language appears in Article 23 of the International Covenant on Civil and Political Rights (G.A. Res. 2200, U.N. GAOR, 21st Sess., Supp. No. 16, at 168, U.N. Doc. A/6316 [1967]), which the United States ratified with reservations, including a declaration that the covenant is not self-executing (see *Cong. Rec* 138 (1992): S4783).[13]

Will the Number of Family-based Immigrants Be Limited?

Ruritania must also decide whether to place numerical limits on family-based immigration (or any immigration for that matter). Numerical limits have obvious practical significance: they typically lead to waiting periods, and these backlogs should prompt the Ruritanian lawmaker to reexamine which family relationships should count. At a more fundamental level, the decision whether to adopt numerical limits is a very telling feature of any country's immigration policy, because it reflects basic attitudes toward immigration.

Germany does not numerically limit family immigration, even though it has established family reunification categories that are more restrictive than those in the United States; instead, its control of immigration is qualitative. This absence of quantitative control is consistent with Germany's "not an *Einwanderungsland*" self-image. As a country that is not a "country of immigration," immigration is an extraordinary phenomenon rather than an ordinary flow that must be regulated through numerical limits.

In this regard, the German law permitting immigration by ethnic Germans *(Aussiedler)* from Eastern Europe and parts of the former Soviet Union provides an interesting contrast to the rest of German immigration law. The influx of ethnic Germans represents the one immigrant flow that is not regarded as extraordinary, at least in that this group is both sizable and officially expected to achieve full political and cultural integration. Unsurprisingly, then, ethnic Germans make up the only group for which German law numerically limits admissions (Basic Law, Art. 116 [1]; Bade 1994, 148–49, 165–66; Kanstroom 1993, 155, 164–67).[14]

Whereas aliens may enter Germany as soon as their eligibility is established, all immigrants to the United States except "immediate relatives" are subject to numerical limits. Table 3.1 shows immediate relative admissions to the United States in Fiscal Year 1993.

Table 3.1 United States: Immediate Relative Admissions, FY 1993

Spouses	145,843
Parents	62,428
Children	46,788
Total	255,059

Source: INS 1993, 17 (table B).

Subject to exceptions and adjustments that are too detailed to cover here, the family preferences are limited to a combined 226,000 admissions annually. Table 3.2 shows allotments and admissions in FY 1993:

Table 3.2 United States: Family Preference Admissions, FY 1993

	Category Allotment[15]	Admissions
1st preference	23,400	12,819
2d preference	114,200	128,308
3d preference	23,400	23,385
4th preference	65,000	62,264
Total	226,000	226,776

Source: INS 1993, 17 (table B).

Just as the near absence of numerical limits in Germany reflects its self-image, U.S. limits reflect a recognition that family reunification is an ordinary part of an immigrant flow that is itself ordinary. (In contrast to family-based immigration, the absence of numerical limits on asylum in the United States reflects the view that asylum constitutes extraordinary relief for extraordinary cases.) These contrasting self-images help to explain why U.S. law sets up broader family reunification categories than those in German law and then employs quantitative controls in addition to qualitative ones in order to limit and shape the immigrant population.

What Delays in Family-based Immigration Will Be Considered Unacceptable, and What Remedies Will Be Adopted?

If Ruritania numerically limits family-based immigration, it may find that demand exceeds supply, resulting in long delays. This has been the recent U.S. experience; as of January 1993, 3.2 million aliens worldwide were waiting for family preference visas (U.S. Dept. of State 1993).

Setting different limits for different family-based categories will cause variations in waiting times. In November 1995 first preference visas for immigration to the United States were available immediately. In contrast, permanent residents' spouses and unmarried minor children who received second preference visas in November 1995 had been waiting since July 1992. Permanent residents' unmarried adult sons and daughters who received second preference visas had been waiting since June 1990. Those who received third preference visas had been waiting since April 1993, and those who received fourth preference visas had been waiting since September 1985 (U.S. Dept. of State 1995). Steadily growing demand makes it likely that much longer waits will confront those who apply now.

Waits may be even longer if Ruritania, like the United States, limits immigration from any single country. Natives of countries where demand exceeds the per-country limit of about twenty-five thousand annually will face longer waits before entering the United States than will similarly situated applicants from other countries. For example, Filipino fourth preference immigrants who received their visas in November 1995 had been waiting since September 1977 (U.S. Dept. of State 1995).

Ruritania may consider whether to reduce these backlogs. One argument against doing so is that family-based immigration is self-multiplying through a "chain migration" process. Chain migration occurs when each immigrant petitions for his or her qualifying relatives, each of whom petitions for their relatives in turn. In the United States, this pattern is associated most often with sibling immigration, for the simple reason that U.S. citizens and permanent residents who wish to sponsor new immigrants typically have multiple siblings.

Studies suggest that considerable chain migration occurs and that it has played a key role in the dramatic shift toward Asian and Latin American immigration.[16] These studies also suggest, however, that chain migration has not led to a Malthusian geometric explosion in immigration. First, citizens can sponsor relatives far more easily than permanent residents can. For example, citizens can sponsor siblings, but permanent residents cannot. As a result, new immigrants must first naturalize for chain migration levels to rise. Second, not all qualified entrants wish to immigrate (Borjas 1990, 180–82; "The 'Explosiveness' of Chain Migration" 1989, 797; Jasso and Rosenzweig 1986, 291). Third, while some chain migrants come as immediate relatives, others—including the siblings that seem to prompt the greatest concerns—enter in categories that are numerically limited. In spite of these constraints on chain migration to the United States, however, Ruritania should pay attention to categories and numerical limits. For example, chain migration potential may prompt Ruritania to maintain numerical limits for certain categories (particularly siblings). Or Ruritania may lower limits or even eliminate certain family categories altogether.

An argument *for* taking steps to reduce the backlog is that long waits may lead to increased levels of undocumented immigration.[17] This view derives support from analyses that show a strong correlation between undocumented immigration and family connections in the receiving country (Cornelius 1990, 227, 235).

The persuasiveness of this argument depends not only on the causal link between backlogs and waiting times but also on

Ruritania's ability and desire to control undocumented immigration. The argument that backlogs should be cut in order to reduce undocumented immigration may be more persuasive in countries like the United States, where there is considerable reluctance to adopt strong enforcement measures to control undocumented immigration, than it would be in more enforcement-oriented societies.

Distinct from this goal of reducing causes of undocumented immigration, the Ruritanian lawmaker may simply find the waits unacceptably long because of the hardships they impose on families. The German Federal Constitutional Court has suggested that numerical limits requiring family members to wait for significant periods of time would "disproportionally" impair the constitutional interest in family unity. Therefore, the court further suggested, waiting periods would be unconstitutional under the same reasoning that prompted the court's decision (discussed above, under Are Family-based Criteria Constitutionally Limited?) to strike down the three-year waiting period for spouses of certain permanent residents (see 76 *BVerfGE*, 65–66). In the United States, such constitutional arguments are much less likely to prevail.

Regardless of the analysis under Ruritanian constitutional law, the Ruritanian lawmaker may consider raising the ceiling on family-based admissions. An increase may be a logical outcome of negotiations among Ruritanian lawmakers; e.g., perhaps the consensus will be to increase overall admissions enough to satisfy all interest groups that want more visas for their constituents. As Peter Schuck has observed, enactment of the 1990 Immigration Act was largely attributable to a key sponsor's "successful logrolling strategy, which sought to increase the numbers in all admission categories, making the pie large enough so that it would no longer seem worth fighting over the relative size of the various slices" (Schuck 1992, 37, 88).

It is equally likely, however, that Ruritanian political forces will favor reduced levels of family-based immigration. Recent U.S. developments illustrate this option. In June 1995 the Commission on Immigration Reform proposed an overall reduction in legal immigration from the current level—between 800,000 and 900,000 annually—to 550,000.[18] Family-based admissions for "immediate relatives" and the four family preferences would be reduced from about 482,000 in FY 1993 to 400,000 annually. These visas would be allocated primarily to spouses and minor children of citizens. Remaining visas would go to parents of citizens and then to spouses and minor children of permanent residents.[19]

Even if the political climate allowed limits to be raised to cut the backlog, the Ruritanian lawmaker might conclude that it is sound policy to keep immigration levels down, long waiting periods notwithstanding. While delays cause hardship, the very existence of a long queue proves that immigrants would prefer to wait than not to get in at all.

This argument against raising the limit can be taken one step further. Once it is clear that no more visas are forthcoming, a long wait becomes—somewhat paradoxically—an argument for eliminating the preference altogether. This reasoning played a role in the Commission on Immigration Reform's recommendation to eliminate the fourth family preference for siblings of citizens. The commission believes that the fourth preference cannot play a meaningful role in family reunification if it admits siblings only after they have waited between ten and eighteen years.

Ruritania may also adopt a more moderate approach to these backlogs, by examining the backlogged categories more closely and redefining them to limit eligibility to closer family members. This would shorten waits and result in more effective family reunification (but only for family members who continue to qualify). In keeping with this approach, an earlier version of what became the 1990 Immigration Act would have limited the fourth family preference to "never-married siblings" (S. 2104, 100th Cong., 2d Sess., S. Rep. 100–290 [26 Feb. 1988]; see also S. 358, 101st Cong., 2d Sess., S. Rep. 101–55 [19 June 1989]).

The United States Congress has adopted similar responses to the second preference backlog for spouses and children of permanent residents. This backlog is considerably shorter than the fourth preference backlog for siblings of citizens. However, because the second preference backlog includes a closer family tie—spouses and children—many find it more troubling than the fourth preference backlog.

The 1990 Immigration Act divided the second preference into two subgroups: 2A for spouses and children (i.e., unmarried and under twenty-one) and 2B for unmarried adult sons and daughters. The act then reserved 77 percent of the visas for spouses and children, cutting their waiting times but increasing those for adult unmarried sons and daughters (see INA § 203 [a] [2]). The act also called for 75 percent of the 2A visas to be distributed without regard to per-country limits. Another proposal, which was part of an earlier version of the 1990 act but deleted before the act's passage, would have limited the second preference to permanent residents' unmarried children under the age of twenty-six (see S.358 [sponsored by Senators Kennedy and Simpson], approved by the Senate, 13 July 1989).

The Commission on Immigration Reform's approach to the 2A backlog would go further and reallocate additional visas for spouses and minor children of permanent residents. First, the commission recommended eliminating the 2B family preference altogether. Second, in order to create more openings for 2A applicants, it recommended eliminating the current first family preference for adult, unmarried sons and daughters of citizens, the current third family preference for adult, married sons and daughters of citizens, and the current fourth family preference for siblings of citizens.[20] Third, the commission recommended that 150,000 additional visas be made available annually on an interim basis until the 2A backlog of about 1.2 million applicants is eliminated.

Finally, some of those who find these long waits troubling have suggested that qualified immigrants should be permitted to enter or stay in the United States while they wait. Congress adopted this response to the family unity problems caused by the legalization provisions of the Immigration Reform and Control Act of 1986 (IRCA). Many families included some individuals who legalized and others who were ineligible, many of whom were spouses and children.[21] IRCA did not grant derivative status to spouses and children, but section 301 of the 1990 act gave them voluntary departure for extended periods and work authorization to cover their waits (Guendelsberger 1993, 45, 46–50). Similarly, the Spousal and Children Immigration Act of 1993, S.618, would have created a new nonimmigrant category that would allow permanent residents' spouses and children to enter as visitors while waiting for immigrant visas (see also H.R. 4275, digested at *Interpreter Releases* 1992, 602). Proponents of these remedies see them as humanitarian measures that allow family members to immigrate while holding the line on non-family-based immigration. These remedies also address the concern that long waits lead to undocumented immigration. At the same time, however, these remedies suggest that a formal revision of admission rules would be a more straightforward solution to the problem.

In Sponsoring Immigrant Relatives, Will Citizens Be Preferred over Resident Aliens?

The U.S. second preference backlog also raises an even more basic issue: whether to treat differently the family reunification interests of citizens and resident aliens. Germany generally admits spouses and children to join both citizens and resident aliens. Absent numerical limits, different waiting times do not arise. In U.S. law, numerical limits force permanent residents' spouses and children to wait in the second preference queue. More harshly, married sons and daughters, parents, and siblings of permanent residents are entirely ineligible for family-based immigration. In contrast, numerical limits do not apply to citizens' spouses, minor children, and qualifying parents. Unmarried adult sons and daughters do not face a waiting period given current supply and demand.[22]

Congress could cut the second preference backlog by treating resident aliens more like citizens. John Guendelsberger (now a member of the Board of Immigration Appeals) has proposed that "immediate relatives" be redefined more broadly, to include permanent residents' spouses and children under eighteen. Like "immediate relatives" under current law, this broadened group would be preferred over more distant relatives of citizens. Under Guendelsberger's proposal, all family-based immigration would then be subject to a numerical limit, but the limit would be higher than it is under current law (Guendelsberger 1988, 88–90).

The Commission on Immigration Reform's recommendations at first seem to adopt Guendelsberger's general approach. As noted above, the commission would eliminate the current first, third, and fourth family preferences (for unmarried and married adult sons and daughters and siblings of citizens). In FY 1993 these three preferences together accounted for about 98,000 immigrants. If the preferences were eliminated and the overall level of family admissions remained fairly constant, these visas would be freed for spouses and minor children of permanent residents. As noted above, however, the commission also proposed legal immigration reductions of about 82,000 below the FY 1993 level. If this proposed reduction becomes law, only a modest number of visas will be available for reallocation.[23]

While U.S. family-based immigration categories prefer citizens over permanent residents, INA § 203 (d) and similar derivative status provisions ensure that only a small percentage of permanent residents' spouses and children must wait to enter. Those who must wait are typically either people who became spouses and stepchildren of a permanent resident alien after that alien acquired permanent resident status or sons and daughters who were twenty-one years of age or older when a parent became a permanent resident.[24] In many cases, an alien has already had permanent resident status for a period of time before acquiring spouses or stepchildren, so he or she can naturalize in well under five years and then use the family reunification categories for citizens. As explained under What Delays in Family-based Immigration Will Be Considered Unacceptable, and What Remedies Will Be Adopted? above, many spouses and children of aliens who legalized under IRCA also did not have to wait, because those spouses and children received voluntary departure and work authorization.

The fundamental issue here is whether it is wrong to treat citizens and resident aliens differently for family reunification purposes. This, in turn, prompts an inquiry into the meaning of citizenship and resident alien status in Ruritania. Ruritanian citizens may enjoy a broad range of significant rights and privileges that resident aliens do not. Ruritania may view these differences as permanent, thus regarding resident alien status as a permanent rather than transitional stage for the individual alien. If so, Ruritania's laws would make naturalization difficult or impossible. If Ruritania also adopts jus sanguinis citizenship principles, resident alien status will carry over to later generations. If this is the case, it would be understandable for Ruritania to treat citizens and resident aliens differently and to reject equal sponsorship rights for resident aliens as devaluing Ruritanian citizenship. However, this sort of objection would probably not be made if other significant differences existed between the relative positions of citizens and aliens in Ruritanian law and society.

Alternatively, Ruritania may consider resident alien status a transitional stage toward citizenship through routine naturalization. Differences may exist between the status of resident aliens and citizens, but those differences would not be regarded as permanent. Under this view of resident alien status, one could argue persuasively that long waits are unacceptable because the adversely affected resident aliens are more clearly members of Ruritanian society. While Ruritanians might still believe that equal sponsorship rights for resident aliens would devalue Ruritanian citizenship, the devaluation would be different; it would occur because conferring equal family reunification rights on resident aliens would eliminate a significant incentive to naturalize (Ueda 1994, 128 [discussing family reunification as an incentive to naturalize]).

Such an incentive exists in the United States, on account of the growing second preference backlog. Rather than wait for a second preference visa, many permanent residents will find it faster to naturalize and bring in a spouse and/or children as "immediate relatives" of citizens (or under first or third preference if the children turn twenty-one). It would be consistent with a transitional view of resident alien status for Ruritania to maintain unequal family reunification rights for citizens and resident aliens, while making sure that Ruritanian citizenship is available to those who wish to naturalize.

Will Different Perspectives on the "Family" Be Accommodated?

Will Perspectives on the "Family" in the Sending Country Be Accommodated?

"Family" can mean many different things, and a wide gulf often separates understandings of the term in sending and receiving countries. In the United States, Germany, and many other Western industrialized countries, the prevailing concept is the "nuclear family": spouses, children, and parents. Elsewhere, "family" may include grandparents, aunts and uncles, cousins, parents-in-law, relationships created by marriage, and perhaps multiple spouses.

Ruritania's approach to these differences will have significant immigration consequences. First and most obviously, defining "family" eligibility more broadly will mean increased overall immigration, and/or decreased immigration in other categories, and/or longer waits for those who are eligible. More fundamentally, Ruritania's approach will reflect and communicate—both to new immigrants and to those who are already citizens and resident aliens—its expectations about assimilation and integration. These expectations help explain why the United States is reluctant to recognize family ties beyond those to one spouse, children, parents, and siblings. Similar expectations may also account for German law's even more restrictive view of the "family."

U.S. immigration law declines to recognize any marriage that would be unlawful in the United States, e.g., polygamous marriage, regardless of whether such a marriage would be allowed or even typical in the sending country.[25] Similarly, German law does not recognize polygamous marriages for immigration purposes (Bamberger 1995, 38). On the other hand, the Ruritanian lawmaker may hesitate to insist that immigrants conform to all aspects of Ruritanian courtship customs. For instance, Ruritania may decide to recognize arranged marriages, in which the partners have limited personal contact beforehand, even if such marriages are not within prevailing Ruritanian customs.

More difficult to analyze are relationships, such as grandparent-grandchild, that may be the functional equivalent of a recognized relationship. In addition to expectations about assimilation and integration—especially conformity to Ruritanian notions of the "family"—hesitation to add to demand may play a major role if Ruritania decides not to recognize extended family relationships.

Even if functional equivalency could be determined on a country-by-country basis, it may be difficult and/or prohibitively expensive for Ruritania to make subjective determinations that would merit public confidence. Family-by-family functional equivalency determinations would be even more difficult and would also run the risk of unacceptable intrusions into family privacy ("Note" 1991, 1640).[26] Functional equivalency determinations also require the legislature and higher-level agency officials to delegate discretionary authority to lower-level officials.

These lower-level officials may lack sufficient background and training, yet there may be no way to review their decisions effectively. These are serious issues of process and institutional competence.[27]

These considerations notwithstanding, German law grants residence permits *(Aufenthaltserlaubnis)* to family members other than spouses and unmarried children when doing so is necessary to avoid extraordinary hardship (AuslG § 22). In the United States, by contrast, the INA enumerates recognized family relationships, and the courts have consistently rejected attempts to use surrogate family relationships to meet statutory requirements.[28]

Will Nontraditional Families and Other Variations Within the Receiving Country Be Accommodated?

Similar issues arise with regard to nontraditional understandings of "family" within the receiving country. As with transnational differences, family-by-family determinations of functional equivalency would pose problems of cost, privacy, and delegation of discretionary authority. Categorical recognition of additional relationships—such as grandparent-grandchild—would raise different issues. Viewed categorically, such relationships would be too distant to qualify for immigration, even though some may be emotionally closer than sibling relationships. Decisions to include or exclude such relationships will turn on the Ruritanian government's perception of whether changes would lead to an increased demand for immigrant visas, especially in light of waiting times.

Categorical recognition of other relationships may also run into substantive difficulties. For example, in the United States a Ninth Circuit panel in *Adams v. Howerton* (673 F.2d 1036, 1039 [9th Cir.], cert. denied, 458 U.S. 1111 [1982]) held that a homosexual marriage cannot be recognized for immigration purposes, even if it is valid under applicable state law. *Adams* derived this substantive view largely from the statute (which was repealed in 1990) that made homosexuals excludable from the United States. Regardless of the wisdom of that decision, *Adams* reminds lawmakers that immigration criteria reflect not only a society's expectations about assimilation and integration of new immigrants but also its expectations in all areas of the public and private lives of its members.

Adams can also be seen as presenting federalism issues. If Ruritania, like the United States, has a federal system of government that reserves much family law to state or local legislative jurisdiction, it will need to decide to what extent federal immigration law will recognize local law determinations of family relationships. This concern arises not only with controversial topics like homosexual marriage but also with heterosexual marriage, adoption, legitimation, and many other legal acts that contribute to the formation of a "family."

A number of U.S. cases are generally consistent with *Adams*. For example, in *Kahn v. INS* (36 F.3d 1412, 1414–15 [9th Cir. 1994]), a federal appeals court held that state law does not conclusively determine whether family ties (in *Kahn* a common-law marriage) exists for purposes of waiver of deportation under INA § 212 (c). In more ordinary situations, however, federal immigration law in the United States routinely relies on state family law, which just as routinely varies from state to state.

What Will Be the Procedures for Deciding Eligibility?

Once Ruritania allows family-based immigration, it will need to resolve a number of procedural issues regarding eligibility. These are largely the same issues—relating to cost, privacy, and delegation of discretionary authority—that arise in connection with different perspectives on the "family." These issues are the most difficult to resolve when family-based immigration is premised on volitional acts, such as marriage, divorce, and adoption.

The U.S. struggle with "sham marriages" is instructive. For discussion's sake, let us assume some agreement on the substantive definition of a "sham marriage."[29] Until 1986 the Immigration and Naturalization Service (INS) sought to detect sham marriages as part of the initial process of granting immigration benefits based on marriage. Standard procedures included interviewing the husband and wife separately to see if their answers about various aspects of their married life were consistent. For many observers, such intrusive and potentially offensive interviews—which often occurred without effective supervision, even within the agency—raised serious policy and constitutional concerns ("Note" 1986, 1238).

Congress shifted course when it enacted the Immigration Marriage Fraud Amendments (IMFA) of 1986 (Pub.L. 99-639, 100 Stat. 3537, 3543). Under IMFA, if an alien receives permanent resident status based on a marriage (to a citizen or permanent resident) that is less than two years old, then the alien receives permanent resident status on a "conditional" basis only.[30] This conditional period lasts two years from the time the alien becomes a permanent resident. The condition is removed, and the permanent resident status made indefinite, only if the citizen or permanent resident spouse and the alien spouse jointly file a petition with the INS within the final ninety days of the two-year conditional period. This joint petition must attest to the bona fides of the marriage. If the marriage has been judicially annulled or terminated during this period or if the spouses fail to petition, conditional status is terminated, and the alien spouse becomes deportable unless he or she qualifies for one of several possible waivers.

In FY 1993 the INS processed 91,258 of these cases and granted indefinite permanent resident status in 81,810 of them (INS 1993, 70–71 [table 22]). While the approval rate is high, it is noteworthy that over 10 percent were not approved. Moreover, the principal affirmative requirements—that the couple generally must remain married for two years and file a joint petition—are likely to deter sham marriages that might have been more readily attempted under the old system. Interviews are still standard procedure when an alien spouse first applies for conditional permanent resident status. However, IMFA has reduced the perceived need for the objectionable separate interviews for husband and wife that were routine before 1986. Based on anecdotal evidence, the INS actually interviews only a small percentage of the couples who file joint petitions two years after conditional status is granted.

On other hand, IMFA may be inducing overly sanguine government reliance on the joint petition. While those who would perpetrate sham marriages may find the task more complex, the joint petition requirement has not necessarily made detection by the INS more likely. Moreover, it is clear that IMFA introduced new problems. The most troubling of these is that it gives the petitioning citizen or resident alien spouse tremendous power over the alien spouse. Until the INS adjudicates the joint petition, the petitioning spouse can refuse to cooperate for a variety of reasons having nothing to do with the bona fides of the marriage. In some cases, the alien can remove the condition and acquire indefinite permanent resident status without the cooperation of the citizen or permanent resident spouse. For example, waivers are available in cases of "extreme hardship" to the alien spouse, for certain marriages "entered into in good faith," and for battered spouses. However, IMFA sets out a standard of proof for waivers that alien spouses often cannot meet. This situation is especially troubling in abusive relationships (Anderson 1993, 1401, 1416–22; Calvo 1991, 627–28).

Ruritania must also consider whether constitutional or super-legislative norms constrain its procedures for determining eligibility for family-based immigration. For example, would a law allowing the Ruritanian government to refuse admission without a statement of reasons violate the constitutional rights of either petitioning citizens/resident aliens or would-be immigrants? As with the substantive admission criteria discussed under Are Family-based Criteria Constitutionally Limited? above, the answer depends, first, on whether there is a constitutional interest in family reunification and, second, on whether constitutional claims are taken seriously in immigration cases. In spite of the plenary power doctrine, U.S. courts will often hear procedural due process claims, but generally not in cases involving first-time entrants, even if they are spouses of U.S. citizens (see, e.g., *United States ex rel. Knauff v. Shaughnessy,* 338 U.S. 537 [1950]).

Will Family Ties Affect the Application of Exclusion or Expulsion Grounds?

Ruritania must decide whether family ties will affect the application of grounds for exclusion or expulsion. In the United States, an alien who fits into an eligible immigration category may still be barred from admission if any of the exclusion grounds in the INA apply. However, the INA allows waivers of some exclusion grounds for aliens, especially if they are relatives of citizens or permanent residents. For example, the exclusion ground for membership or affiliation with "the Communist party or any other totalitarian party" may be waived for a parent, spouse, son, daughter, brother, or sister of a citizen or for a spouse, son, or daughter of a permanent resident. The waiver may be granted "for humanitarian purposes, to assure family unity, or when it is otherwise in the public interest if the immigrant is not a threat to the security of the United States" (INA § 212 [a] [3] [D] [iv]).[31]

Family ties also temper the application of deportation grounds in the INA. A permanent resident's application for a discretionary waiver of exclusion or deportation under INA § 212 (c) depends heavily on "family ties" and "evidence of hardship to the respondent and family if deportation occurs" (Matter of Marin, 16 I & N Dec. 581, 584–85 [BIA 1978].) Similarly, discretionary suspension of deportation under INA § 244 (a) depends largely on whether deportation would "result in extreme hardship" to the potential deportee's citizen or permanent resident spouse, parent, or child. Moreover, INA § 241 (a) (1) (H) provides that deportation for fraud or misrepresentation may be waived in some cases for an alien who is the spouse, parent, son, or daughter of a citizen or a permanent resident.

In German law as well, family ties provide some protection against the expulsion *(Ausweisung)* grounds set out in AuslG § 46. For example, expulsion decisions consider the consequences for family members who lawfully reside in Germany with the alien who is in expulsion proceedings (see AuslG § 45). Aliens living with family members who are German citizens enjoy special protection from expulsion *(besonderer Ausweisungsschutz)* (see AuslG § 48 [1]). This special protection also applies to minor aliens living with their parents or a sole custodial parent (see AuslG § 48 [2]).

The interpretation and enforcement of similar Ruritanian laws may present constitutional issues not unlike those that may affect family-based admission rules in Ruritania. Again, the key questions are whether there is a constitutional interest in family reunification and whether that constitutional interest is recognized in immigration cases. In the United States, the plenary power doctrine applies with less force to deportation than to exclusion, but courts remain reluctant to hear constitutional challenges to substantive deportation criteria (see *Harisiades v. Shaughnessy*, 342 U.S. 580 [1952]). In the family context, U.S. courts have generally rejected the claim that deportation of a citizen child's resident alien parents is unconstitutional because it amounts to the "de facto deportation" of a U.S. citizen.[32] The German Federal Constitutional Court has taken a different approach. As mentioned in Are Family-based Criteria Constitutionally Limited? above, German constitutional law does not treat immigration cases as analytically distinct from cases that do not involve immigration issues. In a 1979 decision, the court reviewed the validity of deporting for a five-year period a Turkish citizen who had been convicted of selling four kilos of hashish (Judgment of 18 July 1979, 51 *BVerfGE* 386 [1979], discussed in Neuman 1990, 54–57). The court held that Article 6 of the Basic Law protects marriages between aliens and between aliens and German citizens and therefore decided that the deportation order had to be proportional to the perceived harm to the public interest if the alien were not deported. On the facts, the court found that a five-year deportation period for a serious drug-related crime met this standard (see also Judgment of 10 Aug. 1994, *BVerfGE* [3. Kammer des 2. Senats] 2 BvR 1542/94, *Neue Juristische Wochenschrift* 3155 [1994] [Article 6 may protect against the deportation of an unsuccessful asylum applicant who has an illegitimate German citizen daughter]).

Several recent decisions from the European Court of Human Rights have taken a similar approach that recognizes family unity as a possible ad hoc bar to deportation. For example, *Moustaquim v. Belgium* (13 E.H.R.R. 802 [1991]) involved a Moroccan national who had lived in Belgium from the age of one until his deportation at the age of twenty as a result of his twenty convictions for crimes including aggravated theft and assault. The court ordered a trial two-year suspension of this deportation order, reasoning that it was "disproportionate to the legitimate aim pursued" and therefore in violation of his right to family life under Article 8 of the European Convention for the Protection of Human Rights and Fundamental Freedoms.[33]

What Share of Total Legal Immigration Will Be Family Based?

Once again, Ruritania can look to the United States and Germany for lessons in both methodology and policy.

How Will the Family-based Share of Total Immigration Be Measured?

United States

U.S. law's strong emphasis on family reunification is obvious when one compares the number of family-based admissions with the number of admissions in other categories. In FY 1993 employment-based categories accounted for 147,012 admissions, and there were 33,468 admissions in the "diversity" category for immigrants from countries with low rates of immigration to the United States. In contrast, the combined total of immediate relatives (255,059), the four family preferences (226,776), spouses and children of legalized aliens (55,344), and children born abroad to alien residents (2,030) was 539,209 admissions. Thus family-based admissions appeared to account for about 75 percent of the total of 719,689 immigrant admissions subject to the overall numerical cap in the 1990 act.[34]

In fact, an even greater number of admissions may be characterized as family based, because of the derivative status for spouses and children under INA § 203 (d) and similar provisions. Table 3.3 shows that about 46 percent of the immigrants admitted in FY 1993 under the employment-based preferences were spouses and children of the principal qualifying workers or investors. Similarly, spouses and children accounted for about 39 percent of admissions in the diversity category.

Table 3.3 United States: Employment and Diversity Admissions, FY 1993

	Principals	Spouses	Children
1st preference	8,023	5,870	7,221
2d preference	13,801	9,451	6,216
3d preference	53,630	14,910	19,149
4th preference	3,576	1,880	2,702
5th preference	196	136	251
Total employment-based	79,226	32,247	35,539
Total diversity admissions	20,544	5,709	7,215

Source: INS 1993, 35–37 (table 5).

Table 3.4 shows that 36 percent of admissions in the family-based categories themselves were spouses and children with section 203 (d) derivative status, not principal qualifying aliens.

Table 3.4 United States: Family-based Admissions, FY 1993

	Principals	Spouses	Children
1st family preference	9,636	n/a	3,183
2d family preference (2A)	84,483	n/a	14,121
2d family preference (2B)	23,221	n/a	6,483
3d family preference	6,475	5,667	11,243
4th family preference	20,983	14,014	27,267
Total family-based	144,798	19,681	62,297

Source: INS 1993, 33–34 (table 5).

Total family-based admissions in FY 1993 numbered 619,919, or roughly 86 percent of the total of 719,689 immigrant admissions subject to the numerical cap. This is the sum of: (1) 539,209 admissions for immediate relatives, the four family preferences, spouses and children of legalized aliens, and children born abroad to alien residents; (2) 67,786 spouses and children admitted under the employment-based preferences; and (3) 12,924 spouses and children admitted in the "diversity" category.

One key question, of course, is just what "family-based" admissions means? I have been using a broad definition that includes any individual immigrant who relies on family ties for lawful entry. Arguably, I should define the term more narrowly to exclude those who enter with derivative family status. But is there any difference between an employment-based immigrant's spouse and children who enter under the second family-based preference (who should clearly count as family-based admissions even under the narrow definition) and an employment-based immigrant's spouse and children who enter with derivative status? There may be a difference in admission priority, but it is harder to see a difference for the purpose of measuring "family-based" admissions from a policy perspective.

In light of the widespread perception that the 1990 act increased the emphasis on employment-based selection criteria, the figures regarding the family-based share of immigration to the United States are particularly striking. The 1990 act increased employment-based immigration almost threefold, from 54,000 to 140,000 visas. However, it also raised the overall numerical cap, without giving any serious consideration to modifying the derivative status provisions.

The same pattern holds true for other immigrant categories that fall outside the numerical cap. The largest of these, refugees and asylees combined, accounted for 127,343 admissions in FY 1993. The criteria for selecting overseas refugees prominently feature family ties.[35] And once refugees are selected, their spouses and children enjoy derivative status. In FY 1993 72,468 applicants actually qualified as refugees and asylees, and 54,875 (about 43 percent of total refugee/asylee admissions) were the spouses and children of the principal applicants. Selection criteria for other categories, such as Amerasian children, also consider family ties (cf. *Interpreter Releases* 1994, 1637 [family relationships are considered in granting parole to Cubans under the September 1994 U.S.-Cuba agreement]). When all legal immigration is considered, family-based admissions account for between 75 and 80 percent of the total number of legal immigrants to the United States.

Germany

Although Germany generally does not impose numerical limits on immigration, it is possible to assess the relative weight that immigration policy places on family reunification. One key measure would be the number of entrants under the family reunification provisions in AuslG §§ 17–27, as compared with the number of aliens in other categories who lawfully take up indefinite residence.[36]

Asylum is one path to legal residence in Germany that has recently received prominent attention both inside and outside Germany. Before significant changes in German asylum law took effect in 1993, the number of asylum applicants in Germany had risen dramatically: from 51,493 in 1979, to 103,076 in 1988, to 256,112 in 1991, and to a high of 438,191 in 1992 (Federal Ministry 1993, 59). In 1993 the number of applications dropped dramatically: from 224,000 between January and July 1993 to 98,500 between July 1993 and January 1994 (Hailbronner 1994, 166, citing Deutsches Bundesministeriums des Innern, *Asyl-Erfahrungsbericht 1993*, 15 Feb. 1994).

While the sheer number of applications and the German response to them attracted considerable attention, my inquiry must focus on the number of applicants granted asylum. That number, when compared with family-based admissions, begins to answer the question of what relative weight German law places on asylum as an immigration criterion. In recent years, well under 10 percent of asylum applications were approved. In addition to this figure, one should consider at least the following: (1) asylum applicants who were denied asylum (or in some cases never applied) but are still allowed to stay in Germany indefinitely for humanitarian or other reasons; and (2) refugees admitted from outside Germany, mainly from Southeast Asia and South America (approximately 38,000 to date).[37]

In assessing the relative weight given to family reunification, the comparison should also include several other categories, among them (1) ethnic Germans from Eastern Europe and parts of the former Soviet Union *(Aussiedler)* and (2) nationals of other European Community countries, who may enter and reside in other EC countries under various EC agreements. For all of these categories independent of the express family reunification provisions in AuslG §§ 17–27, it is important to know how many admittees are family members with derivative status rather than aliens who qualify as principals. For example, the approximately 100,000 asylees now living in Germany are accompanied by about 130,000 dependents (Federal Ministry 1993, 77).

How Will Family-based Immigration Be Balanced Against Immigration Based on Other Criteria?

In the United States, a number of writers have advocated curtailing family-based immigration in favor of greater emphasis on other criteria, including skills and investment (Briggs 1992, 244–55). Some have advocated a "point" system, similar to those used in Canada and Australia, to assess the desirability of each would-be immigrant based on numerous factors, including language ability and employment-related skills (Borjas 1990, 223–24 [discussing advantages and disadvantages of a point system]). Legislation proposed in Congress for an "immigration moratorium" would dramatically curtail family-based immigration by those who are not "immediate relatives" of U.S. citizens (see, e.g., H.R. 373, 104 Cong., 1st Sess. [1995]; S. 160, 104 Cong., 1st Sess. [1995]; S.2448, 104 Cong., 1st Sess. [1995]). As noted above, the Commission on Immigration Reform has recommended significant reductions in family-based immigration. However, it has also recommended that employment-based immigration be reduced in about the same proportion, to 100,000 per year, down from the current level of 140,000. These proposals raise difficult empirical issues. In the United States, one leading economic analysis concluded that the current emphasis on family-based immigration has caused immigrants' skill levels to decline, thus reducing U.S. income by approximately $6 billion annually (Borjas 1990, 222). Other studies have reached different conclusions (Bach and Meissner 1990, 15). Another observer has responded to calls for a greater emphasis on skills with a different sort of empirical skepticism: that it is difficult to identify needed skills and to match foreign workers with domestic employers (Schuck 1991, 29–33).

Others have suggested that family ties produce hidden but significant economic benefits by providing the social and economic networks that are necessary for effective integration into the receiving country's society and economy. Thus family ties compensate for lack of skills, and focusing solely on immigrants' skill levels underestimates their economic contributions (Meissner 1990, 53–58; Bach and Meissner 1990, 15).

A related but broader point is that family-based and economic selection criteria overlap. This means that selection under one set of criteria is inevitably influenced by the other set. Put differently, many aliens who immigrate under employment-based criteria may also have family ties in the receiving country. Since family ties give would-be immigrants superior general labor market information as well as information about specific potential jobs, these immigrants often enjoy a competitive advantage in obtaining employment-based immigrant visas (Bach and Meissner 1990, 55).[38] Thus many choose to immigrate under employment-based preferences instead of family categories, either because the family ties are not recognized for immigration purposes or because immigration in a family category takes longer.

The implications of this overlap between family-based and economic selection criteria are as difficult to analyze as the overlap itself. If many immigrants who qualify under the employment preferences do so because of their family ties, family reunification may account for even more than 75 to 80 percent of total legal immigration to the United States. It would then follow that even significant reductions in the nominal share of family-based immigration would still allow family ties to play a significant role in immigration selection. The corollary is that increasing the nominal share of employment-based immigration will not correct any economic loss stemming from an overemphasis on family-based criteria because family ties will still play a significant role.

Beyond these empirical issues, more basic questions need asking: To what extent should economic benefit define national self-interest? In turn, to what extent should national self-interest define immigration law and policy? Economic analysis helps us measure the fiscal impacts of immigration policy (Borjas 1990, 220–21). Many believe that it should also drive immigration policy making, while others consider economic concerns to be secondary, insignificant, or too speculative to matter. Especially among those who choose to deemphasize or disregard economic analysis, family reunification assumes a unique and sometimes irresistible rhetorical power.

How Will Family-based Immigration Affect the Ethnic Composition of Ruritanian Society?

The recent history of immigration to the United States suggests that family reunification can significantly alter the ethnic composition of the receiving country. From the 1920s to 1965, legal immigration to the United States occurred under the "national origins" system, which tied numerical limits for sending countries to each country's contribution to the immigrant flow in the late nineteenth and early twentieth centuries. Under this system, Europeans accounted for over half of all legal immigrants to the United States in the period from 1951 to 1960 (INS 1993, 27 [table 2]). When Congress abolished the national origins system in 1965, it expected fewer immigrants to come to the United States from northern and western Europe and more to come from southern and eastern Europe. Instead, immigration from Europe waned in general, and Asian and Latin American immigration increased dramatically (Reimers 1992, 74–76, 89–91; Reimers 1983). In FY 1993 over 75 percent of legal immigrants came to the United States from Asian and Latin American countries (INS 1993, 28 [table 2]).

What role did family-based immigration play in this shift? Some of the criticism of family-based immigration has called it "nepotism" that benefits a small number of citizens and permanent residents (Graham 1991, 9). But family-based categories favor those who have immigrated recently. They do not help those—for example, many Europeans today—whose many relatives in the United States arrived in past epochs of immigration history.

The end of the national origins system in 1965 did not lead immediately to dramatic changes in the immigrant flow. While a number of family-based categories had existed before 1965 (Ueda 1994, 25), one consequence of the national origins system was a relatively small number of Asian-Americans who could file the necessary petitions for close relatives in the period immediately after 1965. At first, more Asians immigrated under the employment-based categories. Family preferences did not contribute to the marked growth in Asian immigration until later, when these new immigrants began to petition for their relatives to be allowed to join them (see generally DeJong, Root, and Abad 1986, 598). Although the shift toward Latin American immigration occurred somewhat differently because the preference system did not apply to immigration from Western Hemisphere countries until 1976, the general pattern was similar.

This pattern suggests that family-based immigration did not cause the ethnic shift. The real causal factors included: (1) a rise in demand from Asia and Latin America caused by volatile economic and political conditions; (2) employment-based categories that accommodated this increased demand; (3) a simultaneous decline in European demand; and (4) the end of the national origins system, which would have kept demand-related shifts from occurring. Nevertheless, family-based immigration did accommodate the new demand and dramatically magnified the shift that occurred.

In the political arena, efforts to modify the role of family reunification in immigration policy are often viewed as attempts to modify the ethnic composition of the current immigrant population (Schuck 1992, 73 ["Hispanic organizations, in coalition with the AFL-CIO and other ethnic and denominational groups, lobbied vigorously to protect and increase family preferences" in the 1990 act]). However, a shift away from family-based immigration would not necessarily reverse present ethnodemographic trends. Greater emphasis on employment-based immigration could well lead to increased immigration from India, the Philippines, and other countries with an educated population eager to emigrate. If lawmakers want an ethnic mix in the immigrant pool that contradicts demand patterns, they may need to select immigrants directly by country of origin.

How Will Family-based Immigration Affect the Integration of Immigrants into Ruritanian Society?

Families can provide the social and economic support crucial for integration into the receiving society. Without family support, immigrants can remain sojourners, never considering themselves permanent residents or potential citizens (Hing 1993, 44–49, discussing gender ratio and family formation among Chinese-Americans before 1965).

Integration fostered by family reunification often has distinctive characteristics. Family-based immigrants may be integrated into the smaller and often insular sphere of an immigrant enclave, as opposed to the larger receiving society (see generally Holden 1988, 288). In contrast, single immigrants may be more likely to distance themselves from their native societies and put down entirely new roots that allow them to be absorbed into the receiving society. Such integration may occur through intermarriage, for example. Indeed, immigrant families may be more difficult to integrate than lone immigrants precisely because they must be integrated as families. Moreover, it may be impossible to integrate a critical-mass community of immigrant families without changing the character of the receiving society. Fundamental questions at this point include: What do we mean by "integration"? Does "integration" mean "equal opportunity" in a "multicultural society" or something akin to the classical (and arguably mythical) "melting pot"?

Family reunification not only affects the degree and character of integration in the receiving country, it also raises the stakes for integration policy. A receiving society's failure to integrate families leaves it with a larger group of residents who live separately. The result may be social and economic costs much greater than those attributable to not integrating sojourners. In this regard, a receiving country that generously reunites families must also take seriously the need to integrate them.

If Ruritania wants to integrate its immigrant families, its citizenship laws can play an important role. Significant levels of family-based immigration would make more sense if combined with a jus soli citizenship law, as in the United States, that can assure the next generation of at least legal equality. In contrast, significant family-based immigration combined with a jus sanguinis citizenship law, as in Germany, will lead to a large population of resident aliens separate from the rest of the receiving society. This can be tempered to the extent that resident alien status approximates citizenship status (both legally and socially) and/or resident aliens can naturalize fairly easily.

In Germany, neither condition is present. The trend is toward easing naturalization rules, but routinely acquired legal integration without social integration is likely to trivialize naturalization, not solemnize it. Germany's amended citizenship law, which took effect on 1 July 1993, makes naturalization easier for many aliens who were born in Germany or have resided there for a long time.[39] A revised draft German citizenship law was expected by the end of 1994, but as of this writing it remains the topic of ongoing negotiations (Federal Ministry 1993, 37–40).

A different approach, which would be consistent with easier naturalization, would be to enhance resident alien status. Debate in Germany has focused on the right to vote. For example, in 1990 the Federal Constitutional Court issued two decisions holding that the Basic Law does not allow aliens to vote or to stand as candidates in federal, *Land,* or local elections (Federal Ministry 1993, 29–31).[40] However, other enhancements might make the legal position of resident aliens in Germany more like permanent resident status in the United States.

Conclusion

In deciding how some part of Ruritanian immigration policy might be based on family reunification, lawmakers must confront at least the ten questions discussed in this essay. For each question, there is wide variety of possible answers. Those in the United States and Germany show that the choices are exceedingly complex. Wise family immigration policy depends on harmony with the assumptions that underlie a country's immigration law, its legal process traditions, and ultimately its very concept of nationhood.

Notes

*I am indebted to the members of working group 1 of the the Joint German-American Project on Migration and Refugee Policies sponsored by the American Academy of Arts and Sciences and the German-American Academic Council Foundation, especially Hans-Joachim Cremer, for their collegiality and insightful suggestions. I would also like to thank Ann Estin and Margaret Taylor for their insights on the topic and Tracy Ashmore, Craig Barber, Melissa Decker, John Griffin, Daniel Horne, and Judith Smith for excellent research assistance and very helpful comments on earlier drafts.

1. With apologies to Rudolf B. Schlesinger, Hans W. Baade, Mirjan R. Damaska, and Peter E. Herzog, *Comparative Law: Cases—Text—Materials*, 5th ed. (Mineola, N.Y.: The Foundation Press, 1988), 337.

2. Other writers cited throughout this essay have analyzed specific aspects of family-based immigration.

3. The INA is codified in title 8 of the United States Code; for example, section 201 (b) (2) (A) is 8 U.S.C. § 1151 (b) (2) (A). This essay follows convention by citing INA rather than title 8 section numbers.

4. I consider the commission's recommendations more fully below, under What Delays in Family-based Immigration Will Be Considered Unacceptable, and What Remedies Will Be Adopted? and In Sponsoring Immigrant Relatives, Will Citizens Be Preferred over Resident Aliens?

5. The "accompanying or following to join" provision does not apply to aliens who receive immigrant visas as "immediate relatives." For example, the spouse of a citizen cannot be accompanied or followed by the spouse's child from a previous marriage, unless the child qualifies as the citizen's stepchild. Similarly, a parent of a U.S. citizen cannot be accompanied or followed under section 203 (d) by a child who is, e.g., the citizen's sibling or stepsibling. One possible reason to omit derivative status for immediate relatives may be to keep a citizen from circumventing the fourth family preference queue by petitioning for his "immediate relative" parents, who would then bring the citizen's siblings as children "accompanying or following to join." But according to Charles Gordon, the omission of derivative status for immediate relatives is "just an oversight in the law" ("Family-Sponsored Immigration" 1990, 216).

6. These requirements are relaxed somewhat if the resident alien has been granted asylum in Germany (see AuslG § 17 [3]).
7. There are exceptions, see AuslG § 18 (2).
8. The relevance of a constitutional right to family unity in the deportation context is discussed below, under Will Family Ties Affect the Application of Exclusion or Expulsion Grounds?
9. A 1986 amendment softened but did not eliminate this distinction between fathers and mothers (see INA § 101 [b] [1] [D]).
10. See also *United States ex rel. Knauff v. Shaughnessy*, 338 U.S. 537 (1950) (alien spouse seeking initial entry has no procedural due process right to exclusion hearing); *Swartz v. Rogers*, 254 F.2d 338 (D.C. Cir. 1958) (Fifth Amendment due process clause does not bar deportation of citizen's alien spouse); *Noel v. Chapman*, 508 F.2d 1023 (2d Cir. 1975), cert. denied, 423 U.S. 824 (1975) (equal protection does not require that permanent residents' family members be allowed to enter while waiting for immigrant visas, in order to approximate treatment of citizens' family members). Cf. *Yepes-Prado v. INS*, 10 F.3d 1363, 1368 (9th Cir. 1993) (under INA § 212 [c], 8 U.S.C. § 1182 [c], "private sexual conduct between consenting adults" may not be considered in deciding an application for waiver of exclusion or deportation).
11. For criticism of the decision by German observers, see Huber 1988; Zuleeg 1988.
12. *Abdulaziz v. United Kingdom*, 7 E.H.R.R. 471 (1985). Article 8 may have stronger application in cases where deportation after a long period of legal residence would mean separation from family members remaining in the country.
13. See also sources cited in Guendelsberger 1988, 73–76.
14. For further background, see Ash 1993, 231–43, 660–61.
15. Unused allotments are generally available for applicants who qualify for the next lower preference. Thus actual second preference admissions in FY 1993 exceeded the allotment of 114,200 because some unused first preference visas were available.
16. How Will Family-based Immigration Affect the Ethnic Composition of Ruritanian Society? discusses this shift more fully.
17. The same concerns about causing undocumented immigration also arise in connection with relatively restrictive immigration criteria, such as those in place in Germany.
18. At the same time, the commission proposed an annual allocation of 150,000 additional visas to clear out current backlogs.
19. The Smith bill, H.R. 2202 (1995), would limit family-based immigration to an even lower level of 330,000 annual admissions, allocated under a priority scheme similar to the Commission on Immigration Reform's recommendations.
20. Cf. H.R. 2202, which also proposes eliminating the fourth family-based preference.
21. Legalization required, among other things, unlawful residence in the United States since 1 January 1982. Many of those eligible to legalize had spouses and/or children who were ineligible because they entered the United States after that date.
22. One bill introduced in Congress in 1994 would have excluded parents from the definition of "immediate relative," instead placing them in a new,

numerically limited preference category (see S. 2533, 103d Cong., 2d sess. [1994]).

23. A more significant reallocation is attributable to the commission's proposal to make 150,000 additional visas available annually to clear out current backlogs.

24. Others might be children born outside the United States (a child born in the United States would be a citizen). A much smaller number would be children under twenty-one who could not obtain exit visas from their countries of last residence to join their parents until they turned twenty-one and thus became too old to qualify as "children" "accompanying or following to join."

25. See Matter of Mujahid, 15 I & N Dec. 546 (BIA 1976) (federal immigration law does not recognize polygamous marriage, even if lawful in alien's home country); Matter of H, 9 I & N Dec. 640, 641–42 (BIA 1962) (same). But cf. Guendelsberger 1988, 57 (discussing a recent French Conseil d'Etat decision allowing a second spouse to remain in France under family reunification provisions when the polygamous marriage was valid in the alien's home country).

26. A similar conflict between fact-finding and privacy arises in connection with "sham marriages," discussed below, in What Will Be the Procedures for Deciding Eligibility?

27. See *De los Santos v. INS,* 690 F.2d 56, 60 (2d Cir. 1982) (referring to difficulties of analyzing foreign countries' legitimation laws).

28. See, e.g., *INS v. Hector,* 479 U.S. 85, 88–91 (1986) (rejecting the argument that the Board of Immigration Appeals had to consider "extreme hardship" to an alien's citizen nieces in deciding her application for suspension of deportation under INA § 244).

29. See *Bark v. INS,* 511 F.2d 1200, 1201 (9th Cir. 1975) (the parties "did not intend to establish a life together at the time they were married").

30. In contrast, German law formerly required a waiting period before admission. For a brief discussion of the German Federal Constitutional Court decision on such waiting periods, see Are Family-based Criteria Constitutionally Limited? above.

31. For similar waivers, see section 212 (h) (single offense of simple possession of thirty grams or less of marijuana) and section 212 (i) (fraud or misrepresentation). Cf. sections 212 (a) (6) (E) (ii), (d) (11) (the alien smuggling exclusion does not apply in some cases and may be waived in others if the smuggled alien was "the alien's spouse, parent, son, or daughter [and no other individual]").

32. See, e.g., *Acosta v. Gaffney,* 558 F.2d 1153, 1157–58 (3d Cir. 1977); but cf. *Cerrillo-Perez v. INS,* 809 F.2d 1419, 1423–26 (9th Cir. 1987) (under INA, the BIA must consider hardship to citizen children who may remain in United States without their deported parents). See generally Friedler 1995, 529–35.

33. See also *Berrehab v. Netherlands,* 11 E.H.R.R. 322 (1988) (deportation of a Moroccan citizen who had lived in the Netherlands for several years and had a Dutch daughter would violate Article 8). Cf. *Djeroud v. France,* 14 E.H.R.R. 68 (1991) (quoting a European Commission of Human Rights' finding that deportation of an Algerian national living in France since the age of one would violate Article 8). See also International Covenant on Civil and Political Rights, art. 23, G.A. Res. 2200, U.N. GAOR, 21st Sess., Supp. No. 16, at 168, U.N. Doc. A/6316 (1967), discussed in Are Family-based Criteria Consti-

tutionally Limited? above: "The family is the natural and fundamental group unit of society and is entitled to protection by society and the State."

34. Under the 1990 act, permanent resident admissions in these three general groups were limited to 700,000 for FY 1992, 1993, and 1994 and to 675,000 starting in FY 1995. Several other groups eligible for permanent resident status—e.g., refugees and asylees—are not subject to a numerical cap. Even though immediate relative admissions are not numerically limited, they count toward the overall numerical cap.

35. Family reunification is covered by priority 3 and priority 5 of the six listed. Priority 3 includes spouses, unmarried sons, unmarried daughters, or parents of a citizen, permanent resident, refugee, asylee, or, in some cases, parolee. Priority 5 includes married sons or daughters, unmarried siblings, married siblings, grandparents, or grandchildren of a citizen, permanent resident, refugee, asylee, or, in some cases, parolee, as well as "more distantly related individuals who are part of the family group and dependent on the family for support" ("Description of U.S. Refugee Processing Priorities" 1993: 7).

36. These statistics are not published, though they may be available unofficially.

37. These statistics are not published, though they may be available unofficially.

38. See also Bach and Meissner 1990, 33: (about 40 percent of admissions under the Canadian point system have relatives in Canada); Borjas 1990, 177 ("immigration is likely to be cheaper for persons with relatives already residing in the United States"); and ibid., 185 (citing studies concluding that individuals with family ties in the receiving country are much more likely to immigrate).

39. According to one source, "In Germany, the 1990 Foreigners Law, and a 1993 government decree, made virtually automatic the naturalization of immigrant children between the ages of 16 and 23 who were born or had lived in Germany more than eight years" (Soysal 1994, 26).

40. The Federal Constitutional Court suggested in dictum that it would be constitutional to allow citizens of European Community states to vote and stand for election in local elections as European Community law may allow. Article 28 of the Basic Law was amended to this effect in 1992.

References

Anderson, Michelle J. 1993. "A License to Abuse: The Impact of Conditional Status on Female Immigrants." *Yale Law Journal* 102: 1401–30 (1993).

Ash, Timothy Garton. 1993. *In Europe's Name: Germany and the Divided Continent.* New York: Random House.

Bach, Robert, and Doris Meissner. 1990. *America's Labor Market in the 1990's: What Role Should Immigration Play?* Series on

Immigration Issues for the 1990s. Washington, D.C.: Immigration Policy Project of the Carnegie Endowment for International Peace.

Bade, Klaus J. 1994. *Ausländer—Aussiedler—Asyl*. Munich: Beck.

Bamberger, Wilhelm. 1995. *Ausländerrecht und Asylverfahrensrecht*. Munich: Beck.

Borjas, George J. 1990. *Friends or Strangers: The Impact of Immigrants on the U.S. Economy*. New York: Basic.

Briggs, Vernon M., Jr. 1992. *Mass Immigration and the National Interest*. Armonk, N.Y.: M. E. Sharpe.

Calvo, Janet. 1991. "Spouse-Based Immigration Laws: The Legacies of Coverture." *San Diego Law Review* 28 593–644.

Cornelius, Wayne A. 1990. "Impacts of the 1986 U.S. Immigration Law on Emigration From Rural Mexican Sending Communities." In *Undocumented Migration to the United States: IRCA and the Experience of the 1980s*, ed. Frank D. Bean, Barry Edmonston, and Jeffrey S. Passel, 227. Santa Monica: Rand Corp.; Washington, D.C.: Urban Institute Press.

DeJong, Gordon J., Brenda Davis Root, and Ricardo G. Abad 1986. "Family Reunification and Philippine Migration to the United States: The Immigrants' Perspective." *International Migration Review* 20: 598–611.

"Description of U.S. Refugee Processing Priorities—FY 94." 1993. *Refugee Reports*, 31 Dec., 7.

"The 'Explosiveness' of Chain Migration: Research and Policy Issues." 1989. *International Migration Review* 23: 797–812.

"Family-Sponsored Immigration." 1990. *Georgetown Immigration Law Journal* 4: 201–19.

Federal Ministry of the Interior. 1993. "Survey of the Policy and Law Concerning Foreigners in the Federal Republic of Germany." A1-937 020/15 trans.

Friedler, Edith Z. 1995. "From Extreme Hardship to Extreme Deference: United States Deportation of Its Own Children." *Hastings Constitutional Law Quarterly* 22: 491–555.

Graham, Otis L., Jr. 1991. "Rethinking the Purposes of Immigration Policy 9." Center for Immigration Studies Paper No. 6, May.

Guendelsberger, John. 1993. "Family Fairness: A Status Report." In *Defense of the Alien* 15: 45–57.

———. 1988. "The Right to Family Unification in French and United States Immigration Law." *Cornell International Law Journal* 21: 1–102.

Hailbronner, Kay. 1994. "Asylum Law Reform in the German Constitution." *Immigration Law: United States and International Perspectives on Asylum and Refugee Status*, joint issue of *American University Journal of International Law and Policy* and *Loyola of Los Angeles International and Comparative Law Journal* 9: 159–79.

Hing, Bill Ong. 1993. *Making and Remaking Asian America through Immigration Policy 1850–1990.* Stanford: Stanford University Press.

Holden, Constance. 1988. "Debate Warming Up on Legal Migration Policy." *Science* 241 (15 July): 288–90.

Huber, Bertold. 1988. "Zur Verfassungsmässigkeit der Beschränkungen des Ehegatten und Familiennachzugs im Ausländerrecht." *Neue Juristische Wochenschrift:* 609–11.

Interpreter Releases. 1994. Vol. 71. Washington, D.C.: Federal Publications.

_____. 1992. Vol. 69. Washington, D.C.: Federal Publications.

Jasso, Guillermina, and Mark Rosenzweig. 1986. "Family Reunification and the Immigration Multiplier: U.S. Immigration Law, Origin-Country Conditions, and the Reproduction of Immigrants." Demography 23: 291–311.

Kanstroom, Daniel. 1993. "Wer Sind Wir Wieder? Laws of Asylum, Immigration, and Citizenship in the Struggle for the Soul of the New Germany." *Yale Journal of International Law* 18: 155–211.

Meissner, Doris. 1990. "Revision of the U.S. Legal System: Toward a Selection System." *In Defense of the Alien* 12: 53–58.

Neuman, Gerald L. 1990. "Immigration and Judicial Review in the Federal Republic of Germany." *New York University Journal of International Law and Politics* 23: 35–85.

"Note: The Constitutionality of the INS Sham Marriage Investigation Policy." 1986. *Harvard Law Review* 99: 1238–54.

"Note: Looking for a Family Resemblance: The Limits of the Functional Approach to the Legal Definition of Family." 1991. *Harvard Law Review* 104: 1640–59.

Reimers, David M. 1992. *Still the Golden Door: The Third World Comes to America.* 2d ed. New York: Columbia University Press.

_____. 1983. "An Unintended Reform: The 1965 Immigration Act and Third World Immigration to the United States." *Journal of American Ethnic History* 3: 9–28.

Schuck, Peter H. 1992. "The Politics of Rapid Legal Change: Immigration Policy in the 1980s." In *Studies in American Political Development,* 6:37–92. New York: Cambridge University Press.

_____. 1991. "The Emerging Political Consensus on Immigration Law." *Georgetown Immigration Law Journal* 5: 1–33.

Soysal, Yasemin N. 1994. *Limits of Citizenship: Migrants and Postnational Membership in Europe.* Chicago: University of Chicago Press.

Ueda, Reed. 1994. *Postwar Immigrant America: A Social History.* New York: St. Martin's.

United States Department of State, Bureau of Consular Affairs. 1993. *1993 Report of the Visa Office.* Washington, D.C.: Government Printing Office.

United States Department of State. 1995. *Visa Bulletin* (Nov.). Washington, D.C.: Government Printing Office.

United States Immigration and Naturalization Service. 1993. *1993 Statistical Yearbook of the Immigration and Naturalization Service.* Washington, D.C.: Government Printing Office.

Zuleeg, Manfred. 1988. "Öffentliche Interessen gegen Familiennachzug." *Die Öffentliche Verwaltung* (July): 587–95.

Chapter 4

Readmission Agreements

Olaf Reermann

Matters relating to asylum legislation and the admission of refugees from the third world, as well as from Central and East European countries are turning into a more and more common problem in Western Europe. The growing gap between the affluent countries and the newly industrializing or poor countries of the third world has led to increasing migratory pressures. This trend has been reinforced by the sweeping political changes in the Central and East European states, the dismantling of previously existing border guard systems, and the simultaneous deregulation of traveling.

Because of its geographical position, its prosperity, and its liberal asylum legislation, the Federal Republic of Germany in particular has become one of the main countries of destination of the east-west migration. More than 70 percent of all asylum seekers entering the member states of the European Union between 1991 and 1994 arrived in the Federal Republic of Germany (see table 4.1). Spain, France, and Italy are increasingly exposed to migratory pressure from the Maghreb and western Africa.

Many immigrants claiming to have suffered political persecution in fact only want to escape the poor conditions in their countries of origin; they expect better economic prospects for themselves in Western Europe. This migratory pressure, which is growing year by year, has been a major preoccupation for both the general public and those working in the field of home affairs

Table 4.1 Development of the influx of asylum applicants to the Western European countries since 1985

	1985	1986	1987	1988	1989	1990	1991	1992	1993	1994	1995	till
Belgium	5.357	7.456	6.000	4.990	7.604	12.964	15.318	17.650	26.883	14.340	8.344	Sep 95
Federal Republic of Germany	73.882	99.650	57.379	103.076	121.318	193.063	256.112	438.191	322.599	127.210	127.937	Dec 95
Denmark	8.698	9.299	2.750	4.416	4.588	5.300	4.609	13.900	14.351	6.651	3.304	Aug 95
France	28.925	26.920	27.672	34.253	61.422	54.813	46.784	26.800	26.508	26.044	16.028	Sep 95
Greece	1.157	1.396	6.950	8.964	5.433	4.400	3.282	1.950	827	"+"	"+"	
Britain	4.899	3.882	4.500	2.252	12.573	30.000	57.710	24.600	28.500	42.200	31.125	Sep 95
Ireland	45	23	+	+	36	+	10	+	100	"+"	"+"	
Italy	5.400	6.500	11.050	6.214	2.245	4.750	23.317	2.500	1.323	1.834	833	Apr 95
Luxembourg	57	82	98	44	87	+	160	+	381	"+"	"+"	
Netherlands	5.644	5.865	13.450	7.500	14.000	21.208	21.616	17.450	35.399	52.576	21.302	Sep 95
Portugal	127	128	450	504	116	100	233	700	2.091	"+"	"+"	
Spain	1.681	1.377	2.500	3.096	1.183	6.850	8.139	12.650	12.615	10.230	2.395	June 95
Total EU	138.822	161.908	132.799	175.309	230.605	333.448	437.290	556.391	471.577	281.085	211.268	
German share of influx to EU	54.36%	61.55%	43.21%	58.80%	52.61%	57.90%	58.57%	78.76%	68.41%	45.26%	60.56%	
Norway	850	2.700	8.600	6.602	4.443	3.900	4.569	5.250	12.876	3.379	789	Jul 95
Austria	6.725	8.639	11.406	16.685	21.882	22.789	27.306	16.238	4.477	5.082		
Sweden	14.500	13.158	18.100	17.985	28.970	28.900	26.489	83.200	37.581	18.640	4.775	Jun 95
Switzerland	9.703	8.546	10.913	16.726	24.425	35.836	41.629	17.960	24.739	16.134	17.021	Dec 95
Finland		0	50	50	200	2.500	2.100	3.600	2.023	849	462	Jul 95
Total Western Europe	167.599	194.951	181.868	233.357	310.515	427.373	539.383	682.639	553.540	325.169	234.315	
German share of influx to western Europe (1 and 2)	45.05	51.12	31.55	44.17	37.07	45.17	47.48	64.19	52.28	39.12	54.60	
By way of information												
Canada	8.400	23.000	35.000	45.000	22.000	36.000	30.500	37.700	20.464	21.701	18.729	Sep 95
USA	20.000	18.900	26.100	57.000	100.000	73.600	70.000	103.500	129.594	142.508	63.791	Jun 95
Australia					500	3.8000	17.000	4.114	4.563	4.215	4.313	Oct 95

Notes: +) = no data available   "+" = estimate

Source: Federal Ministry of the Interior, Secretariat General of the EU and the respective states

in the European states; indeed, it has constituted a real touchstone for Europe's common immigration and asylum policies. The conviction that national immigration and asylum policies no longer suffice to counteract this alarming development efficiently has gained more and more ground. Aware of this, the EU ministers responsible for immigration constantly intensify their cooperation. Until Maastricht this work was carried out within the framework of the ad hoc Working Group on Immigration, which was established by the relevant ministers in London in October 1986.

The Maastricht report of 3 December 1991 on the harmonization of immigration and asylum policies clearly states that, in principle, any immigration policy of the member states has to be restrictive. With the exception of allowing residence on humanitarian grounds, immigration should be limited to cases of family reunification. Otherwise the integration of third country nationals residing in the member states may be jeopardized. In order to deal appropriately with the problems associated with immigration it will be indispensable to view them in connection with their respective contexts. Areas such as labor and human rights policies, development cooperation, and integration policy have a direct impact on a European immigration policy. Efficient mechanisms to coordinate these policies and immigration policy will have to be found at both a national and a European level.

The development of a European immigration policy should focus, on the one hand, on the harmonization of admission and removal policies and, on the other, on finding a common answer to illegal immigration. Apart from efficient border controls, other effective measures that need to be examined include:

- restrictions on the possibilities for illegal immigrants to have access to social institutions and social benefits,
- barriers to illegal employment,
- bans on the legalization of illegal residents, and
- a common expulsion policy.

There is agreement that present migratory movements can only be counteracted by increased economic, social, and financial measures that aim at improving the living conditions in immigrants' countries of origin. Clearly, such measures can only work if there is also coordinated and close cooperation with those countries of origin.

Apart from improving economic situations through appropriate international programs, it is also necessary to raise the awareness that illegal immigration can only be contained and combated through coordinated measures. There is a need for so-called "intelligent border protection," which implies the involvement of neighboring states, in particular those in Central and Eastern Europe, but also of those resulting from the collapse of the Soviet Union. Significant milestones on this path were the Vienna conference in January 1991 (Council of Europe 1991), the Berlin conference in October 1991, and the Budapest conference of 15–16 February 1993. In addition to stricter control of external frontiers, the harmonization of visa policies (in popular parlance, "visa union") is essential. And readmission agreements represent another step toward improved control over migratory movements.

Both the work program adopted in Maastricht for the field of immigration policy and the final communiqué of the conference on coping with uncontrolled migratory movements of 15 and 16 February 1993 in Budapest provide for the conclusion of bilateral and multilateral readmission agreements with the countries of origin and transit. The recommendation agreed to by the ministers in London in 1992 concerning the practical procedure for return adopted by the member states also mentions the need to consider the conclusion of readmission agreements with states concerned.

At its meeting on 28 and 30 November 1993 the Council of Justice and Home Affairs adopted principles for the conclusion of readmission agreements with third countries. These constitute a nonexhaustive set of principles for the conclusion of coordinated bilateral and multilateral readmission agreements among the member states. The aim behind them is to make sure that the member states pursue a uniform line when concluding such agreements. The principles do not only deal with the readmission of a country's nationals but also with the readmission of third country nationals whose residence in the countries concerned is illegal or has become illegal. They also contain provisions regarding the competent authorities, time limits, the obligation to bear the costs incurred, provisions concerning transit agreements, and rules for the issuing of travel documents and for giving proof of nationality, as well as provisions for data protection.

Under the German presidency these principles were summed up in a specimen readmission agreement and adopted by the Council of Justice and Home Affairs at its meeting on 30 November–1 December 1994. In order to ensure the effective implementation of the removal measures, a standard travel document for a single journey was adopted at the same time. On 1 January 1995 all member states of the union began using this standard travel document for the removal of third country nationals. The draft implementing protocol required for the application of the specimen readmission agreement was adopted under the French presidency during the first half of 1995.

The importance attributed to the question of removal is highlighted by the fact that at its meeting of 29 and 30 November 1993 the Council of Justice and Home Affairs decided that in suitable cases European agreements, association agreements (concluded between the EU and individual states or groups of states and laying down preferential treatment in areas such as trade, transport, and customs), and cooperation agreements with third countries should be linked to agreements concerning the readmission of nationals residing illegally on the territory of the member states. Such links would not be automatic but rather dependent on the political considerations in each individual case.

As regards the "institutional" side of connecting association agreements and provisions on readmission, two alternatives seem possible. First, readmission clauses could be inserted directly into association agreements. Second, readmission could be established in separate agreements that would require the simultaneous conclusion of association agreements.

Content of Readmission Agreements

By signing a readmission agreement, parties commit themselves to readmitting to their territory specific groups of people when this is requested by another party.

Taking into consideration the individual reasons for expulsion recognized by the states, this refers to people whose behavior or legal status has been shown to cause serious disruptions in or a threat to the country of residence. As a general rule this applies to people

who entered the contracting state illegally or, after an initially legal entry—perhaps as a tourist with a short-term residence permit—have remained illegally without obtaining an authorization of their stay,

who for reasons regarding the public interest or national security are to be removed, or

whose asylum applications are finally rejected and who do not have a right to stay for any other reason.

Possible readmission agreements between the contracting parties can take the form of agreements that

contain only the obligation for a country to take back its nationals (type 1),

also include a regulation regarding stateless persons of the contracting parties (type 2),

are extended to include the readmission of third country nationals residing illegally on the territory of the other contracting party (type 3), or

are extended to cover transits of third country nationals to their countries of destination through the territory of one of the contracting parties (type 4).

Readmission of Own Nationals (type 1)

This is essentially a contractual reaffirmation of an obligation that already exists under international law. In the past it might have been unclear whether such an obligation for a country to readmit its own nationals existed under international law, as is evidenced by the Swiss and German treaties on the right of establishment and agreements on admission of the nineteenth century, in particular by the Treaty of Gotha of 15 July 1851 (de Claparéde 1911), in which the article referring to repatriation reads

Each party commits itself to readmit at the request of the other contracting party:

a) those persons who continue to be its nationals, and
b) its former nationals as long as they have not yet become nationals of the other contracting party or a third country, even if under national law they have already lost their nationality.

The existence of these treaties illustrates that it was not yet assumed that such an obligation existed under international law.

Today, however, it is regarded as a general rule under international law that every state has to readmit its own nationals to its territory. The obligation for countries to take back their own nationals is such an obvious consequence of the law of nationality and citizenship that it has to be regarded as fully equivalent to it (Plender 1988, 133). Thus there is a danger that treaties providing for the readmission of countries' own nationals when they are no longer entitled to stay in their countries of residence may lead to the assumption that this generally accepted rule of international law is being called into question. States referring to already existing agreements of this kind could refuse to take back their nationals until readmission agreements are concluded with them as well, and they could make the conclusion of such agreements dependent on conditions, in particular economic conditions or the abolition of visa requirements.

It has to be acknowledged, however, that only some illegally residing foreigners voluntarily comply with the duty to leave countries of residence. In view of the often desperate economic situations in their countries of origin and as a result of poor occupational prospects, but also because of threats to minorities in their native countries, the danger of famine, or lives of misery and poverty, many foreigners try to avoid returning home and simply disappear. In addition, many illegal foreigners destroy their travel documents and any other papers that could give evidence of identity and nationality. This makes return more difficult because countries of origin usually allow their nationals to return only if they are able to produce travel documents that clearly prove their identities and nationalities. Many countries are not very cooperative when it comes to taking back their nationals, and they will often express doubts as to whether the people in question are really their nationals or take their time identifying their nationals or issuing their travel documents. Bearing this in mind, it makes sense to exert influence on the relevant states and to conclude readmission agreements with them.

Nevertheless, it is important to recall that the conclusion of such an agreement does not create the readmission obligation. Rather, the agreement serves to point out the responsibility already existing under international law for states to take back their own nationals and thus helps to speed up the whole process. Perhaps most important, the parties agree to forgo formal evidence of nationality as long as that can be validly assumed through other means; in contrast to previous treaties, in other words, readmission agreements reverse the burden of proof. Furthermore, agreements specify that receiving states issue necessary identification without delay if border authorities require such documents.

A prime example of such a mutual readmission agreement is the readmission agreement concluded between Germany and Romania in 1992, including the implementing protocol belonging to it. According to this agreement, Romania takes back its own nationals who are residing illegally in Germany without any formality and in a simplified procedure. Passports for Romanian citizens and other travel documents or identification cards issued by Romanian authorities are accepted as evidence for Romanian nationality as long as they have not expired and are complete. Possession of Romanian nationality may also be validly assumed from passports or other travel documents or identification cards (even after their expiration), driver's licenses, work passes, seamen's passports, reliable statements by witnesses (in particular by Romanian nationals), or statements by the person concerned as long as he or she speaks Romanian.

The agreement has proved successful. Whereas in 1992 103,787 asylum seekers arrived in Germany from Romania, that number amounted to only 73,717 in 1993 and dropped to less than 10,000 in 1994. Under the agreed provision, about 35,000 Romanian nationals were returned to Romania by plane in 1993 after an accelerated procedure. In 1994 the number totaled 25,636.

As for rejections at the border, it is striking that, for example, prior to the conclusion of the readmission agreement with Romania and the amendments to the law on asylum in Germany, from July 1992 to October 1992 out of almost 10,000 Romanians intercepted along the border only 66 were returned (by air), which means less than 1 percent. During the same period in 1994 the number of those intercepted along the border went down to 4,299, something that can be attributed to the preventive effect of the measures. Of these 4,167, or 97 percent, were transported back to Bucharest by plane.

Readmission of Stateless Persons (type 2)

It has proved to be important that readmission agreements also cover those people who during their stays in one signatory country were released at their own request from the nationality of the other contracting party without having acquired another nationality. Several states have released considerable numbers of their nationals from their nationality and subsequently refused to take back these persons on the grounds that the formal nationality no longer exists, which leads them to contest the obligation under international law to readmit these individuals.

The overwhelming opinion today is that according to a general rule of international law no state can evade its obligation vis-à-vis other states to take back its nationals simply by depriving those nationals of their nationality without the consent of their countries of residence (Randelzhofer 1985, 416; Plender 1988). An older interpretation concludes that only the arbitrary deprivation of nationality (e.g., mass releases) or the abuse of law, as in an act in breach of good faith (withdrawal of nationality while a person concerned is abroad in order to prevent his or her return, thus leaving another state in charge of this person; Weis 1956, 49; Weis 1979, 46; Verdross 1950), does not lead to the readmission obligation. Particularly in view of the fact that the modern interpretation is contested by a number of states, it would be advisable to include a clause to this effect into a readmission agreement.

Whereas it has not been possible to insert such a clause into the German-Romanian readmission agreement—the readmission of such people is now settled outside the treaty—a readmission clause has been included in the German-Bulgarian readmission agreement of 1994. This agreement explicitly states that the readmission obligation also applies to those who, at their own request, have been released from the nationality of the contracting partner without their having been promised naturalization by the other contracting partner).

Readmission Agreement (type 3)

Agreements regarding the readmission of third country nationals who have illegally entered the requesting country are not new. At the end of the 1950s and during the 1960s a number of such agreements were concluded between almost all West European states.

Such agreements have become necessary because, in contrast to cases involving countries' own nationals or nationals who have become stateless, no general rule of international law says that a state has to take back third country nationals even against their will and without imposing further conditions if these nationals have traveled illegally from its territory to the territory of the other state. For the time being, intermediate structures are becoming part of international common law. Thus at the Vienna conference of January 1991, at the Berlin conference of October 1991, and at the Budapest conference of February 1992 reference was made to an important principle of international law—i.e., the principle of good neighborly relations—as well as to the resulting obligation for a country to take back people who, coming from its territory, have illegally entered another state (Council of Europe 1991, ch. 13).

The aforementioned treaties of the 1950s and 1960s have not lived up to expectations. Above all, they were concluded prior to the age of today's mass tourism and growing illegal migratory pressure and thus do not serve now and will likely prove even less adequate now that the dismantling of internal border controls between the parties to the Schengen agreement has taken effect (on 26 March 1995) and been implemented within the European Union as agreed in Article 7a of the EC treaty.

Application of the old treaties has shown that the following points are particularly problematic:

- Clear evidence of the prior stay—usually fourteen days—on the territory of the other contracting party has to be provided. In general, identification with the appropriate entry stamps is required.
- The respective authorities examine very carefully whether the country was really entered illegally, i.e., by knowingly bypassing border controls. Entry with forged documents is not regarded as illegal as long as a controlled border

crossing was used, and neither is uncontrolled entry when the person in question was waved through at the border crossing. (It must be acknowledged that, at least during peak hours, perfect border controls are not possible even at controlled border crossings; after all, maintaining a regular flow of cross-border traffic is also important. Perfect border controls at the price of enormous traffic jams and delays do not appear to be suitable and would not be politically acceptable.)

- The circumstances—i.e., the time and place—of the illegal entry have to be described in a detailed and comprehensible way.
- Sometimes people are cross-examined again after their readmission to the other contracting state; in cases of diverging or contradictory evidence, they are, in general, returned to the requesting state. In some cases, even unproved information regarding a stay of more than six months in the requesting state suffices for the person to be returned.

Despite all this, the old treaties are still relevant. The majority contain special provisions regarding interception in border areas. People intercepted in these areas can be handed over to the other contracting party without formality within a few days of their interception. This procedure, which only requires information allowing the border authorities to establish that the person in question has crossed the border without authorization, is very efficient in cases regarding crossings not effectuated at official border crossing points.

To overcome the difficulties outlined here, agreements have been developed that adopt an approach more likely to meet today's requirements. Unlike in earlier agreements, the readmission of people residing without authorization is not made dependent on their illegal entry or on a prior stay in the requested contracting party (en route clause); neither is a time limit imposed on the stay in the requesting state (otherwise usually six months after entry). To these readmission agreements of the so-called second category belongs the Multilateral Readmission Agreement Between the Parties Contracting to Schengen and the Republic of Poland (see appendix).

A readmission obligation exists if a person who does not meet, or who no longer meets, the conditions in force for entry or residence on the territory of the requesting contracting state has traveled from the territory of one contracting state to the territory of the other contracting state. In view of the final objective of the Schengen contracting parties—i.e. the dismantling of internal border controls—the contracting party responsible is the one across whose external border the person has entered. The first frontier to have been crossed that is not common to the contracting parties is deemed to be the external frontier. The agreement also allows for short application and taking-over periods as well as a fast procedure without any formality carried out by authorities, mainly border authorities, designated by the contracting parties.

This readmission agreement led to similar admission agreements between Germany and Switzerland at the end of 1993 and between Germany and the Czech Republic in 1994. In these treaties, however, the readmission obligation lapses if, according to the information available to the authorities of the requesting party, the foreigner in question has stayed for more than a year (Switzerland) or more than six months (Czech Republic) on its territory. To foster practical handling and speed up procedures, the contracting parties have also concluded implementing protocols.

In contrast to treaties in the first category, which provided for readmission within six months of arrival in the requesting state, the point at which authorities first note an illegal entry or stay is now the relevant date. This modification corrects what had been a almost insoluble problem for requesting parties: on the one hand, foreigners used to be able to avoid being returned by disappearing; on the other, they could undermine the application of the agreement simply by stating—and often it was not possible to disprove this—that they had been in the requesting state for more than six months.

Germany was particularly interested in concluding such agreements because in 1993 it adopted the so-called first country concept in its asylum legislation. This provision is based on the idea that a person who is politically persecuted has to seek protection in the first country where this is possible. The third country rule aims at returning the person concerned to the first safe country to which he or she was admitted. Thus it is now possible for such a person to be rejected right at the border, or—if he or she has already entered the territory of the Federal Republic of Germany—to return the person immediately to the safe third country. This presupposes the necessary readmission agreements with neighboring states, in particular with those adjacent to Germany's eastern border: i.e., Poland, the Czech Republic, Austria, and Switzerland.

The principles developed for the multilateral readmission agreements between the Schengen states and Poland, as well as Germany's experience with its eastern partners, have left their mark on three fundamental documents drafted by the member states of the European Union within the framework of their program of action. These include principles for the conclusion of readmission agreements with third countries, decided on at the meeting of the Council of Justice and Home Affairs on 29–30 November 1993; a draft specimen bilateral readmission agreement between a member state and a third country based on these principles; and the standard travel documents for the return of third country nationals. The last two documents (not yet published) were adopted at the council meeting on 30 November–1 December 1994. The draft specimen protocol for the implementation of the readmission agreement, which was also submitted under the German presidency, has not yet been adopted, but it has reached the final stages in this process.

The aim of these agreements is to harmonize such treaties with third countries and to conclude multilateral treaties where possible in order to facilitate the implementation of agreements. (At the moment, national authorities have to deal with several different treaties; there are fifteen different treaties of this kind in Germany alone.)

Negotiations for multilateral treaties take a long time, as can the drafting of multilateral agreements. Once concluded, however, bilateral agreements can be based on the agreed principles and follow the agreed standard text, although derogations to account for special circumstances in the relationship between the contracting parties will, of course, be possible.

Clauses common in the agreements of the first category, such as those regarding the illegal crossing of borders, the en route clause, or clauses concerning a prior stay in the requested state, have been dropped from both the agreed principles and the standard draft. Rules have also been laid down for the expiration of the readmission obligation—for instance, the issuing of a valid residence title in the requesting state or residence of more than a year after the noting of illegal entry and stay in the requesting state. In addition, the new agreements provide for short application and readmission periods and contain regulations on data protection and costs.

In general, further agreements on details are required to supplement readmission agreements and enable the authorities in charge to put them into practice. The details are dealt with in the draft implementing protocol and are above all concerned with possible procedures of mutual notification; the exchange of information, documents, and evidence required for admission; the designation of the authorities in charge of the implementation of the agreement; the determination of the border crossings for the admission; the reimbursement of costs; and the conditions for the transit of third country nationals accompanied by police.

Transit of Third Country Nationals (type 4)

Such regulations may stipulate that a person taken in charge for transit purposes has to be accompanied either by forces from the requesting state or by forces from the state of transit (this will often be in the interest of both states if they want to prevent the person taken in charge for transit purposes from disappearing and either entering the requesting state illegally once again or staying illegally in the country of transit). The costs incurred for the transit to the borders of the country of destination and, if necessary, for the transport back are borne by the requesting party.

The conclusion of separate transit agreements makes sense whenever the country of destination can only be reached after passing through several other states that, although willing to readmit their own nationals, are less prepared to commit themselves to taking back third country nationals who traveled through them before illegally entering the requesting state (for instance, the return of someone through the states A, B, and C to the state D).

The Dublin Convention of 15 June 1990: Sui Generis Readmission Agreements Concerning Asylum Seekers

Apart from these different types of readmission agreements, which can also be combined as required, regulations in the Convention Applying the Schengen Agreement (*BAnZ* 1990) and the Dublin Convention (*Bundesgesetzblatt* 1994, 791) concluded between the member states of the European Community govern the determination of the state responsible for the examination of an asylum application lodged in one of the member states. Both treaties have more or less the same content. There is agreement among the signatory states of the Schengen agreement that the Dublin Convention, on its entry into force, will replace the provisions contained in the Convention Applying the Schengen Agreement.

These conventions are sui generis readmission agreements regarding asylum seekers. They aim, on the one hand, to guarantee every asylum applicant an asylum procedure in one of the signatory states and, on the other, to prevent simultaneous or successive applications for asylum in different countries, i.e., so-called asylum tourism or asylum shopping.

Regardless of the state where the asylum applicant lodges the asylum application, it is, on principle, the state that is responsible for the entry of the asylum applicant into the territory of the community and that is in charge of carrying out the asylum procedure. This so-called graded responsibility follows the criteria laid down in the treaty. Moreover, if a signatory state has given any kind of visa stamp or a residence permit to an asylum applicant, then this state is obliged to handle the asylum application. If several signatory states have granted a residence permit or a visa stamp to the person concerned, then the responsibility lies with the state whose residence permit or visa stamp is the last one to expire. If the asylum applicant entered without the necessary documents, the member state that can be proved to be the one by which the applicant entered is responsible for the asylum procedure. If, on the basis of these criteria, it is not possible to determine the state responsible for the examination of the asylum application, the state where the first asylum application was lodged is charged with its examination.

Thus these agreements entail admission obligations but also the possibility to hand over asylum seekers; the relevant deadlines and modalities for the latter are laid down in implementing provisions.

Experience and Outlook

Have the expectations connected with all these readmission agreements been met, or were they merely aimed at placating a public disturbed by the strong influx of illegal immigrants? From the German point of view, at least, the agreements have served the purpose for which they were intended. As a result of the conclusion of the agreements with Poland and the Czech Republic, these states, which until now have regarded themselves only as states of transit, have begun to adopt efficient control measures along their external borders, making it more difficult for third country nationals to enter their territories and move on to the West European states, in particular to Germany. Furthermore, the agreements have contributed to a growing awareness in the Central and East European states of their responsibility for migratory movements across their borders and for their nationals residing illegally in West European states. (In this context, mention should also be made of the step-by-step introduction of a visa regime agreed on by the West European states for the main countries of origin of illegal immigrants.) The states also now acknowledge that the principle of good neighborly relations implies that each state must be responsible for taking back those foreigners who have traveled to a neighboring country without fulfilling its conditions for entry or residence. Finally, the conclusion of such treaties acts as a deterrent against smugglers of illegal immigrants and thus has led to a reduction in the influx of illegal immigrants; for example, the number of interceptions at the borders to Austria, the Czech Republic, and Poland has declined drastically since the conclusion of these treaties (see table 4.2). In addition, the case of Romania proves very clearly that, apart from stricter border controls in the East and the amendment of the asylum legislation in July 1993, the bilateral readmission agreements and the dialogue with the Central and East European states has had a particularly strong impact.

Table 4.2 Number of Asylum Applicants Registered at
Germany's Borders with Poland, the Czech Republic, and
Austria

	Second Semester, 1992	First Semester, 1993	Second Semester, 1993	First Semester, 1994	Second Semester, 1994
Austria	269	223	91 (73)*	33 (20)	44 (25)
Poland	402	453	386 (158)	454 (275)	545 (320)
Czech Republic	1.336	1.807	378 (322)	91 (54)	70 (46)

*Numbers in parentheses represent applicants who were rejected or returned.

However, the principle of good neighborly relations and the
dialogue with neighboring states were not the only factors leading to the conclusion of these treaties. In connection with the
amendments to asylum legislation, the German government's
declared aim has been not to leave its eastern neighbors, the
Republic of Poland and the Czech Republic, to cope on their own
with the problems of illegal immigration but instead to make
sure that declaring them secure third countries would not place
an excessive burden on them. As a result of these considerations
and in anticipation of a European solution to burden sharing,
Germany is allocating considerable financial resources to the
Republic of Poland and the Czech Republic for constructing
facilities intended for the reception and accommodation of
refugees and asylum seekers, securing the borders, and implementing removal measures. In 1993 and 1994 Germany supported the Republic of Poland with a total of DM 120 million. In
the next few years Germany will grant financial assistance of
DM 60 million to the Czech Republic. The agreements with
Poland and the Czech Republic are the first to put into practice
the kind of international solidarity and fair burden sharing that
is necessitated by the growing migratory movements, in particular in Eastern Europe. They could serve as models for a European system of burden sharing.

Reaching similar agreements with the main countries of origin of the immigrants as well as with states that still regard
themselves as countries of transit will only be possible through
a comprehensive package of measures. The decision made by
the member states of the European Union to link association
agreements with readmission agreements shows that an inte-

gral approach is being pursued for the first time. It has become evident that such an integral approach—i.e., the linking of development aid and economic measures as well as other forms of support to readmission agreements—often makes it easier for individual states to conclude such agreements. Thus if access to international markets is made dependent on interested states adopting measures that prove their international reputation and willingness to cooperate, this will probably enhance the possibility of concluding readmission agreements with them. However, the abolition of visa requirements can be assumed to have been reason enough for Poland to conclude its multilateral readmission agreement with the Schengen states, and the same can be assumed of Lithuania and its signing of a readmission agreement with Denmark.

Generally speaking, it would be beneficial if the main countries of origin and transit received more substantial support than in the past for both the readmission of their own nationals and the readmission of third country nationals who illegally moved on to other countries.

So far, however, Germany's revamping of its relationships with Poland and the Czech Republic has not yet inspired widespread movement toward a European policy of solidarity and burden sharing with the main countries of origin and transit. The approaches outlined by the ministers responsible for immigration matters in their report to the European Council on immigration and asylum policies as well as the statements contained in the so-called Flynn Report of 24 February 1994 still need to be more widely applied.

Appendix: Agreement Between Belgium, Germany, France, Italy, Luxembourg, the Netherlands and Poland on the Readmission of Persons in an Unauthorized Situation*

Agreement

on the readmission of persons in an unauthorized situation

The Governments of the Kingdom of Belgium, the Federal Republic of Germany, the French Republic, the Italian Republic, the Grand Duchy of Luxembourg, the Kingdom of the Netherlands and the Republic of Poland, hereinafter called the Contracting Parties,

- in carrying out a common visa policy of the Contracting Parties bound by the Schengen Agreement of 14 June 1985.
- in order to offset the burden likely to result from the movement of travelers not subject to a visa requirement who are nationals of the Contracting Parties to the present Agreement,
- wishing to facilitate the readmission of persons in an unauthorized situation in a spirit of cooperation and on a basis of reciprocity,
- with the intention of inviting the Governments of other States to accede to the present Agreement,

Have agreed as follows:

Article 1

1. Each Contracting Party shall readmit to its territory, at the request of another Contracting Party and without formalities, any person who does not fulfill or who no longer fulfills the entry or visit conditions applicable within the territory of the requesting Contracting Party provided that it has been established or is assumed that the person has the nationality of the requested Contracting Party.
2. The requesting Contracting Party, shall readmit the person on the same conditions if subsequent checks show that the person did not have the nationality of the requested Contracting Party at the time of leaving the territory of the requesting Contracting Party.

Article 2

1. At the request of a Contracting Party, the Contracting Party whose external border was the point of entry of the person who does not fulfill or who no longer fulfills the entry or visit conditions applicable within the territory of the requesting Contracting Party shall readmit that person to its territory without formalities.

2. For the purposes of this Article, external border means the first border crossed which is not an internal border of the Contracting Parties within the meaning of the Schengen Agreement of 14 June 1985 on the gradual abolition of checks at common borders

3. The readmission obligation referred to in paragraph 1 of this Article shall not exist in the case of a person who, when entering the territory of the requesting Contracting Party, is in possession of a valid visa or residence permit issued by that Contracting Party, or who, after entry, has been provided by that Contracting Party with a visa or a residence permit.

4. Where the person referred to in paragraph 1 of this Article has a valid visa or residence permit issued by a Contracting Party, that Contracting Party shall readmit the person to its territory without formalities at the request of the requesting Contracting Party.

5. For the purposes of paragraphs 3 and 4 of this Article, residence permit means any authorization of whatever nature issued by a Contracting Party and giving the right to stay on its territory. This definition shall not cover temporary admission to stay in the territory of a Contracting Party during examination of an application for asylum or for a residence permit.

Article 3

1. The requested Contracting Party shall be required to reply within a maximum period of eight days to any requests for readmission submitted to it.

2. The requested Contracting Party shall be required to take charge within a maximum period of one month of the person whom it has agreed to readmit. That period may be extended at the request of the requesting Contracting Party.

Article 4

The central or local authorities responsible for dealing with requests for readmission shall be designated by the Ministers with responsibility for border controls and notified to the Contracting Parties through diplomatic channels no later than the date of signing of this Agreement or of accession thereto.

Article 5

1. The provisions of this Agreement shall not stand in the way of application of the provisions of the Geneva Convention of 28 July 1951 relating to the Status of Refugees, as amended by the New York Protocol of 31 January 1967.

2. The provisions of this Agreement shall not call into question any obligations arising from Community law for those Contracting Parties which are members of the European Communities.

3. The provisions of this Agreement shall not stand in the way of application of the provisions of the Schengen Agreement on the gradual abolition of checks at common borders or to application of the provisions of the Convention applying that Agreement signed on 19 June 1990 and of the Dublin Convention of 15 June 1990 determining the State responsible for examining applications for asylum lodged in one of the Member States of the European Communities.

Article 6

1. This Agreement shall be signed without being subject to ratification, acceptance or approval, or subject to ratification, acceptance or approval, followed by ratification, acceptance or approval.

2. This Agreement shall apply provisionally as from the first day of the month following the date of its signing.

3. This Agreement shall enter into force on the first day of the second month following the date by which any two Contracting Parties have expressed their consent to be bound by the Agreement in accordance with the provisions of paragraph 1 of this Article.

4. In the case of each Contracting Party which subsequently expresses its consent to be bound by the Agreement, the latter shall enter into force on the first day of the second month following receipt of notification by the depository.

Article 7

1. The Contracting Parties may decide by common accord to invite other States to accede to this Agreement. Any such decision shall be taken unanimously.

2. There may be provisional accession to this Agreement once it provisionally applies.

3. This Agreement shall enter into force for an acceding State on the first day of the second month following the deposit of the instrument of accession with the depository by that State and no sooner than the day of entry into force of this Agreement.

Article 8

1. Any Contracting Party may notify the depository of a proposal to amend this Agreement.

2. The Contracting Parties shall adopt any amendments to this Agreement by common accord.

3. Any amendments shall enter into force on the first day of the month following the date on which the last Contracting Party consented to be bound by the amendments to this Agreement.

Article 9

1. Each Contracting Party may, after consultation with the other Contracting Parties, suspend or denounce this Agreement on serious grounds by notification addressed to the depository.
2. Any suspension or denunciation shall take effect on the first day of the month following receipt of notification by the depository.

Article 10

The Government of the Grand Duchy of Luxembourg shall be the depository of this Agreement.

In witness whereof, the undersigned, duly empowered to this effect, have hereunto set their hands.

Done at Brussels, this twenty-ninth day of March in the year one thousand nine hundred and ninety-one, in a single original, in the Dutch, French, German, Italian, and Polish languages, all five texts being equally authentic, which shall be deposited in the archives of the Government of the Grand Duchy of Luxembourg.

For the Government of the Kingdom of Belgium
For the Government of the Federal Republic of Germany
For the Government of the French Republic
For the Government of the Italian Republic
For the Government of the Grand Duchy of Luxembourg
For the Government of the Kingdom of the Netherlands
For the Government of the of the Republic of Poland

Joint Statement

On the occasion of the signing of the Agreement on the readmission of persons in an unauthorized situation on 29 March 1991 in Brussels, the Contracting Parties state that they undertake:

- not to apply the procedures of the Agreement in the case of nationals of third countries where it has been established that such persons entered the territory of the requesting Contracting Party before the date of provisional application of the Agreement;
- not to refer to the procedures of the Agreement in the case of nationals of one of the States which are Signatories to the Agreement, where it has been established that such persons entered the territory of the requesting Contracting Party before the date of provisional application of the Agreement.

The Contracting Parties reaffirm their commitment to take back their nationals in accordance with the general principles of international law.

Done at Brussels, this twenty-ninth day of March in the year one thousand nine hundred and ninety-one, in a single original, in the Dutch, French, German, Italian, and Polish languages, all five texts being equally authentic, which shall be deposited in the archives of the Government of the Grand Duchy of Luxembourg.

For the Government of the Kingdom of Belgium
For the Government of the Federal Republic of Germany
For the Government of the French Republic
For the Government of the Italian Republic
For the Government of the Grand Duchy of Luxembourg
For the Government of the Kingdom of the Netherlands
For the Government of the of the Republic of Poland

Minutes

At the time of signing of the Agreement on the readmission of persons in an unauthorized situation, the Contracting Parties bound by the Schengen Agreement of 14 June 1985, hereinafter referred to as the Contracting Parties, made the following joint declarations:

1. Declaration re Articles 1, 2 and 5(2):

   At the request of a Contracting Party, the Contracting Parties will coordinate their positions on the procedure for handing over an alien in compliance with the objectives of the Convention applying the Schengen Agreement of 19 June 1990, in particular regarding immediate handing over in a way that involves the least possible burden on the Contracting Parties in accordance with Articles 1 and 2 of the Agreement on readmission. In doing so they will provide the compensation for any financial imbalances which is referred to in Article 24 of the Convention applying the Schengen Agreement of 15 June 1990.

2. Declaration re Articles 2 and 5(3):

   The readmission obligation on the Contracting Parties which results from the readmission Agreement is provisionally limited to nationals of the Republic of Poland. The readmission obligation will be extended to the nationals of other States by decision of the Executive Committee set up by Article 131 of the Convention applying the Schengen Agreement of 19 June 1990, when the latter has entered into force and, in the period preceding that entry into force, of the Ministers with responsibility under national law.

3. Declaration re Articles 8 and 5(3):

   The Contracting Parties agree that on entry into force of the Convention applying the Schengen Agreement of 19 June 1990, they will examine together whether the readmission Agreement requires adaptation.

4. Declaration re Articles 9 and 5(3):
   In the case of suspension or denunciation of the readmission Agreement by one of the Contracting Parties the other Contracting Parties may also suspend or denounce this Agreement.

Done at Brussels, this twenty-ninth day of March in the year one thousand nine hundred and ninety-one, in a single original, in the Dutch, French, German, Italian, and Polish languages, all five texts being equally authentic, which shall be deposited in the archives of the Government of the Grand Duchy of Luxembourg.

For the Government of the Kingdom of Belgium
For the Government of the Federal Republic of Germany
For the Government of the French Republic
For the Government of the Italian Republic
For the Government of the Grand Duchy of Luxembourg
For the Government of the Kingdom of the Netherlands

*Ad Hoc Group Immigration, Brussels, 18 Jan. 1993 (22.01) (OR. f), SN 1907/1/92 (WGI 1032), Rev 1., erd/PT/ldb, Annex.

References

BAnZ 1990. No. 217.

Bundesgesetzblatt 1994. II.

Council of Europe. 1991. "Conference of Ministers of the Movement of Persons from Central and Eastern European Countries, Vienna, 24—25 January 1991." MMP (91)7 Vienna, 25 Jan.

de Claparède, Alfred. 1911. *Die völkerrechtliche Repatriationspflicht in ihrer Entwicklung, dargestellt an den sie betreffenden Verträgen der Schweiz und des Deutschen Reiches*. Doctoral dissertation. Würzburg.

Plender, Richard. 1988. *International Migration Law*. Rev. 2d ed. Dordrecht (u.a.). Nijhoff.

Randelzhofer, Albrecht. 1985. "Nationality." In *Encyclopedia of Public International Law,* ed. R. Bernhardt. Instalment 8. Amsterdam: North Holland.

Verdross, A. 1950. *Völkerrecht* 2d ed. Vienna: Springer.

Weis, P. 1979. *Nationality and Statelessness in International law.* 2d ed. Alphen aan den Rijn, The Netherlands; Germantown, USA; Sÿthoff & Noordhoff.

_____ . 1962. *Staatsangehörigkeit und Staatenlosigkeit im gegenwärtigen Völkerrecht.* Lecture given to the Berliner Juristische Gesellschaft, 29 June, Berlin.

_____ . 1956. *Nationality and Statelessness in International Law.* 1st ed. London: Stevens.

Chapter 5

Migration Return Policies and Countries of Origin

Rosemarie Rogers

This paper addresses the strategies available to host countries to encourage, facilitate, or force the return of migrants whose entry was earlier welcomed or tolerated with the expectation that their stays would be temporary. I consider five types of migrant populations: "temporary workers" or "guest workers"; persons granted temporary asylum in developing countries; persons granted temporary asylum in industrialized countries; rejected asylum seekers in developing countries; and rejected asylum seekers in industrialized countries. How effective are the various return measures that have been used by the host countries? Are the financial and other costs of these programs worth the effort? In what ways have migrants, policymakers, and the public in the host countries, the home countries, and third countries, as well as the relevant international organizations, reacted to different programs? In short, how viable are such measures?

For this analysis I draw on statistical and other reports by governments, international organizations, and NGOs; on secondary sources; and on interviews with migrants, researchers, officials in host and home country governments and international organizations, and service providers to migrants. In some cases, a lack of data is not surprising because the programs are relatively new; in other instances, a lack of data seems to reflect

---

inadequate record keeping or perhaps an unwillingness on the part of authorities to bring the data together or to publish them. In order to evaluate the effectiveness of return programs for European guest workers, it would be helpful to know in all cases the incidence of spontaneous returns; however, precise information is not always available. Yet, such a lack of data is not an obstacle to analysis when returns under specific programs number in the hundreds or low thousands, while the number of spontaneous returns was larger by at least one or two magnitudes. Other data are unavailable as well. For example, I do not know how many migrants, including rejected asylum seekers and those granted asylum on a temporary basis who were expected to leave a Western host country, have "disappeared" among the general population—that is, have become illegal residents.

This paper examines all types of return policies that have been used with respect to the five populations mentioned earlier. Such policies range from return incentives to return assistance to various forms of forced return. The line between return incentives and return or reintegration assistance is not always clear. Indeed, when host countries, third countries, or international institutions institute programs that appear to be intended as return incentives (programs aimed at convincing migrants to return when they otherwise would stay, or to return earlier or voluntarily when they otherwise might return at a much later date or would have to be returned by force), those offering the programs usually refer to them as return "aid."

One condition that distinguishes return incentive from return assistance programs is that the former frequently involve a deadline by which the migrants must apply if they are to be eligible for the benefits—an element of pressure that is absent in the latter programs. The deadline is either inherent in the life of the program itself (i.e., it is announced that the program will cease to exist after a certain date) or it refers to the date by which the migrants' status changed (for example, a program may be available to unemployed migrants for a certain number of months after termination of their employment or to rejected asylum seekers for a certain period after they were apprised of the negative decision). However, I have also included in my discussions of return incentives some programs that did not involve a deadline, primarily because they seem to have been perceived as return incentives by migrants or by policy-makers in the home country.

Return incentive programs were primarily developed in the context of the guest-worker migrations in Western Europe and the Comprehensive Plan of Action in Southeast Asia. An element that characterizes all such programs for European guest workers is the fact that they were instituted unilaterally by the host countries, rather than in cooperation with the sending countries.

In general, the involvement of the international community in return programs tends to be considerable in developing countries but is almost absent in industrialized countries. This is the same as saying that it is considerable in most situations of forced migration (or in situations where a claim of forced migration has been made, as in the case of Vietnamese and Laotian asylum seekers who were "screened out"). With respect to labor migrants, therefore, it is not surprising that a recent instance of decisive involvement by the international community concerned precisely a situation of forced migration and of return to developing countries, i.e., the flight or expulsion of temporary migrant workers from Kuwait and Iraq.

Temporary Workers, Guest Workers

There is a tension in all contexts of intended temporary migration between assuring rotation of the foreign workforce and responding to the needs of the migrants and their employers. If a migration is to remain truly temporary, it is best for the host country to grant only limited economic rights (for example, to tie the migrants to one employer or withhold a part of their earnings until their departure), to grant even fewer social rights (for example, to set restrictions on family reunification or keep the migrants' children out of host country schools), and to grant no political rights. Contracts are offered only after the migrants have returned home for a certain period of time following the expiration of the earlier contracts.

It is not difficult to understand why there would be pressures for permanence: employers must reconcile the frequent turnover of workers with their need for a skilled and experienced labor force and may resist having to pay what they consider to be unnecessary transportation costs; lack of predictability of the labor supply creates insecurity and potential costs; government bureaucracies must deal with a substantial enforcement problem; and the migrants prefer to have the greater freedom that comes with longer residence.

In the 1970s the South African mines, with their system of "oscillating migration," experienced all these tensions (Böhning 1981; Stahl 1981; Curtin 1978; Wilson 1976; Hance 1970). One response to this was the creation of a system of reemployment guarantees and bonuses aimed at encouraging foreign migrants to return to their previous jobs after their several months of enforced residence at home (Elkan 1978). Another response was to diversify the sources of foreign labor. A third was to reduce reliance on foreign miners by employing more native workers.[1] Even with the application of strict measures of control, however, some migrants remained in the country illegally (World Bank 1977).

The oil-rich countries in the Middle East, which for decades have relied heavily on foreign labor, have been relatively more successful in assuring rotation than has Western Europe, with its "guest-worker" populations that were recruited primarily in the 1960s and 1970s. Migrant workers in the Middle East are frequently tied to a specific employer. Family reunification is permitted only for migrants who earn substantial incomes. The Middle Eastern host countries have also increasingly diversified their labor supply, from the Arab world to South Asia to East Asia. Nevertheless, the 1975 Kuwait census already showed that substantial proportions of the Jordanian and Palestinian migrant populations had been in the country for more than five or even ten years and recorded close to 100,000 Jordanian and Palestinian children resident in the country as having been born there (Birks and Sinclair 1980, 52). Today such a pattern can be found in all Middle Eastern host countries and for other migrant groups, despite restrictions on integration.

Still, the insecurity of the migrant populations' status in these countries was demonstrated by the forced exodus of foreigners from Kuwait, Iraq, and Saudi Arabia (Yemenis) during the 1990 and 1991 Gulf crisis. These events gave rise to an untypical "return program" for labor migrants. More than one million migrants left or were expelled from Kuwait and Iraq in the wake of the Iraqi invasion of Kuwait in 1990 and Saddam Hussein's defeat following the Allied intervention in 1991 (IOM 1992, 14). Although these people were not refugees, i.e., they were not threatened by their own governments or deprived of their governments' protection, their "flight" from the host countries represented a humanitarian emergency. Their exodus was as chaotic as that of many refugees fleeing violence in their own countries, and their return home had to be assisted like the mass returns of refugees—although return in this instance was prompted by a negative change in the conditions in the host country rather than by a positive change in the conditions in the home country. The international community stepped in to assist those returning to home countries beyond Jordan, mostly workers from South Asia. Some left through Iran and Turkey; over 700,000 returned home through Jordan (UNDRO n.d., 1). They were efficiently helped by local authorities, their own embassies, the United Nations Disaster Relief Office (UNDRO), other organizations within the UN system, the International Labour Organisation (ILO), and the International Organization for Migration (IOM). Many individual countries, as well as the European Community, funded the returns.

In Western Europe, rotation systems exist for seasonal migrant workers. These systems are uncontroversial when short-term contracts are involved, as with migrants working in the harvest, e.g., in southern France. However, in Switzerland, where seasonal workers have been widely used in construction, tourism, and other sectors and where many, if not most, contracts permit a maximum stay of nine months, there has been a tension between reliance on a restrictive rotation system, on the one hand, and the need to respond to migrants' and employers' preferences, on the other. Since the mid-1980s it has been possible to commute seasonal permits into annual permits after four years of seasonal employment in Switzerland, provided that within this period the migrant worked for the maximum of thirty-six months (Leimgruber 1992, 13).[2] Today Switzerland is moving altogether away from its heavy reliance on seasonal workers in order to bring its migration policies into line with those of other West European countries.

From the initial introduction of guest-worker systems in Western Europe after World War II (which occurred at different points in time in the various host countries, depending on their economic situation and the existence of alternative sources of labor), migrants who were granted yearly permits were permitted to renew them within their host countries without having to return home. In principle, it would nevertheless have been possible to enforce rotation simply by refusing to renew a permit when a further extension would have enabled the migrant to obtain a more protected residence and work status. For example, in Switzerland a year-round migrant becomes a permanent resident after ten years, and since 1971 Germany has granted five-year extensions of work permits to migrants who have worked there for five previous years. However, Switzerland abandoned its rotation policy in 1958 (Leimgruber 1992, 11), and Germany never formally enforced rotation, although in policy discussions the "rotation principle" was consistently referred to throughout the 1960s and early 1970s.[3]

Over time, all West European host countries gradually eased restrictions on family reunification, so that by the time recruitment stopped in 1973/74 this process was a given. Family reunification in fact accelerated in the 1970s as a consequence of the halt to recruitment. Thus any increased return of workers in 1973/74 was soon offset by additional arrivals of migrants' family members. This was a clear indication that the settling process of much of Western Europe's foreign population, already begun in the preceding years, was intensifying. Some host countries sought to slow the process through a number of restrictive measures,[4] but the enforcement of returns was not an option. Hence the question arose whether governments might be able to offer incentives to encourage a substantial number of migrant workers to return home with their families, with the stipulation that they would not be able to return to the host country.

Return Incentive Programs[5]

The first host country to institute a return incentive program was France. Called *aide-au-retour,* the program was designed in 1977 for unemployed migrants from southern Europe (except Italy, an EC member), North Africa, and sub-Saharan Africa. The offer consisted of 10,000 francs for the returning breadwinner; the same amount for a spouse who was separately eligible, or 5,000 francs for one who was not; 5,000 francs for each dependent child; and the coverage of travel costs. In order to qualify, migrants had to apply within a certain time period after becoming unemployed. Four months after the program's inception, the offer was extended to employed migrants, and the deadline for application was dropped. The program was criticized by the sending countries and by advocacy groups in France: it had been unilaterally instituted and did not take the needs of the sending countries into account; the initial time pressure implied an element of coercion; the return bonus was too small to help the migrants to reestablish themselves at home; participating migrants lost important social benefits in France; and the program's legal basis was questionable (it had been instituted through a government circular). In fact, the program was declared unconstitutional in 1979, but it continued to operate until 1981 (France 1985, 82).

The program's effects were modest numerically and differed from what had been expected. Of the 60,000 workers who used it, less than one-quarter were unemployed; and of the total of 94,000 beneficiaries (workers and family members), a full 65 percent were Portuguese and Spanish. It had been hoped that the program would particularly attract migrants from the Maghreb and other parts of Africa—those considered to be the most difficult to integrate (Manfrass 1986, 76–77; "Rückkehrförderung ausländischer Arbeitnehmer in Frankreich" 1982).[6] Total return flows from France during these years amounted to approximately 70,000 per year.

In 1984 the French National Immigration Office (ONI) instituted another program of "reintegration aid" for unemployed foreign workers (except citizens of EC countries) and workers whose firms has requested permission to lay them off. At this time the program is still in existence. Originally it too required that the unemployed apply before a specific deadline, but this requirement again has been dropped. Applicants must have a "project" for their reinsertion into the home country (for example, opening a small shop or certain work in agriculture), but ONI officials admit that projects are discussed seriously only if the returnees request the office's help with their plans. The aid package consists of a cash payment by the French insurance office, state funds directed toward realization of the migrant's project and toward transportation and moving costs, and—in the case of those threatened by layoffs—a contribution by the employer (beyond the obligatory severance pay).

Although the program is again presented as return "aid," a manager in a French firm who had worked with ONI to conceptualize the aid package suggested in a 1985 interview that, whatever its name and the details, the new program was merely the old *aide-au-retour* incentive scheme in a new wrapping: its purpose was to get rid of as many unskilled, poorly integrated foreign workers as possible. How successful has the program been? The number of applicants was highest (13,873) in 1985, during the program's first full year of operation. Since then, the number has declined steadily, remaining well below 1,000 in each of the last five years for which data are available (1989–93). Officials at the Office for International Migrations (OMI, formerly ONI) suggest that the decline in the number of applicants is due to the poor state of the economies of the migrants' home countries, the excellent benefits the migrants receive in France, the fact that some returnees' projects were unsuccessful, and to awareness on the part of migrants in France that some beneficiaries have regretted their decisions and have in fact sought to return to France. Between 1984 and 1993, the total number of migrant worker beneficiaries was 31,648; when family members are added in, a total of 71,623 persons left with the help of the program. This number is exceedingly small if the program is evaluated as a *return incentive*, but obviously the program does provide some assistance to a subset of returning migrants. It probably also plays a role in satisfying public opinion (Manfrass 1986; "Immigration et présence étrangère de 1984 à 1986" 1987; France 1987, 1993, 1994; interviews with ONI [OMI] officials in 1985, 1990, 1994).

In Germany, return incentives were not used until 1983, several years after the institution of the first French return program. (A German state government had experimented with such a system in the 1970s, but the federal government had come out against it.) The centerpiece of German return policies in the 1980s was the "Law to Support (Enhance/Subsidize) Foreigners' Willingness to Return" *(Gesetz zur Förderung der Rückkehrbereitschaft von Ausländern)* promulgated on 30 November 1983 (Hönekopp 1987b). It consisted of two major instruments:

1. "Immediate repayment of workers' contributions to social security". Deadline for application, 30 June 1984. Available to workers who were eligible for such repayment, albeit normally only after a two-year waiting period. (This provision did not apply to citizens of EC-member countries and of countries with which the Federal Republic had bilateral social security agreements, notably Yugoslavia and Spain.) The eligible population included Turks, Portuguese, Moroccans, Tunisians, and Koreans, among others. The beneficiary (but not necessarily his family) had to leave Germany and was not allowed to return there in subsequent years to take up work.

2. "Return aid". Deadline for application, 30 June 1984. Available to workers from former recruitment countries outside the EC (Portugal, Spain, Turkey, Yugoslavia, Morocco, Tunisia, and Korea) who had become unemployed between 30 October 1983 and 30 June 1984 as a result of a complete or partial shutdown of their place of work or who had been forced to work short hours for six months or more. Beneficiaries had to leave Germany with their spouses and dependent children and were not permitted subsequently to return to Germany to take up work. Return aid amounted to DM 10,500 for primary beneficiaries and DM 1,500 for each eligible child. Full aid was granted only if the application was filed no later than four weeks after the worker became unemployed or became eligible for aid due to short hours. A penalty was assessed for each month's delay in application.

In addition to these benefits, returning foreigners who had received repayment of their social security contributions were able to withdraw their government-subsidized savings before maturation and without penalty and to receive severance pay. Also, in conjunction with the offer of return aid, those interested in returning were offered advice concerning general conditions for return and opportunities for economic reintegration, including opportunities for self-employment. Unlike the financial offers, which had involved a time limit, consultation services for returnees were introduced for the indefinite future.

One final program permitted returning foreigners to access funds paid into special German savings plans for housing construction and to use these funds in foreign countries even before their maturation date. This program also had no deadline.

As in the French case, the return programs instituted in Germany had relatively little effect on the number of returns recorded. The German programs were not extended beyond the original deadline.[7] Applications for "immediate repayment of workers' contributions to social security" numbered approximately 135,000, with 120,000 positive decisions. Among these 120,000 positive decisions, 93,000 involved Turkish applicants and 14,250 involved Portuguese applicants; these Turkish and Portuguese applicants received an average of DM 21,870 and DM 22,780, respectively (Hönekopp 1987b, 296–97). "Return aid" was sought by 16,920 applicants and ultimately granted to 13,694 (Hönekopp 1987b, 298).

After analysis of available official data, Elmar Hönekopp concluded that the offer of return aid alone was relatively unsuccessful in encouraging migrants to return. This is evidenced in part by the very light use made of the program by unemployed Spaniards and Yugoslavs, who were not eligible for repayment of social security contributions. Hönekopp concluded further that the offer of immediate repayment of social security contributions, with or without additional return aid, influenced more the timing than the volume of returns: although 247,000 citizens of former recruitment countries—especially Portuguese, Turks, and Tunisians—left Germany in the first nine months of 1984, which is 133,000 more than in the same time span in the previous year, a considerable number of migrants (variously estimated to be as high as 60,000–80,000) appear to have *postponed* their intended returns after discussions of return aid began in 1981. On the other hand, returns by members of the same migrant groups in the same time span in 1985 only amounted to 77,400, suggesting that returns may also have been *hastened* by the existing law. Taking into account these two factors, as well as the probability that there was less undercounting of exits during the period in which the law was valid, the estimated number of foreigners for whom the law functioned as a pure return incentive is, by Hönekopp's calculations, 133,000 minus 40,000 minus 20,000 minus 28,000, or a total of only 45,000.

The Belgian government promulgated a return incentive scheme in 1985. This program was designed to be valid for three years. As with the French and German programs, it was intended for migrants from non-EC member countries (and also excluded Portuguese and Spaniards). Applicants had to have been unemployed for at least a year. Of 67,326 registered unemployed foreigners in Belgium in 1984, 26,963 came from non-EC member countries. Those who accepted the "reinsertion bonus" (which amounted to 312 times the daily unemployment compensation, plus 50,000 Belgian francs for spouses and 15,000 Belgian francs for each child) had to leave Belgium with their families ("De terugkeergedachte" 1984; Frey 1986, 50–51). Between 1 August 1985 and 1 June 1987, 175 out of 384 applications were accepted, leading to the departure of 510 foreign workers and dependents to Turkey, Morocco, Tunisia, and Algeria (Dumon and Michiels 1987, 61–62).

The Dutch parliament rejected proposals for a return bonus scheme in the 1970s. With the introduction of its "minorities policy" in the early 1980s, the Dutch government came out strongly in favor of settlement of the labor migrants. At that time, a return aid scheme that had been in existence for almost a decade was closed down for reasons of cost and, it was argued, so that migrants would not receive the wrong signals concerning promotion of return. Nevertheless, in 1985 the Dutch government unilaterally instituted two new return programs. These involved no deadlines but prohibited remigration to the Netherlands by the returnees. The sending countries reacted to these policies with concern and suspicion (see, for example, "Retornar desde Holanda" 1988), as they had also done with the French and German schemes.

The first Dutch program offered coverage for travel and moving costs, as well as subsistence costs for the first three months in the home country. Under the second program, it was possible for foreign citizens aged 55 years or more who had been unemployed for at least six months to return home without losing their unemployment benefits. Returnees under this program received a reduced benefit (the exact amount varied according to the cost of living in each particular country) until the age of 65, at which time they became eligible for their pensions. By 1 May 1987, 531 Turkish and 113 Moroccan families had made use of these provisions ("Retornar desde Holanda" 1988; Sociaal en Cultureel Planbureau 1987, 19).

Lastly, Switzerland and Sweden did not offer return incentives: such programs would have been inconsistent with Sweden's strong emphasis on migrants' integration and contrary to the Swiss policy of still taking in a number of "new" migrants on annual contracts every year.[8]

Migrant-sending countries reacted to all these return incentive programs with considerable alarm. Official and quasi-official statements that the 1980s were not a time to return home—or at least not a time to return home without specific plans—abounded. For example, a magazine for Spaniards abroad published by the Spanish government emphasized, "Many [emigrants], even if they wish it, cannot return to Spain right now, given the economic and social crisis situation experienced by the Spanish economy" (Sturckow y Gonzalez 1986, 27). A report on a German-Turkish symposium on the occupational integration of the second generation in Germany and Turkey also advised migrants not to return: "Return incentive policies are against Turkey's interests. Return is also against the interests of the returnees. In Turkey there are no institutions for reintegration that could assist returns. The bilateral agreements between Turkey and the Federal Republic do not work well. So far no reintegration assistance project has come to fruition. Therefore the future of the second generation of Turkish migrants ... remains in the Federal Republic" (Akcayli 1987, 21.).

Return Assistance and Development Projects

Home countries have always offered some minimal help to returning migrants, e.g., easing import duties, permitting migrants to keep foreign currency accounts, and providing information about housing, schools, and the labor market. A good description of these programs during the early period of the European labor migrations can be found in van Gendt (1977). Host countries have offered various professional training programs, credit and consulting to migrants who wished to become self-employed, and, in the 1980s, programs that would help the reintegration of second-generation returnees, especially with regard to schooling. Most, but not all, of these programs were formulated in cooperation with organizations in the sending countries or were based on formal bilateral agreements with the sending country governments.

France had one of the first job-training programs for prospective returnees *(formation-retour)*. Between 1975 and 1980 this program had 1,625 participants, at an approximate cost of 47,000 francs over a ten-month period per participant (Frey 1986, 42–43). As the unemployment rate rose, however, French policymakers were no longer satisfied to offer only this program; they decided in 1977 to devise a proper return incentive scheme—the return bonus program discussed above.

Germany has offered various forms of reintegration assistance to prospective returnees. Take Greece, for example: In 1980 Germany and Greece concluded an agreement[9] concerning Germany's role in assisting the reintegration of Greek migrants who wished to return home. In 1987 professional training leading to employment either in Germany or in Greece was offered to young Greek migrants. The German organizers of this program sought appropriate apprenticeship opportunities through the local labor offices in Germany, but some of the training also took place in Greece (Lenske 1988). Similarly, from 1986 to 1988 Germany offered Turkish youths a two-year training program in the hotel sector, which was to lead to firm employment in Turkey. This program served thirty participants (Germany, Der Bundesminister für Arbeit und Sozialordnung 1986). More generally, the German government has, with the aid of a consulting firm, made a systematic effort to supply potential return migrants with information and advice concerning return opportunities (ISOPLAN 1983–present).

The Netherlands launched a program in 1974 to explore whether foreign migrants and their savings could play a role in efforts to ameliorate the root causes of labor migration, i.e., the need for economic development in the home countries. The REMPLOD (Reintegration of Emigrant Manpower and the Promotion of Local Opportunities for Development) project was responsible for investigating how the Dutch Ministry of Development Cooperation could extend development aid to five labor-sending countries in a way that would involve returning migrants (and their savings) in newly generated projects. However, within two years, research in Turkey, Morocco, and Tunisia (which resulted in a number of excellent books) led investigators to conclude that the project should be terminated and that instead the ministry's development assistance should be reoriented toward employment creation in the broadest terms, without reference to labor migrants.

Although this recommendation was accepted, a small proportion of REMPLOD funds was nevertheless dedicated to assisting individual migrants' return projects. The resultant program (NCB-IMOS) was administered by the Netherlands Center for Foreigners and was well conceived: it required that participants have good qualifications and considerable financing on their own, as well as carefully designed and appropriately documented project plans (elaborated in cooperation with authorities and consultants in the home countries) in economic sectors that promised success. Once these criteria were met, the program offered advice and subsidized credits toward the realization of the returnees' projects. These returnees, as a result, became self-employed and created additional jobs (often for family members). However, although the program was able to show good results in the sense that most of the returnees it had supported were successful, it was terminated by the Dutch government in 1984. After almost eight years, the enterprises thus created numbered only in the low hundreds (more were at different stages of planning). It was argued that this result did not justify the high cost of the program and, furthermore, that the emphasis on return was not in the spirit of the Netherlands' new "minorities policy" (Rogers 1988).

In Belgium, impecunious labor migrants who wish to return home have been included in a modest return assistance program offered since 1984. This program has served primarily asylum seekers (both those rejected and those with pending claims) who wish to return. Such migrants are offered a small amount of cash and moving and travel costs. The program will be discussed in somewhat more detail later in this paper ("De terugkeergedachte" 1984; Frey 1986, 50).

There were also instances in which individual migrants initiated development efforts. One particular example dealing with Turkish migrants should be mentioned because it eventually came to involve the cooperation of the host country, Germany. In 1967 a Turkish engineer working in Cologne conceived the idea that Turkish workers could establish enterprises at home, which would create new jobs and lessen the need for out-migration. This goal was to be achieved by the migrants buying shares in the to-be-established companies, which would later pay dividends to the investor. Since the price of the average share was relatively small, the number of shareholders needed to start a company was far larger than the number of jobs created; therefore investment was not likely to create a return incentive, something Turkey wished to avoid.

Among the considerable problems encountered by the fledgling companies were the following: the sites for the new plants and the technologies to be used in them were often not optimal; Turkish law did not properly accommodate such initiatives; the requirement that founding capital be deposited in Turkish rather than foreign currency made the companies victims of inflation before they were even established; managers were often poorly prepared for their jobs; and there were instances of outright fraud.

The Turkish government was slow to support these companies, but the German government, through its Ministry of Development Cooperation, seized on the opportunity. Among the components of the so-called Ankara Agreement of 7 December 1972 was the provision of credit and consulting services to workers' companies. Other parts of the agreement concerned the training of workers for semiskilled and skilled positions; training of skilled workers for foreman and managerial positions (in conjunction with job offers from Turkey); and credit and consulting arrangements for workers to aid them in founding, with their own savings, small individual enterprises. However, although it had ratified the agreement, the Turkish government seems to have feared that the proposed measures might serve as return incentives. It therefore used the instrument only to support workers' companies, and even so, the credit fund for this purpose was not activated until the mid-1970s.[10]

The Turkish workers' companies did not meet with great success in the long run. Although 223 companies were functioning in the early 1980s, only 28 did so at more than 69 percent capacity. With approximately 15,000 jobs created, most of the 345,000 shareholders (Sen 1986, 45) could in any case not expect to find employment, but more importantly, the wages paid for these jobs were below what most returning migrants would have found acceptable. Only a handful of the companies paid dividends (Sen 1987, 12). By the end of the 1980s many shares were being bought up by banks and large companies. In 1985 a special Turkish-German program was established in an attempt to save at least some of the enterprises; these efforts continued into the 1990s (see, for example, Development Bank of Turkey 1990). The model of the Turkish workers' companies has not worked.[11]

Concluding Remarks

West European return incentive programs, which were instituted unilaterally by the host countries, were not popular with governments in the migrants' home countries. They were often aimed at "weaker" members of the labor force (the unemployed); at least this was the case when they were initially formulated. Furthermore, they frequently involved a deadline. Migrants who participated in the programs were expected to return home for good, usually with their families. However, these returnees rarely had the opportunity to go home for any length of time beforehand to "try out" a return or at least to explore in some detail the possibilities for reintegration (although France appears to have been more lenient than the other countries in this respect). Several studies highlight the negative aspects of such a policy. In the 1980s research on returnees from Germany to Turkey showed that at most 50 percent of the respondents in a given sample had created or found employment; some studies found considerably lower proportions (Hönekopp 1987b; Akcayli and Sen 1987).

It is not surprising that spokespeople for home country governments warned migrants not to make return decisions hastily. Migrants were implored to plan their returns carefully, to weigh carefully what they were giving up in terms of social benefits and entitlements by leaving the host country, and to know precisely whether they could buy into pension schemes in the home countries.

With the enlargement of the European Community, the various financial return aid programs became more and more unambiguously aimed at those nationalities considered to be particularly difficult to integrate: Turks, citizens of the Maghreb countries, and (in France) black Africans. The number of migrants using such programs has been quite small; in some instances it seems that the programs have been used mainly by migrants who would have returned in any case. Presumably policymakers had higher expectations for their programs; however, part of the schemes' purpose may also have been to placate domestic public opinion, which often seeks to make foreign workers into scapegoats for the host countries' unemployment problems.

The experience of second-generation migrants who were caught up in these returns suggested that history ironically was repeating itself: the return policies affecting their lives have been, in many ways, as ad hoc as the policies of sending and receiving countries ten or twenty years earlier when labor migration was encouraged. Just as some of the migrants, as well as their older relatives and friends, experienced all the problems associated with "lateral entry" into the school and occupational training systems in the host countries, so they became upon their return "lateral entrants" into similar systems in their "home" countries. Many of them had not wanted to return, but the return aid offered by the host countries stipulated that dependent children had to return with their parents.[12]

Reintegration assistance by the host countries, which is not necessarily easily distinguishable from return incentives, has also been used only sporadically. The best-designed programs are expensive. Furthermore, decisions to return are influenced much more by the economic situation in the home countries or by family matters than by return incentives, and the success and quality of returns are influenced much more by the state of the home countries' or regions' economies than by reintegration assistance (see, for example, the interesting contrasts among return experiences to different regions in Italy, analyzed in Gentileschi and Simoncelli 1983).

The above assessment suggests some questions that may be relevant to new, post–cold war West European policies concerning labor migration from Eastern Europe. Since the end of the cold war, several West European countries have entered into agreements with East European countries regarding temporary employment, sometimes combined with occupational or language training. In his paper in this series (see "The New Labor Migration as an Instrument of German Foreign Policy," ch. 6 in vol. 2), Elmar Hönekopp reports on five such programs for Germany: project-tied work, seasonal work, work involving border commuting, a guest-worker program, and a special program for the employment of nurses. The guest-worker program is intended to provide temporary workers an opportunity to gain skill and language training. It is designed for persons aged eighteen to forty years, with contracts ranging in length from one to one-and-a-half years. Quotas for individual sending countries add up to a total of approximately 10,000. In 1994 about 6,000 European workers were employed under this system.

These programs are somewhat unexpected in light of the West European countries' unsatisfactory experience with guest-worker systems in the past (in the sense that many "temporary" workers became long-term settlers), high unemployment rates and considerable antiforeigner sentiment in the host countries, and in the case of Germany, the high overall volume of immigration and the need to come to terms with the consequences of unification. It therefore seems reasonable to ask whether reasons other than perceived manpower needs can explain the decisions to start new guest-worker programs. One argument for such programs appears to be the desire to assist the new democratic states in Eastern Europe by relieving some of the pressures on their labor markets, although, given the low numbers involved, these programs may represent more a sign of good will and encouragement than substantial assistance. The extent to which the proposed skills and language training will contribute to the home countries' development is also questionable. Are these programs intended in part as quid pro quos for the East European countries' fledgling participation in a coordinated European asylum process? Some argue that the new guest-worker programs, together with various other programs such as those regarding seasonal work or border commuting, may help to curb illegal migration.[13] However, the pool of potential illegal migrants is far larger than can be accommodated by small guest-worker programs. Given this, why do the host countries not simply restrict themselves to employing seasonal workers and border commuters?

Is there reason to assume that the current programs will have different outcomes from the programs of the 1960s and 1970s? New legal arrangements, such as readmission agreements between host and sending countries concerning the citizens of these countries themselves, have been concluded. These stipulations are not really necessary, however; a country has the obligation to take back its own citizens whether or not a bilateral agreement exists to this effect. In the earlier years, the host countries had the option of not renewing workers' contracts upon their expiration. During a time of labor shortages and continued economic growth, they elected not to exercise this option, so by the time of the recruitment stops, the settling processes were already ongoing. Indeed, migrant settlement was one of the reasons for the recruitment stops. Given the different economic situation today, as well as the earlier lessons learned, will the guest-worker programs of the 1990s have a different outcome from those of thirty years ago? Perhaps not, because economic considerations and "lessons learned" would have been arguments against the reinstitution of such programs in the first place.

Refugee Repatriation from Asylum Countries in the Third World

In the last decades, three approaches to asylum have been used in different world regions.

In the Western industrialized countries, asylum has generally been granted on a permanent basis. These countries have rarely had to deal with mass flows, except for the outflows of Hungarians in 1956 and of Czechs and Slovaks in 1968 and the various movements of Cubans to the United States since 1959. Individual status determinations based on the refugee definition embodied in the 1951 UN Convention Relating to the Status of Refugees and its 1967 Protocol therefore served the West well until the 1980s, when the flows of asylum seekers began to increase substantially. Nevertheless, in these host countries the grant of asylum is still usually considered permanent. (In the United States, for example, asylum seekers who have been recognized as refugees may change their status to that of permanent resident after one year.) Essentially, refugees become immigrants. Consistent with this, the host country governments usually make no effort to encourage returns.[14]

Some developing countries have pursued a second approach, granting asylum on a temporary, short-term basis using mass determinations and a broader refugee definition and making this grant of asylum contingent on third-country resettlement. Examples of this approach can be found in the countries of Southeast Asia that received asylum seekers from Indochina, especially from Vietnam, between 1975 and 1989. The changes that have recently occurred in these systems and the resulting issues concerning returns of asylum seekers today will be discussed further below.

Most developing countries have adopted a third approach, granting asylum, based on mass determinations, for an indefinite period of time, but with the understanding that eventually the refugees will go home. Examples are Pakistan (with respect to Afghan refugees) and much of Africa (where some refugee situations date back to the 1960s). In the developing countries (except for Southeast Asia today) a broader criterion for determining refugee status has been added to that of individual persecution: essentially, flight from violence (for example, in civil wars).

Since opportunities for local integration—at least in the full legal sense—are scarce and there is little third-country resettlement of refugees from most developing countries (Rogers and Copeland 1993), repatriation remains the sole option for most of these refugee populations. It is therefore useful to examine the role played by host countries and the international community in the return of refugees from and to developing countries.

With the end of the cold war and, concomitantly, of the proxy wars involving the superpowers, hopes for large-scale repatriations increased. (The UN High Commissioner for Refugees optimistically referred to the 1990s as the "decade of repatriation.") Numerically significant return movements have indeed occurred in Central America, and to Afghanistan, Cambodia, Mozambique, South Africa, and other countries. However, these returns have been more problematic than the oft-cited examples of successful returns, such as those to Zimbabwe in 1980 and more recently to Namibia.

When returns become possible, refugee communities often send a number of their members to the home country to assess the situation. Return movements tend to be refugee-initiated; some refugees return without assistance by the international community. Today, however, the logistic, economic, administrative, and political challenges of mass returns are such that the involvement of international actors has come to be routine. International organizations and NGOs not only provide assistance but perform important protection functions as well. Such support is needed because today most repatriations occur in the face of two major difficulties: first, the home countries are often not yet fully at peace (Stein 1992; Larkin, Cuny, and Stein 1991), and second, the infrastructure of these countries has been devastated by protracted conflicts.

Repatriation Under Conflict

In situations where peace in the home country is not fully assured, UNHCR faces a question of timing. Its traditionally conservative policy of waiting until conditions are "right" may be thwarted by any one of the actors involved. Asylum countries sometimes pressure refugees to return, e.g., by cutting rations or allowing security to deteriorate in the camps, as Ruiz (1992, 8) reported with regard to some of the Afghan camps in Pakistan. When such "inducements" occur, the line between voluntary and forced returns is hardly clear. Home countries may be eager to see refugees return; they view such movements as building confidence and enhancing the prospects for a stronger peace. A recent example is South Africa. Guatemala has come to tolerate refugee-initiated returns as "proof" that its human rights record is improving. Finally, the refugees themselves may not wish to wait any longer; they may decide to return whether or not the international community is ready to provide assistance and protection.

UNHCR has become more flexible in responding to such situations. Rather than insisting on repatriation under the classical tripartite agreements (formulated when, in its judgment, the appropriate time for returns has come), it has been willing to offer some help also under imperfect circumstances. As Ruiz reported with respect to the still dangerous situation in Guatemala in 1993, for example: "UNHCR says that, given the situation in Guatemala, it is not promoting voluntary repatriation at this time, but respecting and responding to the refugees' decision to return by doing what it can to facilitate the return— at the refugees' request" (Ruiz 1993, 10).

Another observer notes that UNHCR's terminology concerning repatriation itself has changed; the emphasis has shifted from "voluntary repatriation" to "repatriation in safety and dignity" to, in 1995, "safe and lasting repatriation" (Bill Frelick, U.S. Committee for Refugees, seminar at Tufts University, Medford, Mass., 1995).

A further issue concerns the willingness of donor countries to fund repatriations and some necessary short-term development efforts when peace in the home country is still uncertain. True peace increases the probability that development projects will succeed, but development may also contribute to prospects for peace. Donor countries seem to prefer to play it safe and wait for peace to be established first. In Central America, after the peace process was initiated in 1987 through the Esquipulas II agreement, the International Conference on Central American Refugees (CIREFCA) launched a return process (combined with some local integration) that was remarkably successful. Donor countries, especially the Nordic countries and Italy, were willing to fund not only the repatriations but also a number of short-term development projects that would enhance the prospects for these repatriations to succeed (Rogers and Copeland 1993). On the other hand, Operation Salam in Afghanistan was never adequately funded, because donors were legitimately wary of committing funds for development while prospects for peace were still uncertain (Ruiz 1992).[15]

Development Needs

In the 1990s there is hardly a country or region to which refugees and internally displaced persons return that has not been devastated by war and neglect. There is a desperate need to rebuild the infrastructure of these countries because the communities to which refugees return must be at least minimally viable in order for returns to succeed. In many countries of return, land mines are a major threat to the population's physical security. Another central concern is the availability of land: in some contexts (Mozambique, Guatemala), complex land issues must be sorted out. Contingency plans for secondary migrations must also be made.

One can distinguish three levels of need for assistance, which differ in degree of immediacy and scope. First, returning refugees need travel assistance (registration, transportation, reception centers in the home country) and aid packages (composed variously of food, tools, seeds, building materials, and so forth) that will allow them to begin their reintegration in the home country. Refugees who may not have been officially registered in the asylum country—especially "self-settled" refugees—may nevertheless wish to participate in the organized repatriation; they are likely to be given the opportunity to register at this time in order to benefit from the assisted returns. UNHCR personnel typically monitor the safety of the returnees in the home countries for one or two years after their return.

UNHCR's plans for the Cambodian repatriation—especially the choice of a return package that involved the provision of agricultural land—turned out to be ill conceived and unworkable (Robinson 1992). In the end, most returnees received a cash grant. More general difficulties surrounding repatriation planning include the fact that those who return have often not farmed in more than a decade, the lack of occupational preparation among many of the younger generation, the fact that returning refugees may have become accustomed to better sanitation and health care than they will find in the communities to which they return, and the loss of skills on the part of traditional healers (for example, among the Khmer population).

Second, in order to forestall excessive remigration by returnees —to the capital city or for a second time across a border—there is a need for at least minimal improvements in the infrastructure of the communities to which they return. In Nicaragua, UNHCR sponsored some innovative activities toward this end: i.e. quick impact projects (QIPs), which are relatively inexpensive grassroots development projects executed in a few months under the auspices of local NGOs. The goal of such projects is to respond to a return community's most immediate physical needs (for example, road or bridge repair to provide access to markets, the building of simple dispensaries, repair of school buildings, or provision of livestock; UNDP/UNHCR CIREFCA Joint Support Unit 1993). These efforts seem to have been successful. QIPs have since been used in Cambodia and Mozambique as well as in other countries of return.

In the long run, far more ambitious development efforts are called for. It is a domestic political challenge for the industrialized countries to respond on this third level, now that many of the countries that generated refugees have lost their strategic interest. The U.S. Committee for Refugees (1994, 61) notes with respect to Mozambique:

> USCR visited Mozambique in April–May 1993 and issued a report. ... USCR warned in its report that the resettlement of 5.7 million uprooted Mozambicans 'promises to be one of the most difficult repatriations ever undertaken' and concluded that returnees 'will find that home isn't what it used to be' due to the staggering destruction left behind by the war.
>
> 'Many returnees will find no towns, no markets, no schools, no health clinics—virtually nothing with which to reintegrate,' USCR reported. 'They will have no choice but to rebuild an entire economic and social structure from scratch' in what may be the world's poorest country.

In Central America, UNHCR has been successful in involving UNDP in return and development projects and in linking the development of returnee communities to longer-term development efforts.[16]

Concluding Observations

Ideally, refugee repatriations should take place after full peace has been achieved in the home countries. This ideal is not always met; many refugees return to still-volatile situations. This circumstance notwithstanding, it can be argued that repatriations have been successful, at least in terms of sheer numbers moved. In 1993 more than 1.6 million refugees were voluntarily repatriated; in 1994 the number was 2.7 million (U.S. Committee for Refugees 1994. 43; 1995, 45).

The international community's assistance in these repatriations has been essential, although some repatriations have involved gross mistakes in planning. For example, UNHCR miscalculated the availability of land for refugees returning to Cambodia. The comparative benefits of cash grants—the option that was finally chosen by many Cambodian returnees—as opposed to other return packages still remain to be studied adequately. It must also be recognized that, in nearly all cases, some refugees will not return; although they may not receive formal offers to become integrated into the asylum country, they are tolerated (at least for the time being) or have become "invisible."

Over the last decade(s) new norms have evolved concerning refugee repatriation. First, it has become accepted practice for UNHCR to offer refugees protection within the home country for some period of time after the returns have taken place. In addition, in responding to both positive and negative pressures for repatriation, UNHCR has become somewhat more flexible in its practices, more willing to make compromises. Furthermore, returnee populations today consist not only of recognized refugees, but also of people "in refugee-like situations"—people who left for reasons similar to those of the refugees but who were never recognized as such[17]—as well as of internally displaced and demobilized soldiers. Reflecting these changes, the focus of repatriation assistance has shifted from the exclusive needs of returned refugees to the needs of impacted communities.

What follows after returns and immediate reintegration have been accomplished? Long-term reconstruction of devastated countries cannot be the responsibility of UNHCR, which lacks both the expertise and the necessary funding to engage in such activities. Other international agencies must become involved, but to date they have not usually taken an interest in refugee populations. UNDP has become active with refugees in Central America, but individuals involved in this program report that this has not been an easy process. UNDP is not an operational agency, and its organizational culture is different from that of UNHCR (Otsea 1992). The World Bank, meanwhile, has so far shown little interest in migration and refugee problems.

International assistance in voluntary repatriation of refugees to developing countries is perhaps the most successful of the various return programs discussed in this chapter. Nevertheless, it must be noted that, although voluntary returns represent the most desirable solution to problems of displacement under ideal conditions (because they signify the reestablishment of the displaced persons' bonds with their home countries), they have, realistically, been too often merely a solution of last resort.

Temporary Asylum in Industrialized Countries

As noted above, when industrialized countries have granted asylum based on individual status determinations, they have usually done so with the expectation that the refugees will remain in the country permanently (or, in the case of some European countries, will ultimately seek resettlement in an overseas immigration country). With few exceptions, the industrialized countries were not confronted with mass movements of asylum seekers during the cold war. They are loath to grant asylum to large numbers of refugees on a *temporary* basis, fearing that they will not be able to enforce the temporary nature of the stay. They have, in fact, no fully developed mechanisms for granting temporary asylum.

The reasons for the countries' concerns are evident. The ethos of liberal democracies—and the memories of World War II—do not support housing temporary refugees in camps for an indefinite period of time. In consequence, if the conflict that generated the refugees' flight is not quickly resolved, these refugees become well integrated into the asylum country. Because of the substantial differential in economic opportunities between the host and home countries, moreover, many refugees may not wish to return home. They will use the fact of their integration as an argument against return. Forced returns in such situations are costly and difficult to effect.

In the past, the West European countries have used a number of ad hoc measures to grant protection to people who did not qualify for asylum based on the strict refugee definition. These measures had various names, including "B status," *Duldung,* and "Temporary Leave to Remain." Despite these terms, such measures generally represented de facto grants of permanent asylum based on humanitarian considerations.

In the 1990s the circumstances surrounding the flow of refugees from the former Yugoslavia, especially Bosnia, have challenged the West European countries to grant *temporary* asylum. The response to this challenge has been mixed. One UNHCR official noted, "Most European states have responded generously to the plight of individuals fleeing the former Yugoslavia, in that two-thirds of all affected States have enacted special legislative or administrative measures to provide temporary legal status to such persons, and many have made special provisions for vulnerable individuals such as former detention center internees" (UNHCR 1995d). Roughly 700,000 persons from the former Yugoslavia have found some form of temporary protection in Europe (3, 6). However, the West European countries have also simultaneously made strong efforts to restrict the entrance of additional Bosnian war refugees, mainly by imposing visa requirements. The solution preferred by these countries has been to have neighboring countries (primarily Croatia) take on ever more of the burden of sheltering refugees. Some West European governments have, in fact, actively sought to convince Croatia to respond in this way, e.g., by offering material assistance (Argent 1992). It remains to be seen how the "temporary" status of the ex-Yugoslavs in Western Europe will be resolved if and when peace returns to the region.

In the United States, temporary asylum status cannot be conferred on people knocking at the country's door. Temporary protected status (TPS)[18] is conferred by the attorney general for a specified time—e.g., for six months—on foreign citizens already present in the country who might suffer bodily harm or exceptional hardship if they return home during that time. The time period can be extended if necessary. People granted TPS need not be asylum seekers; they may have entered the country as students or visitors, for example. They are not permitted to invite their families to join them. Citizens of the same country who arrive in the United States after the date on which the grant of TPS took effect are not eligible for this protected status—an important restrictive feature of the TPS mechanism.

In the 1980s and 1990s TPS and its predecessor, EVD, were offered more than twenty times, with various frequencies of renewal. There is a striking lack of information on the paths taken by beneficiaries after expiration of the grant of TPS or EVD. There has generally been no monitoring of or insistence on returns once conditions in the home countries have improved and the grant of temporary protection has expired.[19]

One of the groups that, in addition to the Cubans, has been knocking on the United States' doors most insistently—Haitians—was kept out for years by the interdiction of vessels carrying asylum seekers. In-country processing of refugee claims was offered for a short period of time. A policy innovation of providing "safe havens" in third countries followed in 1994 and was also extended to Cubans. An official in the Department of State's Bureau for Population, Refugees and Migration referred to these steps as "a mixed policy of providing protection as well as migration control" (McKinley 1994). The use of safe havens is an unsatisfactory policy, however. How long can a Western democratic country keep people in what are essentially detention centers? And barring asylum seekers from access to regular asylum procedures has serious human rights implications.

A critical look at the "safe haven" policy shows that it is not likely to be easily replicated by other potential countries of asylum because of its cost and the difficulty of finding safe haven locations. The creation of safe havens is expensive. To bring persons fleeing by sea to a safe haven on another country's soil, interdiction is necessary; however, interdiction is only an option for countries that have the capabilities necessary to effect it. In the Cuban and Haitian cases, moreover, countries in the Caribbean were not eager to become hosts to large numbers of asylum seekers. The U.S. government therefore had to use persuasive powers at the highest levels to gain cooperation. Some countries also expected generous compensation for opening their territory to such use. In the end, the United States sent most asylum seekers to Guantánamo, to which it has a lease in perpetuity. Lastly, to get the job done fast, the military's services were essential—another expensive requirement.

It can be argued that, with President Aristide's return to power, the Haitian situation has resolved itself, although at the time of this writing there remains a good deal of insecurity in the country. Having been told that they had no other options, most of the more than 14,000 Haitians held at Guantánamo as of August 1994 (U.S. Committee for Refugees 1995, 180) returned to their country "voluntarily." At the end of December 1994, the 4,900 who had refused voluntary repatriation were told that "they had until January 5 [1995] to repatriate 'voluntarily' or the government would return them forcibly" (Frelick 1995b, 18).[20] Of these, 677 "volunteered" to go home, 99 were allowed (based on a cursory "evaluation" rather than a regular asylum screening) to stay until the U.S. embassy in Port-au-Prince could investigate whether it was safe for them to return, and 672 were allowed to remain for other reasons (most were unaccompanied minors or on "medical hold"). The remainder, several thousand, were forcibly repatriated (Frelick 1995b, 18–19). Since the United States did not permit these individuals to have access to the regular asylum process, UNHCR refused to participate in the proceedings (UNHCR 1995d, 4–5).

The situation of the Cubans on Guantánamo is more complicated, since the Cuban government remains unchanged. Frelick (1995b, 27) asks: "Are [the Cubans on Guantánamo] expected to wait, warehoused in indefinite detention until Castro dies?" A permanent solution to the problem of Cuban asylum seekers is needed—most likely, resettlement to the United States and, ideally, to other countries in the region as well. For this to be achieved, the Cubans on Guantánamo will have to be given access to a refugee determination procedure.

Frelick speculates that, despite its mixed experience with "safe havens," the United States plans to use Guantánamo to house other populations in the future.[21] Summarizing the general criticism voiced regarding this policy, he notes, "The eleventh circuit decision suggests that the very purpose of establishing a center offshore is to insulate it from the reach of U.S. law and to minimize the due process rights of the asylum seekers" (Frelick 1995b, 27).[22]

Concluding Observations

When confronted with mass movements of refugees, Western industrialized countries are reluctant to offer temporary asylum on their own soil. This is due to the fact that, unless the situations generating the flows resolve themselves within a short period of time, there are considerable pressures for permanence. Holding camps are not acceptable on German or French or U.S. soil, yet other living conditions permit either integration, which, in turn, becomes an argument for permanence, or a slide into illegal status. Forced returns—which would be legal if the temporary asylees were also given access to regular asylum procedures—are extremely difficult to implement; they are costly (people must be located and then detained until the deportation takes place), and they are unacceptable to many groups in the host country population.

On the other hand, refugee status determination procedures at embassies in the home countries put those who are most deserving of protection at greatest risk. Such procedures are also inappropriate for large numbers of applicants: the apparatus in place is soon overwhelmed, as was evident in Haiti in 1993 and 1994 (U.S. Committee for Refugees 1995, 181). Thus, if a host country wishes to honor the spirit of refugee protection, it cannot use in-country applications as the reason for closing off access to other asylum procedures, whether individual asylum seekers or mass flows are involved.

Providing temporary protection to large numbers of asylum seekers on foreign soil, close to the home country, appears to be an attractive option. In spite of the difficulties discussed above, the Haitian experience may be judged a qualified success, particularly in light of what preceded it (primarily interdiction and summary returns). It benefited from the fact that positive changes occurred in the conditions in the home country within a reasonable time period. However, the process was costly and depended to a large extent on the United States being able to use Guantánamo Bay. It is not clear what locations would be available for similar use by West European countries. Finally, although public opinion in the host country is more likely to accept (or ignore) forced repatriations from "safe havens," the host countries are countervening at least the spirit, if not the letter, of both their own and international laws if they exclude from access to their regular asylum procedures those whom they are protecting.

Rejected Asylum Seekers in Developing Countries (The Comprehensive Plan of Action in Southeast Asia)

Until 1989 countries in Southeast Asia granted blanket temporary protection to Vietnamese and Laotian asylum seekers on the condition that they would be resettled to third countries. The same was true at various times for those who left Cambodia, although at other times Thailand foreclosed access to resettlement to Cambodians, expecting that such a procedure would discourage those without strong reasons for flight from leaving ("humane deterrence"). Between 1975 and mid-1995, 754,253 Vietnamese were resettled from the CPA area,[23] and 320,718 Laotians were resettled from Thailand (UNHCR 1995a, 9).

When outflows from Vietnam increased drastically in 1979 and resettlement offers from the West ceased to keep pace with the numbers of new arrivals, the Southeast Asian asylum countries began to force boats with asylum seekers back to sea. The international community responded to this situation by holding a conference in Geneva, the result of which was that the resettlement countries raised their monthly quotas for Vietnamese refugees and the Orderly Departure Program was instituted, which allowed direct resettlement from Vietnam to the United States and other participating countries.

The international community's response was different in the latter part of the 1980s, however, when the numbers of asylum seekers leaving Vietnam again showed a pattern of increase. It was recognized that by this time many of those leaving the country were fleeing generally oppressive conditions and economic stagnation rather than persecution or generalized violence and that the firm connection among flight, asylum, and resettlement had to be broken.

A 1989 meeting attended not only by representatives of the asylum and resettlement countries but also by other world powers (such as the Soviet Union), as well as, importantly, by Vietnam and Laos, resulted in the Comprehensive Plan of Action for Southeast Asia (CPA).[24] The plan had several components, the most important of which was the decision to break the cycle of blanket asylum and near-automatic resettlement. Asylum countries would henceforth use individual status determinations for asylum seekers from Indochina, based on the refugee definition in the 1951 UN Convention Relating to the Status of Refugees and its 1967 Protocol. Persons with weak claims to protection would be "screened out" (that is, refused refugee status) and would have to return to their home countries (Jambor 1992).[25] It was important for Vietnam, the country with the largest outflows, to agree to take back those who were refused refugee status (something it was unwilling to do at first, citing economic reasons) and to guarantee their safety. For some time, the United States objected to the principle of forced returns (some among the screened-out were refusing to return voluntarily), but, given its own interdiction policy for Haitians, it had little ground to stand on. NGOs voiced concerns about fairness and consistency in the new status determinations. The new system has become firmly established, however, with UNHCR monitoring the returnees' safety in Vietnam.

A major factor in the CPA's success was that the asylum countries established a March 1989 cutoff date for blanket acceptance (Hong Kong had already set one in 1988), after which they began using individual refugee status determinations and requiring the return of those who were screened out (UNHCR 1995a, 3). UNHCR reported in August 1995 that since 1989 72,200 people had returned to Vietnam and more than 23,000 had returned to Laos (UNHCR 1995a, 3), for the most part voluntarily. Still, as of 1 July 1995, 38,313 screened-out Vietnamese asylum seekers remained in camps in first asylum countries in the region, and 167 screened-out Laotian asylum seekers remained in Thailand (UNHCR 1995a, 9). In February 1994 the CPA steering committee targeted the end of 1995 for the CPA's termination and the return of all those found to be nonrefugees (UNHCR 1995c, 1).[26]

Many rejected asylum seekers have been reluctant to return. Some of them incurred debts when leaving Vietnam and know that they will not be able to repay them. Furthermore, having left with the hope of resettlement, many feel that return to Vietnam implies failure. Some who have been in the camps for years have become apathetic and prefer camp life to the economic insecurity awaiting them at home. Others fear that they will be persecuted upon return and feel that they have been unjustly screened out. A few know that they will be prosecuted for earlier criminal offenses. Finally, there is always the hope that the Western resettlement countries may relent and, at the last moment, decide to resettle the remaining camp populations.[27]

What have the asylum countries and the international community done to facilitate, encourage, and, if necessary, force returns? Observers agree that an important element in encouraging returns is simply the provision of trustworthy, reliable information concerning the conditions awaiting the returnees at home, combined with delivery of the unambiguous message that resettlement opportunities will not be forthcoming ("NGO Group Visits Vietnam" 1995; Nickerson 1994). In addition, every returning Vietnamese, adult or child, receives a repatriation grant. The amount of this grant has been as high as $410—considerably more than the average annual wage in Vietnam or Laos (UNHCR 1995a, 9)—but has been lowered over time, presumably with the intention of putting some pressure on reluctant candidates to decide to return sooner rather than later. (In 1993 the $360 grant was reduced to $240; however, those who received their final status determinations after the stipend had been reduced were still awarded $360 if they registered for voluntary repatriation within three months after the final decision [UNHCR 1994c].)[28]

Several specific programs of reintegration assistance for returning asylum seekers have also been implemented in Vietnam. The major programs, which were initiated in 1991 and 1992, are described briefly below.[29] Some of these programs were due to end in 1994, before the anticipated closure of the CPA.

1. UNHCR created a microproject program with a focus on income generation and then shifted more in the direction of supporting infrastructure projects like the QIPs in Nicaragua (UNHCR 1993; Chris Carpenter, speech by the UNHCR Representative in Vietnam to the Ministry of Labor, Invalids and Social Affairs, Do Sun, Vietnam, 10 June 1994, cited in Nickerson 1994). These projects cover a broad range of efforts intended to strengthen the returnee communities, thus serving both returnees and those who never left (UNHCR 1995a, 11). (Unlike the CIREFCA program, however, these projects are not tied to any longer-term development efforts.) Perhaps the projects' unintended consequences are as important as those that were explicitly contemplated: Nickerson notes that they have functioned as useful teaching tools for Vietnamese development planners.

2. The European Community International Program (EC-IP), which began to wind down in 1994, provided various types of aid, including information for asylum seekers in camps (mainly about the program itself); a credit scheme that offered, in cooperation with two Vietnamese banks, loans to returnees and non-returnees for the creation of private sector enterprises; vocational training for returnees; QIP-type microprojects; and health sector development (the building of dispensaries in a number of villages and provision of a year of health insurance for unaccompanied minors). Returnees experienced difficulties in securing loans because of the need to provide collateral, and news about these difficulties traveled quickly back to the camps. Again, the credit scheme provided useful training for bank officials (Nickerson 1994). The provision of health insurance for unaccompanied minors filled an important need and, at the same time, served as a training opportunity for the administrators and health care workers involved. However, the vocational

training offered to returnees was relatively unsuccessful because it was not geared to existing market needs.

3. The Nordic Assistance to Repatriated Vietnamese, a consortium of five Nordic country NGOs, provided extremely important services. It helped reintegrate unaccompanied minors into the Vietnamese educational system through activities that ranged from helping the young people to catch up with the age-appropriate Vietnamese school curriculum to assisting with the construction or renovation of schools in remote areas. This program was due to end in 1994.

4. Finally, the U.S. Department of State's Bureau for Refugee Programs (now the Bureau for Population, Refugees and Migration) has funded reintegration assistance carried out by several U.S. NGOs. The NGOs involved in these programs range from World Vision (more experienced in development work than in reintegration assistance) to the Southeast Asia Resource Action Center (SEARAC, a Vietnamese-American NGO inexperienced in repatriation assistance but familiar with the Vietnamese language and culture) to a consortium of smaller NGOs to the International Catholic Migration Commission (which had earlier run an outreach and training program for rejected Vietnamese asylum seekers in the Philippines). The programs offered have ranged from the provision of medical insurance to tutoring for children to vocational training to support of micro-projects (Nickerson 1994).

In many cases, the assistance provided by the programs described above has been made available to returnees and non-returnees alike. When beneficiaries of insurance schemes were selected from among the nonreturnees, this often caused resentment among those who were not chosen. In general, the number of beneficiaries was relatively small. (For example, Nickerson 1995 mentions that there were "approximately 281 ICM-funded businesses" as of June 30, 1994 [509].)

So far, the number of forced returns has been small, probably in the low thousands. Hong Kong, objecting to the slow pace of voluntary repatriation, has organized several forced repatriations since late 1989. It has also invented a different category of returnees: those who, while not volunteering to return, nevertheless "did not oppose repatriation." Forced repatriations have been organized by the Philippines as well. Today, all actors who are part of the CPA, from the asylum countries to UNHCR to the United States to Vietnam, agree that forced repatriations are justified as a last resort. Until now, such measures seem to have been employed primarily as symbolic acts or trial balloons (e.g., to test the reaction of the United States while it still opposed all forced returns) or in an attempt to create pressure on the camp populations to register for "voluntary" returns. As the CPA winds down, however, forced repatriations may become more widely used.

Concluding Remarks

Although in 1994 some NGOs questioned the fairness of the asylum adjudication process in the various countries of asylum, UNHCR has not found substantiation for allegations that genuine refugees have been screened out, despite the fact that it encourages persons with such claims to come forward so that it can review their cases. Except for Hong Kong, UNHCR has participated directly in the asylum recognition processes of the asylum countries. In addition, it has the authority to recognize refugees under its mandate. In many situations, this represents essentially a third stage of review. It has used this authority most extensively in Hong Kong, where it has recognized as mandate refugees 1,542 persons who had been rejected on appeal by the Hong Kong government. In each of the other asylum countries, there have been fewer than twenty mandate cases (UNHCR 1995a, 4–5).[30]

In the context of the Comprehensive Plan of Action, the international community developed an approach to resolve the situation of rejected asylum seekers who had to leave the camps in Southeast Asia that was similar to its approach to resolving mass returns of recognized refugee populations to their home countries. The basic component of this return program was to offer a stipend to all those who choose to return voluntarily. (In the case of refugee repatriation, the return package has more often consisted of goods in kind.) A number of program beneficiaries who returned to Vietnam with a stipend later remigrated to Hong Kong, presumably to obtain another stipend. Hong Kong dealt harshly with these so-called "double backers", thereby preventing the return stipend from becoming an incentive to remigration.

In Vietnam, UNHCR has monitored the safety of returning asylum seekers in an effort that represents "by far the most complex, far-reaching and systematic individual case follow-up of any repatriation operation to date" (UNHCR 1995b, 9). Between March 1989 and the first half of 1995, it conducted monitoring visits to over 18,000 returnees, about 25 percent of all those who have returned. Based on this examination, UNHCR is satisfied that the returnees are safe, noting, "To date, the overwhelming majority of returnee complaints stem from economic difficulties, bureaucratic problems, or delays in payment of their repatriation grants" (UNHCR 1995, 9).

No definitive evaluations of the reintegration assistance programs that have been offered to a subset of rejected asylum seekers returning to Vietnam are as yet available (see "NGO Group Visits Vietnam" 1995; also Balfour 1993). I therefore do not know whether these programs have acted as return incentives. Their existence has probably made the attitudes in the camps more positive with respect to voluntary returns. Perhaps equally important, these programs have made some contribution to the overall process of Vietnam's reconstruction. They may also have been a means of repaying Vietnam for accepting the return of the screened-out asylum seekers, which initially it was unwilling to do. Since reintegration assistance programs were established before the normalization of relations between Vietnam and the Western countries, they were a means of granting some aid through the backdoor and of training Vietnamese officials (for example, loan officers in banks or employees in insurance companies) in skills that will be increasingly useful and necessary in the country's cooperative relationships with the Western industrialized countries. Finally, they confirmed the returnees' participation in Vietnam's reconstruction process.

Return aid—whether in the form of repatriation grants or more specialized reintegration assistance—will be extended by the international community only if it is perceived as contributing to a real solution to an existing problem, not if the population of potential beneficiaries renews itself continuously through new outflows. The number of Vietnamese seeking asylum in the Southeast Asian host countries has indeed slowed to a trickle since the CPA has been firmly in place. Frelick observes, "From 69,968 Vietnamese boat departures in 1989, the number fell to 32,063 in

1990, 21,870 in 1991, and dropped to 41 in 1992. It thereafter stayed at a much lower level than during the 1980s—139 in 1993 and 338 in the first 9 months of 1994" (1995a, 126, based on data supplied by the Hong Kong government). If people experiencing true fear of persecution (who can and indeed should be screened in under the current procedures) are not deterred from seeking asylum or are still able to leave through the continuing Orderly Departure Program, then a real success has been achieved.

Rejected Asylum Seekers in Industrialized Countries

Table 5.1 shows the number of asylum applications received in thirteen West European countries, Australia, Canada, and the United States since 1983, when the influx of asylum seekers began to increase substantially and to become more diversified by origin, especially in Europe. The total number for Europe—and the noticeably large number for Germany—reached a peak in 1992. As the numbers have increased, however, recognition rates have fallen.[31] It is widely agreed that the asylum channel is being used as an immigration route by people who lack access to West European countries through other means such as close family relationships or a claim to membership in a host country's population on ethnic grounds.

Because of the considerable number of asylum seekers involved, the large total cost of Western Europe's asylum systems (which far exceeds the UNHCR's budget to assist and protect the millions of refugees worldwide), and the difficulty of assuring the return of rejected asylum seekers to their home countries, the asylum situation has been widely seen as being in crisis (see, for example, the quotations in Rogers 1993, 144). Overseas immigration countries have also experienced difficulties in effecting rejected asylum seekers' returns. In addition, the United States in particular is dealing with a large backlog of applications.

Asylum seekers in Europe are supported by the receiving states while their applications are pending. They may be housed and fed in group accommodations or given stipends. Some obtain permission to work. In contrast, in the United States, asylum seekers who are not granted work authorization also do not

Table 5.1 Asylum Applications in Participating States, 1983–1995

	1983	1984	1985	1986	1987	1988	1989	1990	1991	1992	1993	1994	1995
Europe													
Austria	5,900	7,200	6,700	8,700	11,400	15,800	21,900	22,800	27,300	16,200	4,356	n/a	n/a
Belgium	2,900	3,700	5,300	7,700	6,000	5,100	8,100	13,000	15,200	17,754	28,883	14,340	11,409
Denmark	800	4,300	8,700	9,300	2,800	4,700	4,600	5,300	4,600	13,884	14,351	6,651	5,112
Finland	n/a	n/a	n/a	n/a	50	50	200	2,500	2,100	3,634	2,023	849	849
France**	14,300	15,900	25,800	23,400	24,800	31,600	60,000	56,000	46,500	28,872	26,662	26,044	19,085
Germany	19,700	35,300	73,900	99,700	57,400	103,100	121,000	193,000	256,000	438,191	322,599	127,210	129,517
Italy	3,000	4,500	5,400	6,500	11,000	1,300	2,200	4,700	31,700	2,588	1,571	1,834	1,732
Netherlands	2,000	2,600	5,700	5,900	13,500	7,500	14,000	21,200	21,600	20,346	35,399	52,516	29,258
Norway	200	300	900	2,700	8,600	6,600	4,400	4,000	4,600	5,238	12,876	3,379	1,460
Spain**	1,400	1,100	2,300	2,300	2,500	3,300	4,000	8,600	8,100	11,700	12,615	10,230	4,429
Sweden	3,000	12,000	14,500	14,600	18,100	19,600	32,000	29,000	27,300	84,018	37,581	18,640	9,046
Switzerland	7,900	7,500	9,700	8,600	10,900	16,700	24,500	36,000	41,600	17,960	24,739	16,134	17,021
U.K.*	4,300	4,200	6,200	5,700	5,900	5,700	16,800	38,200	73,400	32,300	28,000	42,200	43,965
Subtotal	64,000	98,600	165,100	195,100	172,950	221,050	313,700	434,300	560,000	692,685	549,655	320,027	272,883
Overseas													
Australia**	n/a	n/a	n/a	n/a	n/a	n/a	500	3,800	17,000	4,114	4,589	4,215	5,235
Canada	5,000	7,100	8,400	23,000	35,000	45,000	19,934	36,735	32,347	37,748	21,066	21,710	25,631
U.S.A.**	26,091	24,295	16,622	18,889	26,107	60,736	101,679	73,637	56,310	101,569	151,788	142,508	147,870
Subtotal	31,091	31,395	25,022	41,889	61,107	105,736	122,113	114,172	105,657	143,431	177,443	168,433	178,736
Grand Total	96,491	129,995	190,122	236,989	234,057	326,786	435,813	548,472	665,657	836,116	727,098	488,460	451,619

*Please note that, except for 1995, the yearly data for the UK have been adjusted to include dependents.

**Please note that the data for Australia, France, Spain, and the USA refer to principal applicants and do not include dependents.

receive support from the government. They may be helped by family or friends, or they work without permission. Some asylum seekers who have tried to enter an asylum country without proper documents are placed in detention. Whereas in the last years the European countries have substantially reduced their backlogs of applications, as of this writing this process has been much slower in the United States.[32]

There is considerable agreement in the international community that two conditions must be fulfilled if an asylum system using individual status determinations is to be viable: the adjudications must be both fair and prompt, and returns must be enforced (UNHCR 1995d). Otherwise, the system will be emasculated: If it offers asylum seekers a relatively comfortable life and economic opportunities, it will attract persons with weak claims because of the time they may spend in the host country during the application and appeals process. This, in turn, will penalize those in genuine need of protection by unnecessarily prolonging their ambiguous status while many false claims are processed. It will create arguments against the departure of rejected asylum seekers because integration will take place during the protracted determination process. Finally, it is likely to create an illegal population when individuals are refused refugee recognition but are not forced to leave.

Some European governments have created programs to aid rejected asylum seekers to return to their home countries after receiving a negative decision. These programs generally apply also to asylum seekers who wish to withdraw applications that are under consideration. The programs are administered either by the governments themselves or through the International Organization for Migration (IOM). However, unlike in the Southeast Asian asylum countries, where rejected asylum seekers are housed in camps and can be easily reached by information programs, in Western Europe return aid programs are not widely advertised. They are also far more modest. Most importantly, this weak carrot has been complemented by an even weaker stick: voluntary returns are generally not monitored, and forced returns are difficult to implement and occur infrequently, though apparently they are growing in number.

In 1991 France instituted a return aid program for people who have been asked to leave the country (which includes, but is not limited to, rejected asylum seekers). The program offers coverage of return travel and a small grant that essentially amounts to pocket money (as of 1994, 1,000 francs were given to each adult and 300 francs were given to each child). Furthermore, as part of the program, a file on each of the returnees is created and sent to an NGO or to a branch office of the French Office for International Migrations in the migrant's home country in the hope that these organizations will at least assist the returnees by providing useful information (interview with an OMI official, Paris, 1994). In 1991 255 rejected asylum seekers were granted aid under this program; in 1992 the number was 856 (France, OMI 1993, 159–61). Small numbers of accompanying family members were also involved. There is also a special fund to finance return projects of rejected asylum seekers, but between 1991 and 1994 only a handful of returnees had applied for aid from this fund.

The Belgian return program (Reintegration and Emigration Programme for Asylum Seekers in Belgium, or REAB), instituted in 1984 and administered by IOM, targets three populations: asylum seekers whose applications are under consideration, rejected asylum seekers, and other migrants with insufficient means who desire to return permanently to their home countries or to migrate to a third country that has offered to accept them. The aid offered under this program is similar to that of the French program. Utilization of the program has been extremely modest: between 1983 and 1993 107,420 asylum seekers entered Belgium, but between 1984 and 1993 only 4,465 persons used the program. About 44 percent of program beneficiaries between 1984 and 1992 were asylum seekers with applications in process, 41 percent were rejected asylum seekers, and 15 percent were other migrants. In 1993 the proportions were 31 percent, 58 percent, and 11 percent, respectively (data supplied by Mr. H. Vandamme, IOM Brussels, 24 June 1994.) Germany and the Netherlands have recently instituted similar programs (REAG and REAN), although the specifics of implementation vary: in Belgium, for example, beneficiaries are accompanied by IOM officials to their place of departure, but in Germany this is not the case.

In general, little is known about the steps taken by asylum seekers after they have received notification that they have been rejected. How many return home on their own? How many move on to another country? How many remain in the host country illegally? And how many are deported? The number of deportations from Western asylum countries is generally low. In Germany, however, deportations of rejected asylum seekers increased from 5,583 in 1990, to 8,232 in 1991, to 10,798 in 1992, and to 35,915 in 1993 (Germany, Bundesministerium des Innern 1994, 51). In the United States, separate figures on rejected asylum seekers are not available in published form. The total number of deportations from the United States was 36,686 in 1993. Of these, however, 20,033 deportations occurred because applicants had been convicted of criminal or narcotics violations or for reasons related to such violations, and another 14,456 people were deported because they had entered the country without inspection (U.S. Immigration and Naturalization Service 1994, 164). Although some asylum seekers enter without inspection, it is likely that most of those who are deported are labor migrants.[33]

Increasingly, however, the West European countries are relying on neither return incentives nor deportations to effect the returns of rejected asylum seekers; rather, they are trying to keep asylum seekers out. Current measures go far beyond attempts to rationalize the asylum process within the EU by formulating clear rules as to which state is responsible for hearing a particular person's asylum claim and by ensuring that asylum applications cannot be lodged in more than one EU member state (as is foreseen in the Dublin Convention). They include accelerated status determination procedures, visa requirements, the imposition of sanctions and fines on air and sea carriers that accept passengers without proper travel documents, "safe third country" and "safe country of origin" rules, and the detention of asylum seekers in "transit zones." Some countries even require rejected asylum seekers to leave the territory while a negative decision is being appealed (the so-called nonsuspensive effect) (Berthiaume 1995, 7–9). All these measures are problematic. They risk barring genuine refugees from access to all West European countries' asylum systems and returning them to danger in their own countries.[34] In the United States, the barriers are less high, although carrier sanctions had been introduced earlier than in Europe, and in 1995 the United States and Canada agreed in principle to the mutual application of the safe third country rule.

It is UNHCR's position that it will support industrialized countries' efforts to deport people who have been found not to be refugees, provided that these individuals have had full access to internationally accepted asylum procedures. At present, this condition is far from being universally met (see, for example, the statement by the director of UNHCR's Regional Bureau for Europe, quoted in Berthiaume 1995, 7).

Concluding Remarks

The Western industrialized countries, which were the magnet for Vietnamese and Laotians who sought asylum in the CPA region, are now themselves asylum countries sought out by both genuine asylum seekers and de facto economic migrants from other parts of the world. Characterized by a high economic standard and offering few opportunities for regular immigration, these countries have seen their asylum channels used by large numbers of applicants who lack strong claims to asylum. However, unlike in Southeast Asia, asylum seekers in the West are not kept in camps. It has therefore proven difficult to repatriate those whose claims are rejected. The United States, Canada, and Australia do not offer any return incentives or return aid to asylum seekers. A few European countries have made some efforts in this direction, but the amounts offered are small, and the utilization of these programs has been negligible. In order to be effective, offers of aid would have to be inordinately high, far higher than would be tolerated by the economies of or public opinion in any Western industrialized country.

Forced returns are difficult and costly. Long-term detention (throughout the entire application process) is contrary to the ethos of liberal democracies, although today it is being applied in some cases. It is also expensive. It would hardly be feasible for the Western asylum countries to detain asylum seekers in the numbers in which they have been arriving since the mid-1980s. Yet this is the best way to ensure that rejected asylum seekers will be available for deportation. And despite their costs—in terms of dollars as well as lack of support by some publics— deportations have a payoff if they serve as a deterrence to future migrations by other asylum seekers with unfounded claims.

Instead of pursuing a more aggressive deportation policy, many Western industrialized countries—particularly those in Europe—have opted to make access to asylum channels more difficult, i.e., to keep asylum seekers out, if possible. This is a disturbing trend, because these methods keep out not only frivolous asylum seekers but also those in genuine need of protection. Berthiaume (1995, 10) summarizes and quotes a statement by Dennis McNamara, the director of UNHCR's Division of International Protection, on this point: "Dennis McNamara ... agrees that in their eagerness to bar illegal immigrants, West European governments are weaving a net so tight that legitimate refugees may not be able to get through. 'Nobody—not a single politician—is saying that there is a difference between a refugee and someone who is an illegal migrant,' McNamara says. 'Nobody acknowledges that there are actually very few refugees knocking at their door and that they should be making every effort to find places for them. Instead, they're all being lumped together.'" It should be noted that these new policies are not yet firmly established. Consequently, there remains the likelihood that rules will be reformulated and refined so that flows of asylum seekers with unfounded claims will be controlled, while genuine refugees will be able to make their claims. Kumin (1995, 13) notes:

> While the German government credits the safe third country rule, together with other changes in German asylum legislation, with having brought the number of asylum-seekers in Germany down from a record high of 438,191 in 1992 to 127,210 in 1994, the safe third country rule is coming under increasing judicial scrutiny in Germany and elsewhere. Germany's highest court is expected to rule soon on the constitutionality of the safe third country rule introduced into the German Basic Law in mid-1993. The court challenge comes in the context of cases where the "safety" of Greece and the Czech Republic have been questioned. In the United Kingdom, the "safety" of Germany, France, Austria and Greece as countries of asylum have been subject to scrutiny.[35]

A Review of Conclusions

The return programs discussed in this paper were aimed at two types of migrants. The first type of migrants—the guest workers in Western Europe—are not obliged to return; they have the option of remaining indefinitely in the host country. However, spontaneous returns occur all the time. On different occasions, the host countries have attempted to increase the number of returnees by creating incentives to return and have assisted spontaneous returnees in their reintegration. The second type of migrants discussed are refugees or people who came to the host countries as asylum seekers but were refused refugee status. Those who are given temporary asylum in either developing or industrialized countries are expected to return home when conditions in the home countries change. Rejected asylum seekers are expected to return when they have received a definitive answer from the host country authorities (albeit possibly after one or more appeals).

Return incentive programs for guest workers have generally had very limited success. When the economic situation in the home countries is poor, the offers are not sufficiently large to convince significant numbers of guest workers to leave. When the differentials between host and sending countries are relatively small, there is, in any case, a substantial volume of spontaneous return migration (although I do not wish to suggest that only economic considerations influence migration decisions), and return incentive programs seem to be used primarily as reintegration assistance by migrants who have already decided to return.

The programs analyzed in this paper were often aimed at the weakest groups, the unemployed. The fact that many of these programs were later extended to other populations is an indication of their relative lack of success with the original target group. Furthermore, since they were generally instituted and promoted unilaterally by the host countries and involved deadlines that put pressure on the migrants to make quick decisions, they were hardly welcomed by the sending countries. The domestic political benefits of host governments being seen to deal firmly with a perceived problem were perhaps as important as any economic benefits that accrued to the host country.

Return assistance programs can be justified on humanitarian grounds and as a way of repaying migrants and home countries for benefits they brought (as a group) to the host countries. Such programs cannot be clearly distinguished from return incentives; discussing policymakers' motives in instituting them would be speculation. However, they usually involve some bilateral cooperation. Some European examples show that, even so, sending countries were often suspicious of such programs. One of the problems was that the migrants did not have the option of trying out their returns; remigration was generally not an option. However, this was true of spontaneous returns as well.[36]

In developing countries, the provision of return assistance to forced migrants has been an important element in making returns and reintegration possible. The clearest examples of this are the large refugee repatriations, during which the logistics of transportation alone make the involvement of UNHCR and the international community necessary. Return packages are essential in such instances. Of course, there are many details of repatriation planning that could be rethought and perhaps handled more flexibly, but, on the whole, return assistance to refugees in developing countries comes closest to being a success story among the policies discussed in this paper.

Various forms of return aid have also played a crucial role in the voluntary returns of rejected asylum seekers from Vietnam and Laos under the umbrella of the CPA. The return stipends offered have had some of the characteristics of return incentives: they were progressively lowered (leading potential beneficiaries to wonder whether they would be further lowered in the future), and for some time two different amounts were offered, with eligibility for the higher amount dependent on whether persons applied within a specified, short time after receiving a negative response to their asylum requests. The support provided by the grants has been much needed. Most screened-out asylum seekers took economic risks in leaving their home countries and were not able to accumulate savings while in the camps.

The asylum countries have a right to deport these migrants. Although such deportations are much easier to arrange in developing countries than in industrialized countries because the migrants are living in camps, there are costs attached to forcing returns. There have therefore been consistent attempts to encourage voluntary returns. Some question whether UNHCR should be so heavily involved in the return of nonrefugees (administering return stipends, monitoring the returnees' safety in Vietnam, administering one of the reintegration programs). The situation has often been incorrectly represented in the mass media and in discussions as one in which refugees (not *non*refugees) were given no other option but to return against their will.

The reintegration assistance available in Vietnam does not seem to reach the majority of returnees. As has become a practice in refugee repatriations in developing countries, a part of the assistance is targeted at the local communities (including nonreturnees). The content of the programs varies. An interesting element is due to the unintended (or at least unadvertised) consequences of some programs, i.e., they have afforded valuable experience and on-the-job training to the Vietnamese officials who were involved in administering them.

The situation is far more difficult in industrialized countries. The industrialized countries hesitate to grant temporary protection to large numbers of asylum seekers, because, unless the situations generating the flows change quickly, most of these refugees may not wish to return home. Solutions open to the industrialized countries include accepting the mass refugee flows and expecting a good deal of settling (not a welcome prospect today), shifting the burden to other countries, creating safe havens on foreign soil (with some or all of the problems discussed in this paper), and intervening in the affairs of the countries that generate the flows (e.g., Haiti). Forcing the returns of people accepted as temporary refugees would create considerable problems of logistics and cost and, above all, political problems (both domestic and foreign).

On the other hand, rejected asylum seekers could be dealt with more aggressively. When the adjudication process is fair and prompt, deportations are justified. If the process is prompt enough, migrants will not be able to use integration into the host society as an argument for being allowed to remain. Given the direction of public opinion today, it is unlikely that substantial return assistance will be offered to these populations. Such offers would create yet another incentive for individuals to seek asylum frivolously. Current return assistance programs, such as those offered by European governments through their own migration organizations or through IOM, have been ineffective. Deportations are costly for industrialized countries, but as long as they do not violate the spirit of refugee and human rights law, they may be worth employing as a deterrent.

Germany has stepped up deportations of rejected asylum seekers and, at the same time, has revised its asylum law. The substantial downward trend in the numbers of asylum seekers recorded in Germany and other countries since the peak of 1992 seems to be primarily attributable to measures designed to keep asylum seekers out of the process in the first place. These procedures risk barring genuine asylum seekers from finding protection. Thus the European countries are at a crossroads: today, the asylum system is under greatest threat on the very continent that saw the birth and first growth of the international refugee regime as we know it.

A subject that has been almost entirely beyond the scope of this paper is the question of how host countries can better address the root causes of unwanted migrations. In the case of European guest workers, underdevelopment in the sending countries was not treated as a major issue when recruitment was at its height. Workers were simply needed in the host countries. Lack of economic growth has slowed spontaneous returns today (of course, some recruitment countries are now members of the European Union), as has the ongoing settling process, despite antiforeigner sentiment and discrimination. Economic development in the home countries would alleviate migration pressures and stem the flow of asylum seekers with unfounded claims.

With respect to those who flee for political reasons, options for various forms of intervention in the home countries should be discussed. Again, this discussion is beyond the scope of this paper. However, it is appropriate to acknowledge the problems involved and the hesitancy on the part of powerful countries to intervene in certain conflicts, even as the concept of sovereignty is undergoing substantial revision.

Notes

1. Between the beginning and the end of the decade, the proportion of foreign workers in the country's mining labor force was reduced from 80 percent to about 50 percent (World Bank 1977; Böhning 1977).
2. The number of commutations of seasonal to annual permits has grown steadily since 1985, from 9,354 in that year to 16,889 in 1991 (OECD 1994, 97).
3. Unlike the other recruitment agreements between Germany and labor-sending countries, the first agreement between the Federal Republic and Turkey (1961) stipulated that the workers were to remain in Germany for no more than two years, after which they would be replaced by new migrants. However, this provision was never enforced and was deleted from the 1964 renewal agreement (Böhning 1980, 48; 1984, 280). Similarly, the German federal government declared in 1972 that it was not acceptable to enforce returns through nonrenewal of residence permits of foreign workers who had been in the country for several years (and who thus were likely to settle)—a principle that had also been upheld earlier by an administrative court in Bavaria (Miller 1986, 71).
4. For example, at one point Germany barred spouses and adolescent children who had come into the country through family reunification from joining the labor market for two years after their arrival, but this measure was soon abandoned. Similarly, Germany and later Belgium experimented with keeping new arrivals from settling in municipalities in which the percentage of foreign workers exceeded a certain threshold. Several countries debated or actually implemented legislation lowering the age limit under which children were allowed to join their parents.
5. This discussion of return incentive programs formulated by various European host countries is merely illustrative. Furthermore, the same type of information is not always available on all programs. The only return incentive programs formulated in a sending country in the context of West European labor migration were relatively unsuccessful efforts by the Algerian government and Algerian enterprises to attract back some of the migrants working in specific branches of French industry (see Rogers 1981, 1984).
6. Shortly before the program's expiration, Portuguese and Spanish migrants were declared ineligible because of their countries' impending entry into the EC.
7. Weil (1991, 212) notes the high cost of the German programs and suggests that this was the main reason why they were not renewed.
8. In the spirit of sharing with the sending countries some of the benefits it had gained from labor migration, Sweden offered the OECD one million kronor to study possibilities of improving economic cooperation between it and Yugoslavia, with special emphasis on underdeveloped areas of Yugoslavia to which migrants might wish to return (see Popovic, Gudic, and Vucinicet 1982). The project was initiated in 1979. As of 1987 it had not produced any concrete proposals, and a Yugoslav letter of that year suggesting how the remaining funds should be used merely proposed "the continuation of research towards finding answers to some questions which have remained outstanding in the previous research."

9. Entitled "Abkommen zwischen der Regierung der Bundesrepublik Deutschland und der Regierung der Republik Griechenland über die Förderung auf Griechenland bezogener Selbsthilfeinitiativen von in der Bundesrepublik Deutschland beschäftigten griechischen Arbeitnehmern und ihrer beruflichen Wiedereingliederung in die griechische Wirtschaft."

10. Later, Turkey did cooperate with Germany in the provision of credits and consulting to migrants who wished to become self-employed (see Sen 1986, 46–47; "Antwort des Staatssekretärs" 1987).

11. In the former Yugoslavia, an initial effort in a Croatian community to collect contributions from migrants toward the improvement of the community's infrastructure developed into a wider program in which migrants extended "loans" to individual enterprises to expand and create new jobs to which the migrants or their family members would have priority claims (Rogers 1981). This effort was soon endorsed and encouraged by the central and republic governments, both in broad, hortatory government statements and by the provision of additional loans from banks and various development funds. The results of the programs were less than encouraging: The enterprises that were economically soundest and those in the most developed regions showed little enthusiasm for the schemes. The enterprises that encouraged loans were often of doubtful economic viability from the start, and a number of them later went bankrupt. Another problem was the frequently poor match between the enterprises' manpower requirements and the qualifications of those migrant-depositors who wished to return for employment there (Rogers 1982). Soon the migrants hesitated to commit their savings for this purpose (Gajski 1987).

12. In a 1986 survey of 218 Turkish children and adolescents who had returned with their parents at ages twelve to eighteen in connection with the German offer of return aid, only 28 percent said that they had wished to return. The rest reported either that they had not actively opposed their family's wish to return (39 percent) or that they had in fact returned against their will (32 percent) (Hönekopp 1987a, 484).

13. According to the SOPEMI report for 1992, such arguments have been expressed in Sweden: It is known that some people from Central and Eastern Europe work in the black market, often after entering as tourists. Some of this movement is organized. Partly to prevent this situation developing, cooperative programs, especially with the Baltic states, are being developed (OECD 1992, 79). The report for 1993 notes that Sweden "entered into bilateral agreements on work practice for young people with Estonia, Latvia and Lithuania" (OECD 1994, 96).

14. The international community has, in exceptional cases, created return programs for refugees who came to an industrialized country either through resettlement or as asylum seekers, when there was a profound change in the home country government and the refugees desired to return. For example, in 1990 UNHCR and the International Organization for Migration (IOM) signed a tripartite agreement with the Chilean government to implement a Voluntary Return and Reinsertion Programme for Chilean Refugees. In 1990 (including in the months before the agreement was in force) 1,774 persons returned to Chile. An additional 1,434 returned in 1991 (IOM 1992, 12–13).

15. In 1992, although large numbers of Afghan refugees returned home, the battle among the different rebel factions for control of Kabul created a newly internally displaced population of about 500,000 and over 60,000 new refugees in Pakistan (Ruiz 1992). In Angola, UNHCR had to suspend refugee repatriations when, despite a 1991 peace agreement, UNITA resumed the war in late 1992 after its leader lost the presidential election (U.S. Committee for Refugees 1995, 50).

16. "The 'Development Programme for Displaced Persons, Refugees and Returnees in Central America' (PRODERE) is the most important project within the CIREFCA framework. It has been financed by the Government of Italy with a contribution of US$ 115 million, and is implemented by UNDP in association with UNHCR, the International Labour Organisation (ILO) and the Pan American Health Organisation/World Health Organisation (PAHA/WHO)" (UNDP/UNHCR Joint Support Unit 1993, 4). PRODERE was created in 1988 in the context of PEC (Special Plan for Economic Cooperation for Central America), in conjunction with the Esquipulas II Accords.

17. In Central America this group was far larger than that of recognized refugees.

18. TPS has been part of U.S. law since 1990; the earlier, similar mechanism of extended voluntary departure (EVD) was an administrative measure.

19. INS officials have stated impressionistically that most Kuwaitis granted TPS have returned home. However, this experience is probably not indicative of what happened with other groups.

20. "The Administration offered modest cash incentives and job training offers [*sic*] for those willing to go home before that date. But behind the carrots, a stick was being brandished: 'Those of you who do not take advantage of these programs *will be required to return to Haiti,* but these enhanced benefits will not be available after that date'" (Frelick 1995b, 18).

21. As Frelick (1995b, 27) reports,

    The government's intent to convert Guantánamo into a permanent safe haven appears evident not only from its actions in early 1995, such as building permanent shelters and concluding a deal with the British to transfer, for a fee, hundreds of Cubans from refugee camps in the Cayman Islands to Guantánamo, but also from a 'civilianization plan' that has been drawn up by the Department of Defense (DOD) ... . The plan outlines in detail three phases for converting the camps into civilian-contracted administration. It says that the 'operation must be capable of supporting a 20,000 migrant population with a surge capacity for an additional 10,000 migrants.'

22. The eleventh circuit asserted that "by bringing the migrants to safe haven, the government has not created any protectable liberty or property interests against being wrongly repatriated and the migrants may not rest a claim of right of counsel and information on the due process clause" (Frelick 1995b, 25).

23. The asylum countries are Hong Kong, Indonesia, Malaysia, Singapore, the Philippines, and Thailand. In addition, a handful of asylum seekers from the two countries also arrived in Japan and Macao. In addition to resettlement from the asylum countries, several hundred thousand Vietnamese

have been resettled directly from Vietnam, primarily to the United States, through the Orderly Departure Program. (Between 1975 and 1994, 1,321,810 Vietnamese were resettled to the United States through the two types of channels; Frelick 1995a, 124).

24. In total, over seventy countries participated in the conference (UNHCR 1995b, 1).

25. Other important elements of the CPA were the following: the resettlement countries would resettle all those refugees in the camps who had arrived before the announced cutoff date (including "long-stayers" who for various reasons had been passed over for resettlement); they would continue to take in people who were to be granted refugee status under the new screening procedures; the Orderly Departure Program from Vietnam would be continued and strengthened; and the principle of temporary first asylum would be safeguarded in Southeast Asia—i.e., host countries would allow asylum seekers access to the new system (vessels carrying asylum seekers would not be pushed back to sea).

26. Termination of the CPA does not imply the abandonment of individual status determinations. New arrivals will be treated "'in accordance with national legislation and internationally accepted practices'" (U.S. Committee for Refugees 1995, 97).

27. This hope is not entirely unfounded. Although the Vietnamese ethnic associations in the United States seem to have accepted the inevitability of return for rejected asylum seekers, articles in the U.S. media periodically criticize this policy (see, for example, Rosenthal 1995), and there was an effort in the U.S. Congress in 1995 to resettle this population (Shenon 1995).

28. A survey on stipend usage conducted by the administrative authority of one Vietnamese province reported a rather high incidence of investment in small business: 30 percent of the respondents reported using the money for the purchase of fishing nets, 15 percent for "other production means," 10 percent for house repair, and 5 percent for boat building and repair. Nickerson notes that this behavior is probably not representative of the entire returnee population in the country (Nickerson 1994). No information is provided about the survey's methodology.

29. Much of this discussion is based on Nickerson 1994 and 1995.

30. It does appear that a number of applicants paid bribes in order to be screened in. Two local persons who briefly worked for UNHCR as consultants were under investigation in 1995 (UNHCR 1995a, 7).

31. Recognition rates based on aggregated data for fourteen West European countries fell from 42 percent in 1984 to 17 percent in 1987, 10 percent in 1990, and 8 percent in 1993 (UNHCR 1994a, 23). Rates based on aggregated data for 1984–1993 for individual countries ranged from 39 percent in Belgium and 28 percent in France to 8 percent in Germany and Sweden, 7 percent in Switzerland, and 3 percent in Spain; the rate for all European countries was 13 percent (UNHCR 1994a, 22).

32. In the United States, 143,118 applications (cases) were filed with asylum officers in fiscal year 1993; at the same time, the number of applications pending increased from 223,709 at the beginning of the year to 333,647 by the end of the year. 1,048 cases were "reopened" in 1993; 5,012 applications (representing 7,464 individuals) were granted, 17,979 applications were

ZZZ

denied, and 11,237 were "otherwise closed" (U.S. Immigration and Naturalization Service 1994, 85).

33. The total numbers of deportations for 1990, 1991, and 1992 were 26,091, 28,759, and 38,202, respectively (U.S. Immigration and Naturalization Service 1994, 164).

34. Accelerated procedures can deprive asylum seekers from obtaining adequate hearings. Those who make the adjudications are often not properly trained. In Belgium, "90 percent of asylum requests are now rejected at the border .... [In France,] two-thirds of asylum-seekers never make it across the frontier" (Berthiaume 1995, 7). Many bona fide refugees find it difficult to obtain visas to enter an asylum country and sometimes also to obtain travel documents such as passports from their own governments. The "safe third country" rule stipulates that asylum seekers may be returned to countries that they have passed through in transit, as long as these countries can offer protection. Some host countries declare any country that has acceded to the 1951 Convention or the 1967 Protocol a safe country. All countries bordering Germany are deemed "safe," so that, theoretically, asylum seekers entering Germany over land no longer have a claim to having their applications considered by the German authorities. Host countries using the safe third country rule do not necessarily check on whether asylum seekers are indeed able to enter the asylum process in the country to which they are returned (Kumin 1995). Applying the "safe country of origin" rule also presents dangers: a country may be "safe" for most of its citizens but not, say, for certain minorities (Romania is an example). "Transit zones," which tend to be detention centers by another name, are unacceptable when asylum seekers are housed there not just for days or weeks but for months or years.

35. The author adds:

> It is likely, however, that safe third country rules are here to stay, in one form or another. Four steps would go a long way toward making them more palatable, from both the legal and humanitarian viewpoints.
>
> • Firstly, the applicant should be able to challenge ... the presumption that he or she could find safety in the third country.
>
> • Secondly, the receiving state should be informed that the individual being sent back is an asylum seeker, and its consent to admit him or her to an asylum procedure should be secured.
>
> • Thirdly, the individual should be informed of the possibility to apply for asylum in the country concerned and of the procedure to follow.
>
> • Lastly, asylum-seekers should not be made subject to safe third country rules if they have compelling reasons for being exempted from them, such as an urgent medical condition or close family ties in the destination state. (Kumin 1995, 13)

36. A more nuanced statement would have to discuss differences in host country policies, not only as formulated on paper but in implementation, and with special exceptions and, finally, special legislation for adolescents who had returned and wished to remigrate.

References

Akcayli, Nurhan. 1987. "Grundsätzliche Bemerkungen zu den Phänomenen von Integration bzw. Reintegration." In *Berufliche Integration der zweiten Türkengeneration in der Bundesrepublik Deutschland und in der Türkei,* ed. Nurhan Akcayli and Faruk Sen, 16–21. Frankfurt: Dagyeli.

Akcayli, Nurhan and Faruk Sen, eds. 1987. *Berufliche Integration der zweiten Türkengeneration in der Bundesrepublik Deutschland und in der Türkei.* Frankfurt: Dagyeli.

"Antwort des Staatssekretärs im Bundesministerium für wirtschaftliche Zusammenarbeit auf die schriftlichen Anfragen Nr. 490, 491, und 492 des Abgeordneten Jochen Borchert (CDU)." 1987. Bonn: Bundesministerium für wirtschaftliche Zusammenarbeit.

Argent, Tom. 1992. *Croatia's Crucible: Providing Asylum for Refugees from Bosnia and Hercegovina.* Issue Paper. Washington, D.C.: U.S. Committee for Refugees, Oct.

Balfour, Frederick. 1993. "Home Again: Repatriation Money Turns Returnees into Nouveau Riche." *Far Eastern Economic Review,* 4 Mar.

Berthiaume, Christiane. 1995. "Asylum under Threat." *Refugees* 101: 3–10.

Birks, J. S., and C. A. Sinclair. 1980. *International Migration and Development in the Arab Region.* Geneva: International Labour Office.

Böhning, W. R. 1984. *Studies in International Labour Migration.* London: Macmillan.

_____. 1981. *Black Migration to South Africa: a Selection of Policy-Oriented Research.* Geneva: International Labour Office.

_____. 1980. "Guest Worker Employment, with Special Reference to the Federal Republic of Germany, France and Switzerland— Lessons for the United States?" Working Paper No. 47. Geneva: International Labour Office, World Employment Programme.

_____. 1977. "Black Migration to South Africa: What Are the Issues?" Working Paper No. 13. Geneva: International Labour Office, World Employment Programme, Migration for Employment Project.

Curtin, P. D. 1978. "Postwar Migrations in Sub-Saharan Africa." In *Human Migration; Patterns and Policies,* ed. W. H. McNeill and R. S. Adams, 188–98. Bloomington: Indiana University Press.

"De terugkeergedachte in de Belgische politiek en het migrantenbeleid." 1984. *Bareel* (special issue on return).

Development Bank of Turkey. 1990. "A Model for the Rehabilitation of Turkish Workers Companies (With a Case Study)." Ankara: Development Bank of Turkey, Feb.

Dumon, W., and L. Michiels. 1987. *Belgique 1986.* Belgian country report for SOPEMI. Paris: OECD.

Elkan, W. 1978. "Labour Migration from Botswana, Lesotho and Swaziland." *African Perspectives* 1: 145–56.

France, Ministry of Social Affairs and National Solidarity. 1985. *1981–1985: Une nouvelle politique de l'immigration.* Paris: Ministere des Affaires Sociales et de la Solidarite Nationale.

France, Office for International Migrations (OMI). 1994. "Les procédures de retour." Office des Migrations Internationales, Paris. Mimeo.

_____. 1993. *OMISTATS: Annuaire des Migrations 92.* Paris: Office des Migrations Internationales.

_____. 1987. *Revenir au Pays?* Flyer prepared for distribution to migrants. Paris: Office des Migrations Internationales.

Frelick, Bill. 1995a. "Needed: A Comprehensive Solution for Cuban Refugees." *Interpreter Releases* 72 (no. 4): 121–29.

_____. 1995b. "Safe Haven: Safe for Whom?" In U.S. Committee for Refugees, *World Refugee Survey 1995,* 18–27. Washington, D.C.: U.S. Committee for Refugees.

Frey, Martin. 1986. "Direkte und indirekte Rückkehrförderung seitens der Aufnahemeländer—Überblick." In *Die "neue" Ausländerpolitik in Europa: Erfahrungen in den Aufnahme- und Entsendeländern,* ed. Heiko Körner and Ursula Mehrländer, 15–63. Bonn: Neue Gesellschaft.

Gajski, Zvonko. 1987. "Zasto nema deviznih kredita." *Vjesnik,* 17 Sept.

Gentileschi, Maria Luisa, and Ricciarda Simoncelli, eds. 1983. *Rientro degli emigrati e territorio: Risultati di inchieste regionali.* Institutes of Geography of the Universities of Cagliari, Naples, Padova, Roma, Trieste, and Udine, Gruppo di Lavoro A. Ge. I. Mobilità della popolazione in Italia. Naples: Istituto Grafico Italiano.

Germany, Bundesministerium des Innern. 1994. "Bericht des Bundesministerium des Innern über erste Erfahrungen mit den am 1. Juli 1993 in Kraft getretenen Neuregelungen des Asylverfahrensrechts (Asyl-Erfahrungsbericht 1993)." Bonn: Bundesministerium des Innern, 25 Feb.

Germany, Der Bundesminister für Arbeit und Sozialordnung. 1986. "Qualifizierungs massnahmen für rückkehrwillige junge Türken im Hotel- und Gaststättengewerbe durch ESB—Gemeinnützige Gesellschaft für berufliche Bildung, Bad Neustadt/Saale." Der Bundesminister für Arbeit und Sozialordnung, Referat IIc 3, Bonn. Mimeo.

Hance, W. A. 1970. *Population, Migration and Urbanization in Africa.* New York: Columbia University Press.

Hönekopp, Elmar. 1987a. "Ausländische Jugendliche nach der 'Rückkehr'—wieder ein Seiteneinsteiger-Problem?" *Mitteilungen aus der Arbeitsmarkt- und Berufsforschung* 20, no. 4: 479–89.

———. 1987b. "Rückkehrförderung und Rückkehr ausländischer Arbeitnehmer—Ergebnisse des Rückkehrförderungsgesetzes, der Rückkehrhilfe-Statistik und der IAB-Rückkehrbefragung." In *Aspekte der Ausländerbeschäftigung in der Bundesrepublik Deutschland,* ed. Elmar Hönekopp, 287–341. Nuremberg: Institut für Arbeitsmarkt- und Berufsforschung der Bundesanstalt für Arbeit.

"Immigration et présence étrangère de 1984 à 1986—Faits et chiffres." 1987. *Actualites-Migrations* (special issue) 170 (23 Mar.).

"Intergovernmental Consultations on Asylum, Refugee and Migration Policies in Europe, North America and Australia (IGC)." 1995. Intergovernmental Consultations, Geneva, 28 Feb. Mimeographed statistics.

International Organization for Migration (IOM). 1994. *Annual Report 1993.* Geneva: IOM.

———. 1992. *Annual Report 1991.* Geneva: IOM.

ISOPLAN. 1983–present. *Der Rückkehrberater: Handbuch für die Beratung rückkehrender Ausländer.* Saarbrücken: Institut für Entwicklungsforschung, Wirtschafts- und Sozialplanung.

Kumin, Judith. 1995. "Protection *of,* or Protection *from,* Refugees?" *Refugees* 101: 11–13.

Jambor, Pierre. 1992. "The Vietnamese Boat People and the Comprehensive Plan of Action: An Innovative Solution for an Enduring Problem." Paper prepared for the Joint ILO-UNHCR Meeting on International Aid as a Means to Reduce the Need for Emigration. Geneva: UNHCR, May.

Larkin, Mary Ann, Frederick C. Cuny, and Barry N. Stein, eds. 1991. *Repatriation under Conflict.* Washington, D.C.: Georgetown University Center for Immigration Policy and Refugee Assistance.

Leimgruber, W. 1992. *Switzerland.* Impact of Migration in the Receiving Countries, ed. L. A. Kosinski. Geneva: International Organization for Migration.

Lenske, Werner. 1988. "Berufliche Bildung junger Griechen." *Informationsdienst zur Ausländerarbeit* 2: 59.

McKinley, Brunson. 1994. "Safe Haven for Boat People in the Caribbean." Fletcher School of Law and Diplomacy seminar series, Critical Issues in International and U.S. Refugee Policy. 5 Oct. Washington, D.C.: Bureau for Refugee Programs, Department of State. Mimeo.

Manfrass, Klaus. 1986. "Rückkehrförderung—Der Fall Frankreich." In *Die "neue" Ausländerpolitik in Europa: Erfahrungen in den Aufnahme- und Entsendeländern,* ed. Heiko Körner and Ursula Mehrländer, 73–86. Bonn: Neue Gesellschaft.

Miller, Mark J. 1986. "Policy Ad-Hocracy: The Paucity of Coordinated Perspectives and Policies." in *The ANNALS of the American Academy of Political and Social Science ("From Foreign Workers to Settlers? Transnational Migration and the Emergence of New Minorities"),* ed. Martin O. Heisler and Barbara Schmitter Heisler, 485 (May): 64–75.

"NGO Group Visits Vietnam, First Asylum Countries, Issues Recommendations." 1995. *Refugee Reports* 16, no. 1: 7–14.

Nickerson, Joshua B. 1995. "Micro-Enterprise Development Schemes as Effective Reintegration Assistance Programs for Voluntarily-Repatriated Vietnamese Asylum Seekers." *Asian and Pacific Migration Journal* 4, no. 4: 493–515.

——. 1994. "Backward Linkages: The CPA and the Repatriation of Vietnamese Boat People." Master's thesis, The Fletcher School of Law and Diplomacy, Tufts University, Medford, Massachusetts.

Organisation for Economic Cooperation and Development (OECD). 1994. *Trends in International Migration.* Continuous Reporting System on Migration (SOPEMI), Annual Report 1993. Paris: OECD.

——. 1992. *Trends in International Migration.* Continuous Reporting System on Migration (SOPEMI), Annual Report 1992. Paris: OECD.

Otsea, Jenifer. 1992. "Returnee Aid and Development. Memorandum to Mr. L. Mebtouche." United Nations High Commissioner for Refugees, Regional Bureau for Latin America and the Caribbean, Geneva, 14 Jan. Mimeo.

Popovic, Pavle, Milenko Gudic, and Jadranka Vucinic. 1982. "Analysis of Past Economic Cooperation Between Yugoslavia and Sweden and Possibilities for Its Improvement, with Particular Orientation on Productive Work Engagement of the Population in Emigration and Insufficiently Developed Areas." Institut za Ekonomiku Industrije, Belgrade. Mimeo.

"Retornar desde Holanda." 1988. *Carta de Espana* 373: 27.

Robinson, Court. 1992. "'Still Trying to Get Back Home': The Repatriation of Cambodian Refugees in Thailand." *Refugee Reports* 13, no. 11: 1–11.

Rogers, Rosemarie. 1993. "Western European Responses to Migration." In *International Migration and Security,* ed. Myron Weiner, 107–46. Boulder, Colo.: Westview.

——. 1988. "Return Migration from Western Europe: The Migrant and the Role of the State." Paper delivered at the Population Association of America's Annual Meeting, New Orleans, 21–23 Apr.

_____. 1984. "Return Migration in Comparative Perspective." In *The Politics of Return,* ed. Daniel Kubat, 277–99. Rome: Center for Migration Studies.

_____. 1982. "Employment Creation through Migrants' Loans to Yugoslavia: Policies, the Innovative Return Migrant, and Prospects for Economic Development." Final report submitted by M. Morokvasic and R. Rogers to the Rockefeller-Ford Research Program on Population and Development Policy. Mimeo.

_____. 1981. "Incentives to Return: Patterns of Policies and Migrants' Responses." In *Global Trends in Migration: Theory and Research on International Population Movements,* ed. Mary M. Kritz, Charles B. Keely, and Silvano M. Tomasi, 338–64. Staten Island, N.Y.: Center for Migration Studies.

Rogers, Rosemarie, and Emily Copeland. 1993. *Forced Migration: Policy Issues in the Post–Cold War World.* Medford, Mass.: The Fletcher School of Law and Diplomacy, Tufts University.

Rosenthal, A. M. 1995. "Voyage of the Damned." *New York Times,* 23 May, A17.

"Rückkehrförderung ausländischer Arbeitnehmer in Frankreich." 1982. In *Kurzberichte,* ed. Institut für Arbeitsmarkt- und Berufsforschung der Bundesanstalt für Arbeit. Nuremberg: Institut für Arbeitsmarkt- und Berufsforschung der Bundesanstalt für Arbeit.

Ruiz, Hiram A. 1992. 1993. *El Retorno: Guatemala's Risky Repatriation Begins.* Issue Paper. Washington, D.C.: U.S. Committee for Refugees, Feb.

_____. 1992. *Left Out in the Cold: The Perilous Homecoming of Afghan Refugees.* Issue Paper. Washington, D.C.: U.S. Committee for Refugees, Dec.

Sen, Faruk. 1987. "Turks in the Federal Republic of Germany: Achievements, Problems, Expectations." Zentrum für Türkeistudien, Bonn. Mimeo.

_____. 1986. "Auswirkungen der Rückwanderung: Remigration in die Türkei." *Informationsdienst zur Ausländerarbeit* 2: 44–47.

Shenon, Philip. 1995. "U.N. Links G.O.P. to Boat People's Riots: Bill Offering Asylum Set Off Melee in Hong Kong, Officials Say." *New York Times,* 24 May, A8.

Sociaal en Cultureel Planbureau. 1987. "Sociale en Culturele Verkenningen 1988." *Cahier* 56: 19.

Stahl, C. W. 1981. "Migrant Labour Supplies, Past, Present and Future; With Special Reference to the Gold-Mining Industry." In *Black Migration to South Africa. A Selection of Policy-Oriented Research,* ed. W. R. Böhning, 7–44. Geneva: International Labour Office.

Stein, Barry N. 1992. "Policy Challenges Regarding Repatriation in the 1990s: Is 1992 the Year for Voluntary Repatriation?" Paper commissioned by the Program in International and U.S. Refugee Policy, The Fletcher School of Law and Diplomacy, Tufts University, Medford, Mass. Mimeo.

Sturckow y Gonzalez, Maximo. 1986. "Iglesia y emigracion." *Carta de Espana* 343: 27.

UNDP/UNHCR CIREFCA Joint Support Unit. 1993. "Questions and Answers about CIREFCA." San Jose, Costa Rica: UNDP/UNHCR CIREFCA Joint Support Unit, Feb.

United Nations Disaster Relief Office (UNDRO). n.d. "Iraq-Kuwait Crisis: The Plight of Returnees." In *UNDRO News Special Supplement.* New York: Office of the UN Disaster Relief Coordinator.

United Nations High Commissioner for Refugees (UNHCR). 1995a. "The Comprehensive Plan of Action." In *Information Bulletin.* Geneva: UNHCR, Aug.

_____. 1995b. *The Comprehensive Plan of Action 1989–1995: A Regional Approach to Improving Refugee Protection.* Geneva: UNHCR, 23 July.

_____. 1995c. "Implementation of the Comprehensive Plan of Action: Appeal for 1995." Geneva: UNHCR, Jan.

_____. 1995d. "UNHCR Protection Consultation." Washington, D.C.: UNHCR, 15 Feb.

_____. 1994a. "Populations of Concern to UNHCR: A Statistical Overview." Geneva: UNHCR, May.

_____. 1994b. "UNHCR Activities Financed by Voluntary Funds: Report for 1993–1994 and Proposed Programmes and Budget for 1995." Part 2, "Asia and Oceania." Section 11, "Vietnam." A/AC.96/825/Part II/11. Geneva: UNHCR, 12 Aug.

_____. 1993. "Implementation of the Comprehensive Plan of Action: Appeal for 1993." Geneva: UNHCR, Jan.

U.S. Committee for Refugees. 1995. *World Refugee Survey 1995.* Washington, D.C.: U.S. Committee for Refugees.

_____. 1994. *World Refugee Survey 1994.* Washington, D.C.: U.S. Committee for Refugees.

U.S. Immigration and Naturalization Service. 1994. *Statistical Yearbook of the Immigration and Naturalization Service, 1993.* Washington, D.C.: U.S. Government Printing Office.

van Gendt, Rien. 1977. *Return Migration and Reintegration Services.* Paris: OECD.

Weil, Patrick. 1991. *La France et ses étrangers: L'Aventure d'une politique de l'immigration 1938–1991.* Paris: Calmann-Levy.

Wilson, F. 1976. "International Migration in Southern Africa." World Employment Programme, Migration for Employment Project Working Paper No. 3. Geneva: International Labour Office.

World Bank. 1977. "Migration from Botswana, Lesotho and Swaziland." Washington Report No. 1688-EA. Washington, D.C.: World Bank.

Chapter 6

Is the 1951 Convention Relating to the Status of Refugees Obsolete?

*Joan Fitzpatrick**

Introduction

The 1951 Convention Relating to the Status of Refugees shows few outward signs of desuetude. In the space of one recent year, the convention and its 1967 Protocol gained ten new parties (UNHCR 1993, ¶ [c]).[1] The total in 1994 stood at 127 increasingly diverse states (Ex. Comm. 1994, 19 ¶ [d]).[2] The Executive Committee of the Programme of the United Nations High Commissioner for Refugees (UNHCR) continually reaffirms the place of the convention and its protocol as the "cornerstone" (Ex. Comm. 1994, ¶ 19 [c]) and the "centre of the international legal framework for the protection of refugees" (UNHCR 1993, ¶ 19[b]). Yet in recent years it has become commonplace to assert that the premises of the 1951 Convention are badly outdated (Helton 1995, 1623, 1627). By the fortieth anniversary of the convention in 1991, T. Alexander Aleinikoff could plausibly wonder whether it should be redesignated a "Convention Emeritus" or at least regarded skeptically as a treaty with a serious midlife crisis (Aleinikoff 1991, 618). The aim of this paper is to explore why the convention's postulated obsolescence is receiving such attention and what this bodes for the future protection of forced migrants.

Thirty years ago, there were grounds to fear that the convention would become obsolete. Its original temporal limitation, extending protection only to refugees affected by events occurring before 1 January 1951 (Article 1A [2]),[3] appeared to destine it for that fate. The drafters of the convention were primarily West European and North American states facing the need to assimilate people displaced in Europe by the Second World War and the ensuing regime changes in Eastern Europe, for whom repatriation was unrealistic. Those states preferred to assume a common set of legal obligations that would not be excessively onerous in domestic political terms. The convention's negotiators were thus reluctant to accept an open-ended obligation, even though they were aware that new refugee crises were arising in China, Korea, and Palestine. The temporal limitation was somewhat misleading, in any case. Post-1951 flows of refugees, such as Hungarians departing en masse after the failed 1956 rebellion, could be protected under the convention by a liberal reading that traced their plight to pre-1951 events. And the 1950 statute of the UNHCR did not limit the competence of that office to pre-1951 flows.

A decade and a half after its signing, the international community took steps to ensure the continued relevance of the Refugee Convention by eliminating the temporal limitation, through the 1967 Protocol. This renegotiation signaled a formal recognition that refugees present an ongoing, evolving challenge. Yet in 1967 the basic premises of the 1951 Convention were not yet seen as outdated. Indeed, the convention's key provisions were simply incorporated into the protocol, including the individualized definition of refugee.[4] This occurred even though decolonization had displaced world war and its aftermath at the center stage of forced migration issues in the 1960s.

The roughly contemporaneous drafting of the 1969 Organization of African Unity Convention Governing the Specific Aspects of Refugee Problems in Africa indicates that policymakers, including the UNHCR, were well aware of the new dimensions of the refugee challenge by the time the protocol was drafted.[5] The OAU Convention expands the refugee definition to encompass a group-based conception.[6] The OAU Convention also specifically addresses relationships between refugee-producing and refugee-receiving states by forbidding refugees to engage in subversive activities from the territory of the asylum state (Article III) and by providing for appeals to "African solidarity" and burden sharing (Article II.4). Yet, like the protocol, the OAU Convention pays homage to the 1951 Convention by adopting its key criteria. The international community has thus repeatedly signaled its reluctance to jettison the 1951 foundation, however creaky it might seem at times, for fear that hoped-for advances might instead dilute standards of protection.

The Refugee Convention is not so much obsolete as incomplete, a condition that has plagued it from the outset. Its drafters included what was possible, not what was required, to create a comprehensive international system to protect forced migrants. Refugee advocates have sometimes attempted to fill key gaps in the convention through progressive interpretation or recognition of extraconventional norms (Goodwin-Gill 1988, 103).

But the increasing suggestions that the convention is an artifact of a past era cannot be ignored. Changes in the nature of refugee flows are often cited as the basis for this assessment, sometimes to justify restricting access to durable asylum. Yet the Refugee Convention is really no more ill-suited to this age than to its earlier ones. The end of the cold war has done less to alter the nature of refugee flows than to transform, in an ungenerous direction, the political dynamic within which the Refugee Convention is applied. A crisis exists not because the convention fails to meet the needs of asylum seekers but because it meets them so well as to impose burdens that are no longer politically tolerable. The claimed obsolescence is thus seen primarily from the perspective of the traditional asylum states.

If not obsolete, however, the Refugee Convention does deal poorly with many pressing aspects of refugee protection. The challenge for policymakers and refugee advocates is to identify and cure those flaws in the convention framework that impede effective protection of today's vast number and variety of forced migrants.

The postulated obsolescence of the 1951 Refugee Convention can be examined from at least five perspectives: (1) the continued vitality of the norm of nonrefoulement, the key substantive provision of the Refugee Convention; (2) the vagueness and manipulability of its other key provision, the refugee definition; (3) the lack of an agreed framework for refugee determination; (4) crucial substantive lacunae or ambiguities, concerning the right to receive asylum, the right of admission, the rights of asylum seekers interdicted at sea, and the right of temporary refuge for forced migrants who do not qualify as convention refugees; and (5) key gaps in interstate obligations, especially burden sharing through admission of refugees, security issues relating to refugee encampments, and dependable financing both of refugee relief and preventive strategies.

Continued Relevance of the Central Norm of Nonrefoulement

Nothing in the passage of time since 1951 has diminished the vital role played by the norm of nonrefoulement in protecting refugees, however defined, from danger. The most enduring contribution of the 1951 Convention is Article 33's articulation of this norm.[7]

Admittedly, Article 33 is subject to qualifications: it may pertain only to those who manage to reach the territory of an obligated state; it extends only to those meeting the refugee definition whose life or freedom would be threatened on their return to the state of persecution; and its protection may be denied to refugees who present a danger to security or who have been convicted of a particularly serious crime.[8] Despite these limits, Article 33 imposes a clear and mandatory obligation on the parties to the Refugee Convention, whose breach may be detected and protested.

While verbal commitment to this central pillar of modern refugee protection remains undiminished, the norm has been affected by two noteworthy developments. One is essentially positive. The UNHCR (Ex. Comm. 1994, ¶ 19 [k–o]) and some regional instruments[9] have sought to expand the scope of nonrefoulement to encompass broader classes of beneficiaries, in particular those fleeing armed conflict or civil strife. This extension of nonrefoulement does not suggest that the convention has lost relevance. By expanding the numbers of people theoretically protected, however, this trend may weaken some governments' commitment to strict respect for the norm.

Evidence of that erosion in commitment may be seen in the second development: the popularity of evasive strategies that enable governments to avoid their obligations without committing direct breaches of Article 33. These strategies involve both narrowing the scope of protection through ungenerous definitions of those entitled to protection[10] and deterrent measures including visa requirements, carrier sanctions, safe third country arrangements, safe country of origin presumptions, and interdiction without screening. All these measures are increasingly popular among states that have long prided themselves on their strict respect for the Refugee Convention.

The apparent disaffection of these key states does not establish that the convention itself is obsolete. Strategies to avoid the obligation of nonrefoulement testify to its continuing power and the accomplishment of those who managed to confer obligatory status on it in 1951. States do not readily admit to a breach of Article 33. When breaches become undeniable, reparatory steps are sometimes taken. The need to assure refugees that they will not be returned to their persecutors remains as compelling as ever, even while forms of persecution alter. Given increasing resistance to full integration of asylum seekers and growing stress on time-limited remedies for persecution, nonrefoulement appears even more suited to these times than to those of the convention's drafting.

The major drawback in the convention's provision on nonrefoulement is its silence concerning the legal status of recipients of Article 33's protection, especially those who cannot be sent to any other place of refuge. That gap is increasingly being filled by national measures conferring tenuous and unstable forms of leave to remain.

Temporary protection measures do not directly violate the prohibition on refoulement, even when they are extended as the exclusive measure of protection to people with unheard but valid claims to refugee status under the convention and protocol. For this reason, the UNHCR finds itself in the awkward position of encouraging temporary protection as a "pragmatic and flexible method of affording international protection of a temporary nature in situations of conflict or persecution involving large scale outflows" (Ex. Comm. 1994, ¶ 19 [r]). Noting the growing reliance on temporary protection to prevent refoulement of victims of both conflict and persecution, the Executive Committee of the High Commissioner's Programme urges that "in providing temporary protection States and UNHCR should not diminish the protection afforded to refugees under those instruments" (Ex. Comm. 1994, ¶ 19 [t]). Unfortunately, little more than nonrefoulement is categorically guaranteed even to convention refugees.

The strength of the nonrefoulement norm is also manifest in a tendency to reiterate it in new international instruments. In its Article 6 (6), the 1988 United Nations Convention against Illicit Traffic in Narcotic Drugs and Psychotropic Substances adopts an approach reminiscent of the traditional political offense exception to extradition, permitting states to refuse extradition requests when "compliance would facilitate the prosecution or punishment of any person on account of his race, religion, nationality or political opinions." The United Nations Convention against Torture and Other Cruel, Inhuman and Degrading Treatment or Punishment takes the stricter approach of forbidding states under Article 3 (1) to "expel, return (*'refouler'*) or extradite a person to another State where there are substantial grounds for believing that he would be in danger of being subjected to torture." While a proliferation of such nonrefoulement provisions might eventually marginalize the Refugee Convention, that effect has not yet materialized.[11]

Vagueness and Manipulability of the Refugee Definition

The convention's focus on individualized persecution based on any of five grounds (race, religion, nationality, particular social group, or political opinion) is widely seen as a cold war relic of little pertinence to contemporary forced migrations. Two criticisms underlie this perception. First, the causes of flight are no longer seen as primarily persecutory. Second, the implicit condemnation of the refugee-producing state, inherent in a finding that a refugee possesses a well-founded fear of persecution, is regarded as ill suited to an era striving to facilitate voluntary repatriation to the maximum degree and in as short a time as possible. During the cold war, the condemnatory aspect of the refugee definition was not a barrier to recognition; indeed, it could serve as a positive inducement to anticommunist asylum adjudicators.

In reality, the refugee definition never accurately described the situation of many of the convention's intended beneficiaries: large groups displaced by the Second World War. Rarely were its criteria applied with stringency and intellectual rigor during the cold war (Collinson 1993, 66). If they had been, many ballet dancers and athletes would not have been able to transfer their loyalties through the device of political asylum. From the outset, aspects of the definition were vague (e.g., the nature of "persecution") (Hathaway 1991a, 99–101) or almost empty of agreed meaning (e.g., the definition of a "social group") (157).

The vagueness of the refugee definition is unsatisfactory not primarily because it imposes undue rigidity. Regrettably, it permits a kind of local option for asylum adjudicators either to permit adaptation to new realities or to deny asylum claims that fail to follow an archaic scenario. During the past four decades, notions of persecution evolved along with concepts of the political, especially with respect to violence against women (Goldberg 1994). Adaptation to these new conceptualizations has been uneven.

More problematic changes have occurred in the nature of the persecutor and the site of persecution of those seeking asylum in the West. The paradigm inspiring the Refugee Convention was the right-wing totalitarian regime of Nazi Germany, which acted on its hatreds with astounding efficiency, thoroughness, and candor. At its drafting, the Refugee Convention was easily directed to victims of left-wing totalitarian governments in Eastern Europe, which manifested similar impulses to root out nonconformist elements by infliction of state terror. In today's chaotic world, however, the identity and motivations of the persecutor are more elusive. Not only have many totalitarian regimes fallen, the state itself has vanished in some refugee-producing locales. Repression comes at the hands of shadowy organizations whose links to state authority are deliberately obscured or who portray themselves as antagonists of the formal state. These groups range from the Bosnian Serb insurgents, to the Interahamwe of Rwanda, to the attachés of Haiti's former military regime, to the Islamic militants of Algeria. Criminal profit motives are increasingly and more visibly linked to the impulse for political dominance.

As the nature and motivations of the persecutor evolve, the definition of persecution may likewise adapt. International responsibility vis-à-vis refugees is theoretically grounded in the notion that, when the state of nationality has defaulted on its protective role, other states may take over for it. The inability of a state to provide effective protection against insurgents has been recognized as sufficient to confer refugee status on the victims of their nonstate violence (Goodwin-Gill 1983, 124–33). Recent trends toward the disintegration of the state may simply signal that the failure of the state protective role is more acute than in the past.

This does not suggest a conceptual gap in the convention. Unfortunately, the elasticity of the definition of persecution depends largely on the political will of the member states implementing it, through their national refugee determination systems. The text of the convention is less inflexible than the generosity of its parties. In an era of retrenchment and fear of incurring illimitable obligations, the pattern in asylum states may be not adaptation to new exigencies for forced migrants but a return to outdated presumptions about persecution. The Justice and Home Affairs Council of the European Union (EU) approved a definition of refugee that excludes victims of nonstate actors, in order to accommodate the rigid views of four of its members, France, Germany, Italy, and Sweden ("EU: Definition" 1995).

Certain disturbing statistics indicate that the adaptability of the refugee definition, rather than ensuring survival of the convention regime, may prove its undoing. While rates of asylum applications have soared, rates of approval have plummeted (Loescher 1993, 98 [table 5-1], 227 n. 84; UNHCR 1995, 196 [drop in approval rate in Western Europe from 42 percent in 1984 to 10 percent in 1993]). In some instances, not only have rates of approval declined, but absolute numbers of asylum grants have decreased while claims escalate (Joly, Nettleton, and Poulton 1992, 35). Given the manipulability of the refugee definition, it is impossible to attribute these dramatic shifts entirely to alterations in the content of asylum applications. National authorities have discretion to tighten criteria, consciously and visibly for deterrent aims, surreptitiously, or even in subconscious reaction to fears of opening floodgates.

Questioning whether this state of affairs reduces the refugee definition to a legal fiction, some commentators have stressed the need to establish uniform interpretation through heavier reliance on objective factors (Arboleda and Hoy 1993, 66). Yet the prospects for substantive harmonization of standards of eligibility, even within the EU's elaborate framework for discussion, still remain remote (Bhabha 1994, 108–9).

Arguably, one dated aspect of the Refugee Convention is its repeated reference to stateless persons, who presented a more severe problem for the world community in the first half of this century. Stateless persons obviously lack the protection of a state of nationality and thus require the protection of an asylum state. Today's chaotic conditions in places such as Somalia and Afghanistan, where national borders remain intact but central authority has suffered a profound breakdown, present an entirely new dimension of "statelessness." The protection needs of refugees fleeing this chaos are different, but not necessarily less severe, than those of the literally stateless, who were a major concern of the convention's drafters.

Lack of A Uniform Framework for Refugee Determination

The Refugee Convention delegates authority to participating states to devise their own refugee determination systems. Until recently, states had little reason to complain of the flexibility granted to them by the convention. European states, however, have grown acutely worried that, with the integration of the EU, disparities in disposition of asylum applications could resonate beyond the state of application. Once granted asylum by any EU state, an asylee would have freedom of movement within the entire union. While the thrust of harmonization to date has concentrated on identifying the state with primary responsibility for entertaining the application, attention has begun to shift toward harmonizing and centralizing decision making. The Justice and Home Affairs Council of the EU has begun the process of promulgating minimum guarantees for asylum procedures, addressing issues such as safeguards for asylum seekers applying at border posts and applications by unaccompanied minors.[12]

Uniformity in substance and process, without reduction to the lowest common denominator, would be advanced by the creation of a central refugee determination agency in which UNHCR would play a prominent role. Given the heightened visibility of immigration in the domestic politics of many industrialized states, however, the chances seem slim for a genuine cession of decision-making authority from state officials to a central agency, especially one inclined to be sympathetic toward asylum seekers.

One cause of disaffection among officials in the traditional asylum states is the enormous cost of refugee determination procedures, estimated to range up to $7 billion total (Hathaway 1991b, 129). Asylum adjudication systems also tend to be plagued by delay, creating backlogs feared to operate as magnets for abusive claims. Arguably, the Refugee Convention's implicit assumption that claims to refugee status would be processed on an individualized basis is a mark of obsolescence, given the unpredicted explosion in asylum requests.

UNHCR has long recognized that individualized procedures may not be feasible in situations of mass influx, and the Executive Committee of the High Commissioner's Programme in its Conclusion No. 22 (XXXII) of 1981 (Ex. Comm. 1981, 18) urged that admission and temporary refuge be granted in such situations. But mechanisms of temporary refuge and group-based status determinations may not be appropriate in situations of mass influx into the industrialized democracies. Bosnian victims of ethnic violence were channeled in large numbers into schemes of temporary protection providing less stable guarantees of sojourn and none of the integrative possibilities of an asylum grant (UNHCR 1994; Kjaerum 1994). While freezing asylum claims for beneficiaries of temporary refuge no doubt saves expense and delay, the prolongation of the war in Bosnia may prove that this was a short-sighted and politically motivated strategy that caused unjustified distress. Many grants of temporary protection do not authorize work or provide for family reunification. When bona fide refugees are frozen out of the asylum system, a serious issue arises as to whether states of refuge are fully complying with their obligations under the Refugee Convention and other human rights guarantees (Kjaerum 1994).

Crucial Substantive Lacunae

In addition to its silence concerning processes for refugee determination, the convention lacks explicit mention of important substantive protections for asylum seekers, including the right to receive asylum, the right of admission, the right not to be denied access to asylum through interdiction at sea, and the right of temporary refuge for nonconvention refugees fleeing armed conflict or internal strife. The UNHCR has striven to address issues such as temporary refuge, nonrejection at the frontier, and interdiction; however, the decentralized nature of the convention's application permits national authorities to impose strained and narrow meanings that deny these vital protections.

The right to seek and enjoy asylum is embraced in the international community's foundational postwar charter of fundamental human freedoms as Article 14 of the Universal Declaration of Human Rights (UDHR).[13] The specter of spurned Jewish asylum seekers turned back toward Nazi Germany, sometimes perishing in consequence, thrust this right into the consciousness of those defining the basic principles of human dignity for the postwar world. Yet the drafters of the UDHR carefully refrained from articulating a right to be granted asylum (Holborn 1975, 163).

When the "soft law" of the UDHR was succeeded by the Refugee Convention, no mention was made of the right to seek and enjoy asylum. The key obligatory provisions (Arts. 31, 32, and 33) assume a situation in which refugees, possibly by irregular means, have managed to arrive at or in the territory of the contracting state. The obligation of states to admit asylum seekers is mentioned only in a recommendation attached to the final act of the conference adopting the convention (see Grahl-Madsen 1980, 139):

The Conference,

Considering that many persons still leave their country of origin for reasons of persecution and are entitled to special protection on account of their position,

Recommends that Governments continue to receive refugees in their territories and that they act in a true spirit of international cooperation in order that these refugees may find asylum and the possibility of resettlement.

The International Covenant on Civil and Political Rights (ICCPR) failed to build on the UDHR's right to seek and enjoy asylum. Article 12 of the ICCPR includes the right to leave any country and the right to enter one's own country but not a right of entry for purposes of seeking asylum. The omission was intentional (Holborn 1975, 228).

When the United Nations General Assembly restated the right to seek asylum two decades after the UDHR in the 1967 Declaration on Territorial Asylum, little progress was made in strengthening a corresponding state duty to respect this "right." Article 1 of the declaration follows the traditional approach, by characterizing asylum as a right of states that other states should not regard as unfriendly. Viewed as an exercise of territorial sovereignty, grants of asylum are inherently discretionary rather than obligatory.

Article 3 (1) of the Declaration on Territorial Asylum did mark an advance by including the right not to be rejected at the frontier. However, Article 3 (1) is undercut by Article 3 (2) permitting states to make exceptions "for overriding reasons of national security or in order to safeguard the population, as in the case of a mass influx of persons." States need only "consider" granting provisional asylum or assisting asylum seekers to go to another state under Article 3 (3).

The relatively weak language of the Declaration on Territorial Asylum is cause for concern especially when viewed in light of the failure of the 1977 United Nations conference to draft a convention on territorial asylum. Certain documents prepared by experts in advance of the conference included a right of provisional admission pending disposition of asylum claims (Grahl-Madsen 1980, 174–75), intended to bolster the effectiveness of nonrefoulement and give real meaning to the right "to seek and to enjoy asylum." The texts actively discussed at the 1977 conference required states to extend the prohibition on nonrefoulement to applicants "at the frontier seeking asylum." However, they also contained an exception for instances of mass influx constituting "a serious problem to the security" of the asylum state (210–11). States invoking this exception were bound only to "consider" permitting the asylum seekers to depart to another state, leaving open the possibility of refoulement of many bona fide refugees.

The time may still not be ripe for obligations more demanding and precise than those agreed to in 1951. But if there are not to be improvements on the question of provisional admission in the 1951 text, it is all the more necessary to understand existing obligations. The UNHCR has repeatedly stressed the importance of provisional admission for asylum seekers arriving as part of a mass influx, even when the bulk of the arrivals may be entitled to no more than temporary refuge. The Executive Committee of the High Commissioner's Programme noted in 1994, for example, that "admission to safety" is an integral aspect of temporary refuge (Ex. Comm. 1994, ¶ 19 [r]).

The territorial reach of Article 33 has become increasingly ill defined. In *Sale v. Haitian Centers Council* (113 S.Ct. 2549 [1993]), the United States Supreme Court imposed a strained interpretation on Article 33 and U.S. immigration law to reach the conclusion that U.S. officials possess unfettered authority to seize and repatriate asylum seekers intercepted outside U.S. territory. Relying on confused passages in the *travaux préparatoires* suggesting an exception to Article 33 for instances of mass influx, the Court concluded that obligations run only to asylum seekers who reach the territory of the asylum state.

The Haitian interdiction policy was particularly stark and troubling but hardly unique in its aim: to control the irregular flow to the industrialized states of asylum seekers from repressive and economically disadvantaged regions. Filings by persons entering irregularly, especially with the assistance of organized smugglers, have become a subject of acute concern. Governments have imposed a wide variety of deterrent measures, apparently with some effect, as application rates began to decline after 1992.

These deterrent measures are acceptable to policymakers even though their impact is indiscriminate with respect to both bona fide claimants and those abusing the asylum system. The public increasingly views asylum claims as inherently abusive and the irregular presence of asylum seekers as a disqualifying lack of respect for order and law.[14] The Refugee Convention places few obvious constraints on the discretion of policymakers to devise deterrent measures. Indeed, both the Schengen and Dublin Conventions carefully recommit their signatories to respect for the Refugee Convention and Protocol. While "safe third country" or "safe country of origin" designations may undermine effective access to asylum, the Refugee Convention does not directly address them.

The Bosnian war has caused a broad shift away from durable asylum. The new emphasis on temporary protection, by European states previously committed to refugee determination premised on the convention, made the convention appear increasingly irrelevant in acute refugee crises. Ironically, Bosnian victims in many cases have stronger claims of persecution within the meaning of Article 1 of the convention than some who successfully fled communist regimes during the cold war. The parallel between the religious and ethnic genocide in Bosnia and that inflicted by the Nazis is so strong that it prompted the U.N. Security Council to establish the first international war crimes tribunal since Nuremberg.

The Bosnian experience also had a profound transformative effect on the UNHCR. That body acceded to the strategy of temporary protection for Bosnian victims. And while the UNHCR had for decades assumed a widened mission to protect not only convention refugees but others in refugeelike situations, the Bosnian war drew it deeply into protection of the internally displaced as well. The UNHCR provided direct material relief to refugees, the internally displaced, and trapped residents of "safe zones." This relief task sometimes compromised the UNHCR's traditional protective role, as UNHCR staff had to negotiate with warring sides to make deliveries of vital supplies (Refugee Policy Group 1994). The withdrawal by Médecins sans Frontières from Rwandan Hutu refugee camps in Tanzania, based on the perception that relief was reinforcing the authority of those responsible for the genocide and postponing an appropriate solution to the crisis,[15] reflects the ethical dilemmas posed by such refugee relief activities.

Waves of often-skilled East Europeans in the period immediately following the Second World War were welcomed as much for their potential contribution to economic development as for their need for protection from persecution. They not only benefited from nonrefoulement but had their paths smoothed toward full integration. Recessionary fears and political/cultural concerns about absorptive capacity have altered this picture, more so in Western Europe but probably to an increasing degree in the United States and Canada as well.

For this reason, the 1951 Convention's detailed guarantees of economic and social rights, especially the right to work, housing, and protection for refugee families, seem almost quaint. While these guarantees continue to be enjoyed by the relative few who receive grants of political asylum, they are increasingly elusive for asylum seekers and those now remitted to temporary protection schemes. The economic and social rights of the convention suggest a dual purpose: to provide a life of minimal dignity during the period of exile and to facilitate the growth of ties that will ease assimilation into the culture and economy of the asylum state.

With emphasis shifting to deterrence of asylum seekers, measures designed to make the life of exile more attractive obviously have lost appeal in official circles. Policymakers in many areas of the world are striving to design conditions of accommodation that will prompt the earliest possible return of refugees to their states of origin. Provisions such as Article 34, inviting states to facilitate the naturalization of refugees, might strike some present-day officials as the product of a bygone era.

Interstate Cooperation

The Refugee Convention's lack of detailed provisions concerning the obligations states owe each other reduces its value as a framework for resolving contemporary refugee crises. The articulated obligations run from the state to refugees who arrive in its territory. There are no duties to relieve other states of the burdens of asylum by providing either financial resources or offers of admission. Financing of the UNHCR remains voluntary, though its tasks have multiplied enormously. Even during the Bosnian crisis, little sense of shared obligation to frontline states was manifested.

It has sometimes been possible to induce compliance with principles such as nonrefoulement through burden-sharing arrangements. Temporary refuge for asylum seekers in Thailand and Malaysia was secured by substantial programs of distant resettlement and financial support for camp operations. The Comprehensive Plan of Action for Indochinese Refugees improved refugee determination processes in exchange for offers of resettlement and promises by refugee-producing countries to crack down on irregular departures.

Efforts to stem flows are attracting increasing attention from industrialized states. "Orderly departure programs," while not intended to choke off flows entirely, place barriers in the paths of asylum seekers. Recent migration agreements between the United States and Cuba provide a startling example of this emphasis on preventing irregular departures. While maintaining a hostile relationship steeped in cold war values, the two countries found a place of mutual accommodation in stemming the tide of asylum seekers. This is especially ironic in light of prior Western emphasis on the right of citizens to leave their own states.

No firm conclusions about possible trends can be drawn from the recent modest success by the United States in inducing nearby states to cooperate in providing extraterritorial prescreening of asylum seekers and, subsequently, temporary refuges without screening. The creation of temporary refuges for Haitian and Cuban asylum seekers at Guantánamo Bay and in Panama do not contradict any indisputable commands of the Refugee Convention (Aleinikoff 1994, 71). Moreover, they appear to provide effective temporary protection for asylum seekers unable to meet the refugee definition. But the violence that afflicted both locales, the contingency of the arrangements, and the disparate treatment of the two groups cast a pall on the experiment (U.S. Safe Haven Camps in Cuba and Panama 1994, 14). The experiment does indicate, however, that cooperative arrangements are possible, at least on a bilateral basis, to control flows of asylum seekers without necessarily undermining fundamental safety.

Finally, events in Rwanda illustrate the complexity and importance of security issues relating to refugee flows. Conditions in the camps in Tanzania and Zaire are not unique, though they have attracted unusual attention. The time may be ripe for more serious discussion about the responsibilities of states of refuge, the international community, and the beneficiaries of refugee protection to ensure that vulnerable elements in the flow are not repeatedly victimized and that refuges do not become menaces to their inhabitants, the territorial state, or the state of origin. The OAU Convention stresses the security aspect to a much greater degree than did the Refugee Convention, which alludes to it primarily in terms of individualized security threats posed by particular refugees.

Conclusion

The 1951 Refugee Convention does not provide answers to all the vexing questions posed by contemporary forced migration. But neither is it obsolete in the sense that it no longer usefully guides state responses to the flight of refugees.

The most enduring contribution of the convention is its elevation of nonrefoulement to the status of an obligatory norm. The principle that refugees should not be forcibly returned to the site of persecution remains as vital today as it was in 1951. The norm has developed beyond the bounds of the convention to cast a protective net over expanded classes of forced migrants fleeing generalized conditions of violence as well as persecution. The persecutory focus of the convention's refugee definition is not as anachronistic as it is sometimes pictured. The definition is elastic and could be adapted to new targets of persecution, new forms of persecution, and new identities of persecutors.

What does seem new is the increasing resistance to the concept of asylum among the states that traditionally prided themselves on their strict compliance with the Refugee Convention. Asylum is not mandated by the convention, but the practice had been for states to grant asylum to persons meeting the convention's refugee definition, at least if no alternate state of refuge was available. The growing emphasis on speedy voluntary repatriation as the "ideal solution to refugee problems" (Ex. Comm. 1994, ¶ 19 [v]) signals a new inclination to prevent the development of enduring ties between asylum seekers and states of refuge.[46]

The convention's reliance on good faith determination of refugee status by participating states contributes to its potential marginalization in an era of retrenchment. While discussions have begun concerning harmonization of substantive standards and the creation of a uniform procedure for status determination, for the moment states retain the ability to undermine the convention through ungenerous implementation. Even more seriously, states are finding it possible to erect onerous barriers of access to asylum seekers without breaching any specific duty under the convention. This trend is the source of legitimate and grave concern to refugee advocates and the UNHCR.

The convention's silence or ambiguity on crucial subjects such as the right to receive asylum, the right of admission, the problem of interdiction, and the rights of those forced to flee the dangers of armed conflict remains a serious limitation. Yet, the present fearful mood among policymakers and publics in the industrialized democracies hardly indicates that the time is ripe for the drafting of a new instrument that would satisfactorily address these questions.

Finally, the convention's focus on the obligations running from each participating state to each individual refugee appears dated in light of recent emphasis on the need for comprehensive cooperative relationships among refugee-producing, first-asylum, and industrialized states. A new framework may well emerge that will displace the convention regime of the past forty years. But until the new thinking achieves concrete form, the Refugee Convention will continue to play a vital role in moderating the impulse of states to focus too narrowly on their own material or security needs, at the expense of their essential humanitarian obligations to forced migrants.

---

*A revised version of this essay was published in volume 9 of the *Harvard Human Rights Journal* in 1996.

Notes

1. The new parties, some joining by succession, were Armenia, Azerbaijan, the Bahamas, Bosnia and Herzegovina, Bulgaria, Cambodia, the Czech Republic, the Republic of Korea, the Russian Federation, and the Slovak Republic.
2. Acceding to the convention in 1994 were Dominica, the former Yugoslav Republic of Macedonia, and Tajikistan.
3. Also encompassed within the refugee definition in Article 1A (1) were those persons considered refugees under the arrangements of 12 May 1926 and 30 June 1928 or under the conventions of 28 October 1933 and 10 February 1938, the Protocol of 14 September 1939, or the Constitution of the Inter-

national Refugee Organization. Article 1B gives parties the option to limit their commitment to people displaced by events occurring in Europe.

4. Article 1 (A) (2) of the Refugee Convention defines a refugee as a person who, owing to a well-founded fear of being persecuted for reasons of race, religion, nationality, membership in a particular social group, or political opinion, is outside the country of his or her nationality and is unable or, owing to such fear, is unwilling to avail him- or herself of the protection of that country, or who, not having a nationality and being outside the country of his or her former habitual residence is unable or, owing to such fear, unwilling to return to it.

5. By 1967 the United Nations General Assembly had on several occasions authorized the UNHCR to extend protection to people who did not meet the Refugee Convention definition but had fled from dire man-made situations. See G.A. Res. 1388, U.N. GAOR, 14th sess., supp. no. 16, at 20 U.N. Doc. A/4354 (1959) (Chinese entering Hong Kong); G.A. Res. 1673, U.N. GAOR, 16th sess., supp. no. 17, at 28, U.N. Doc. A/5100 (1961) (civilians fleeing African countries engaged in independence struggles); G.A. Res. 2039, U.N. GAOR, 20th sess., supp. no. 14, at 41, U.N. Doc. A/6014 (1965) (blurring distinction between refugees strictly within UNHCR's mandate and those outside it).

6. The OAU Convention adopts a dual approach. In Article I.1, it restates the Refugee Convention definition, without geographic or temporal limitations. Article I.2 defines additional classes of refugees, including "every person who, owing to external aggression, occupation, foreign domination or events seriously disturbing public order in either part or the whole of his country of origin or nationality, is compelled to leave his place of habitual residence in order to seek refuge."

7. Article 33 (1) provides that "No Contracting State shall expel or return (*'refouler'*) a refugee in any manner whatsoever to the frontiers of territories where his life or freedom would be threatened on account of race, religion, nationality, membership of a particular social group or political opinion."

8. Article 33 (2) permits states to deny protection to a refugee "whom there are reasonable grounds for regarding as a danger to the security of the country in which he is, or who, having been convicted by a final judgment of a particularly serious crime, constitutes a danger to the community of that country."

9. The OAU Convention and the 1984 Cartagena Declaration are the most often cited instruments adopting this approach.

10. For example, *I.N.S. v. Elias-Zacarias*, 502 U.S. 478 (1992).

11. For example, the Convention on the Rights of the Child addresses the situation of child refugees in its Article 22 but simply guarantees their rights under "other international human rights or humanitarian instruments," presumably including the Refugee Convention.

12. The EU Justice and Home Affairs Council adopted in principle a set of guidelines addressing both of these issues on 10 March 1995 (see "EC Commentaries" 1995). The reaction of the UNHCR was negative, with its legal experts expressing fears that minimum guarantees could be perceived as maximum guarantees (see "EU: UNHCR" 1995).

13. Article 14 (1) of the UDHR provides that "Everyone has the right to seek and to enjoy in other countries asylum from persecution."
14. For example, 72.8 percent of Swiss voters recently approved a referendum granting "sweeping new powers of search, arrest and detention in dealing with asylum seekers and foreigners who enter the country illegally ... The Government says people request asylum knowing they have no chance of getting it, but use the time while their cases are being processed to earn money by dealing in drugs" (*New York Times* 1994, A5).
15. *Seattle Times* 1994, A18.

References

Aleinikoff, T. Alexander. 1994. "Safe Haven: Pragmatics and Prospects." *Virginia Journal of International Law* 35 (1994): 71–79.

———. 1991. "The Refugee Convention at Forty: Reflections on the IJRL Colloquium." *International Journal of Refugee Law* 3: 617–25.

Arboleda, Eduardo, and Ian Hoy. 1993. "The Convention Refugee Definition in the West: Disharmony of Interpretation and Application." *International Journal of Refugee Law* 5: 66–90.

Bhabha, Jacqueline. 1994. "European Harmonisation of Asylum Policy: A Flawed Process." *Virginia Journal of International Law* 35: 101–14.

Collinson, Sarah. 1993. *Beyond Borders: West European Migration Policy Towards the Twenty-first Century.* London: Royal Institute of International Affairs.

"EC Commentaries." 1995. *Social Affairs,* 18 May, LEXIS, EURCOM Library, ECNEWS File.

"EU: Definition of Refugees Adopted by Justice Council a First Step—Gradin." 1995. *Reuter Textline, Agence Europe,* 28 Nov., LEXIS, Intlaw Library, ECNews File.

"EU: UNHCR, ECRE and Amnesty Concerned by EU Minimum Guarantees for Asylum Procedures." 1995. *Reuter Textline, Agence Europe,* 5 Apr., LEXIS, EURCOM Library, ECNEWS File.

Executive Committee of the High Commissioner's Programme. 1981. "Addendum to the Report of the United Nations High Commissioner for Refugees." U.N. GAOR Supp. No. 12A, at 18, U.N. Doc. A/36/12/Add.1.

_____. 1994. "Report of the Forty-Fifth Session of the Executive Committee of the High Commissioner's Programme." U.N. Doc. A/AC.96/839.

Goldberg, Pamela. 1994. "Asylum Law and Gender-Based Persecution Claims." *Immigration Briefings* 94-9 (Sept.): 1–26.

Goodwin-Gill, Guy. 1988. "Nonrefoulement and the New Asylum Seekers." In *The New Asylum Seekers: Refugee Law in the 1980s*, ed. D. Martin, 103–21. Dordrecht: Nijhoff.

_____. 1983. *The Refugee in International Law*. Oxford: Clarendon.

Grahl-Madsen, Atle. 1980. *Territorial Asylum*. Stockholm: Almqvist and Wiksell International.

Hathaway, James. 1991a. *The Law of Refugee Status*. Toronto: Butterworths,

_____. 1991b. "Reconceiving Refugee Law as Human Rights Protection." *Journal of Refugee Studies* 4: 113–31.

Helton, Arthur C. 1995. "The Role of International Law in the Twenty-First Century: Forced International Migration: A Need for New Approaches by the International Community." *Fordham International Law Journal* 18: 1623–36.

Holborn, Louise. 1975. *Refugees: A Problem of Our Time*. Metuchen, N.J.: Scarecrow.

Joly, Danièle, Clive Nettleton, and Hugh Poulton. 1992. *Refugees: Asylum in Europe?* London: Minority Rights Publications.

Kjaerum, Morten. 1994. "Temporary Protection in Europe in the 1990s." *International Journal of Refugee Law* 6: 444—56.

Loescher, Gil. 1993. *Beyond Charity: International Cooperation and the Global Refugee Crisis*. New York: Oxford University Press.

New York Times. 1994. 5 Dec., A5.

Refugee Policy Group. 1994. *Humanitarian Action in the Former Yugoslavia: The U.N.'s Role 1991–1993*. Washington, D.C.: Refugee Policy Group.

"Relief Agency Pulls Out of Rwandan Camp in Protest." 1994. *Seattle Times*, 20 Dec., A18.

United Nations High Commissioner for Refugees. 1995. *The State of the World's Refugees: In Search of Solutions*. New York: Oxford University Press.

_____. 1994. Humanitarian Issues Working Group of the International Conference on the Former Yugoslavia. "Survey on the Implementation of Temporary Protection." 23 June. Mimeograph.

_____. 1993. "Report of the United Nations High Commissioner for Refugees." 48 U.N. GAOR Supp. (No. 12A), U.N. Doc. A/48/12/Add.1.

U.S. Safe Haven Camps in Cuba and Panama. 1994. "A Study in Contrasts." *Refugee Reports*, 27 Oct., 14–19.

Treaties and Declarations

"Convention Against Torture and Other Cruel, Inhuman and
Degrading Treatment or Punishment." Adopted 10 Dec. 1984,
entered into force 26 June 1987. U.N. Doc. A/39/51 (1984).

"Convention Applying the Schengen Agreement of 14 June 1985
between the Benelux Economic Union, FRG and France on the
Gradual Abolition of Checks at Their Common Borders." Done at
Schengen 19 June 1990. 30 I.L.M. 84 (1991).

"Convention Determining the State Responsible for Examining
Applications for Asylum Lodged in One of the Member States of
the European Communities." Done at Dublin 15 June 1990. 30
I.L.M. 425 (1991).

"Convention on the Rights of the Child." Adopted 20 Nov. 1989,
entered into force 2 Sept. 1990. U.N.T.S. 1992/3, 28 I.L.M. 1448
(1989).

"Convention Relating to the Status of Refugees." Done at Geneva, 28
July 1951, entered into force 22 Apr. 1954. 189 U.N.T.S. 137.

"Declaration on Territorial Asylum." G.A. Res. 2312 (XXII), U.N. Doc.
A/RES/2312 (XXII) (1967).

"International Covenant on Civil and Political Rights." Adopted 16
Dec. 1966, entered into force 23 Mar. 1976. G.A. Res. 2200 A (XXI)
(1966).

"Organization of African Unity Convention Governing the Specific
Aspects of Refugee Problems in Africa." Done 10 Sept. 1969. 1001
U.N.T.S. 45.

"Protocol Relating to the Status of Refugees." Done 31 Jan. 1967,
entered into force 4 Oct. 1967. 606 U.N.T.S. 267, 19 U.S.T. 6223,
T.I.A.S. 6577.

"United Nations Convention Against Illicit Traffic in Narcotic Drugs
and Psychotropic Substances." Opened for signature 20 Dec. 1988,
entered into force 11 Nov. 1990. U.N. Doc. E/CONF.82/15 (1988).

"Universal Declaration of Human Rights." G.A. Res. 217A (III), U.N.
Doc. A/810, at 71 (1948).

Chapter 7

Refugee Definition

Rainer Hofmann

Introduction

A key issue in the discussion of refugee law during the last decades concerns the refugee definition as laid down in Article 1 A of the 1951 Refugee Convention: Does it adequately serve the needs of people forced to leave their home countries to escape from persecution? Or should it be modified to match better the profoundly changed patterns of forced transboundary movements of refugees? At the outset, it is interesting to note that the only normative change in the definition—namely, the removal of the temporal and geographic limitations contained in Article 1 A (2) and B of the 1951 Refugee Convention by virtue of Article 1 of the 1967 Protocol Relating to the Status of Refugees—concurred with the drafting of the Organization of African Unity Convention Governing the Specific Aspects of Refugee Problems in Africa that was eventually adopted in 1969. That convention clearly reflects the new dimensions of the refugee issue, in particular in its expansion of the refugee definition beyond the scope of the universally applicable one of 1951/1967. A similar approach resulted in the similarly enlarged refugee definition of the 1984 Cartagena Declaration.

Notes for this chapter begin on page 252.

Since the early 1970s, considerable efforts have been made to convince states outside Africa and Latin America to apply similarly expanded definitions. Although it must be emphasized that—at least during certain periods of time—some states admitted people not covered by the 1951/1967 refugee definition, such action was based either on strictly humanitarian grounds, without recognition of any pertinent legal obligation, or on specific legal provisions (Goodwin-Gill 1986, 901 ff.; Hailbronner 1986, 886 ff.; Hofmann 1987, 2053 ff.). More recently, however, the ever-increasing numbers of people seeking refuge from situations characterized by (civil) war and/or massive violations of human rights or looking for better living conditions have prompted many industrialized states to resort to legal and political actions with a view to stemming the flood. Such actions may be either preventive or repressive: In the former category belong, e.g., the recent—if still inconsistent—practice of the UN Security Council to deem situations likely to result in large-scale transboundary movements of refugees as threats to peace, thus justifying actions under Chapter VII of the UN Charter; the increasing emphasis placed on international cooperation in order to prevent states from conducting refugee-generating policies; and the renaissance of the concept of making financial and other assistance to a state dependent on that state's human rights record. Among the repressive actions can be mentioned the increased efforts to implement international programs of durable solutions such as resettlement in the region of the refugees' countries of origin; voluntary repatriation; and, in particular, the far-reaching changes in national asylum laws and practice. The latter, which encompass, inter alia, the introduction of concepts such as safe countries of origin and safe countries of first asylum, are of considerable relevance for this paper although they do not directly relate to the refugee definition as such. Notwithstanding the recent decrease in the numbers of asylum applications, apparently resulting from such actions, the effects of the wars in the former Yugoslavia revealed, in the European context, the merely limited possibilities of such measures: although the national asylum laws of practically all European states exclude people from the former Yugoslavia (irrespective of whether they originate from any of the war-stricken areas or have left their countries of origin in order to escape from being drafted into the armed forces of their respective countries of origin) from being admitted as refugees in a strictly legal sense, most European states—admittedly, to quite a varying degree—tolerate the presence of such persons on "strictly humanitarian grounds," if only on a temporary or provisional basis. From a legal point of view, this policy, which is at least partly due to the so-far-quite-effective pressure of public opinion, might be characterized as an implementation of the concept of temporary refuge (or protection) (Kjaerum 1994, 444 ff.), which in recent years has become one of the more promising topics in the universal refugee law discussion (Coles 1978/79, 189 ff.). Clearly, there is an urgent need to continue the debate over the fate of the refugee definition.

Refugee Definitions in International Treaty Law

The Refugee Definition of the 1951/1967 Convention System

The refugee definition of Article 1 A of the 1951 Refugee Convention as modified by Article 1 of the 1967 Protocol still constitutes the most important legal basis for international and national refugee law. More than two-thirds of the world's states are parties to these treaties, and it could be argued that the remaining states are also legally bound to respect the refugee definition as constituting customary international law. In addition, this definition forms, either explicitly or implicitly, part of (almost all) national asylum laws that have either incorporated the convention system into the national legal order or based their relevant legislation on it.

At this stage, it is not necessary to embark on a detailed presentation of the contents of the 1951/1967 refugee definition (Grahl-Madsen 1966, 142 ff.; Goodwin-Gill 1983, 24 ff.; Hathaway 1991, passim). It is sufficient to mention here that the definition limits refugees to those with a well-founded fear of persecution on one of five specific grounds ("race, religion, nationality, membership of a particular social group or political opinion"). Various well-known problems of interpretation arise from the definition, such as, e.g., the question of whether the "well-foundedness" of an individual's fear of persecution is to be determined on the basis of objective and/or subjective criteria (Hathaway 1991, 65 ff.), to what extent persecution directed against some members of a group justifies other members' fears of being persecuted themselves (Hathaway 1991, 99 ff.), and how these grounds for persecution are to be interpreted (Hathaway 1991, 135 ff.).

Since the 1951 Convention does not provide for an international institution empowered to interpret, with binding force on all states party to the convention, the contents of the definition, the task is left to the national authorities; this fact inevitably results in differing national practices notwithstanding the considerable efforts by UNHCR bodies to formulate guidelines to ensure uniform application and the increasing importance of comparative research in this field. But the most important problem connected with the refugee definition is structural: although the convention was primarily drafted with a view to protecting future victims of generalized persecution of the type that had occurred in Nazi-dominated Europe and although during most of the cold war era Western states applied it with considerable generosity with regard to people originating from socialist countries, the refugee definition of the 1951/1967 Convention has always—or at least very often—been seen as based on the concept of individualized persecution and thus excluding the notion of group persecution. Even more important, however, is the fact that the concept of individualized persecution necessarily fails to address the new patterns of forced migration that since the early 1960s have become the predominant feature of involuntary transboundary movements of people. Whatever their cause— struggle against colonialism, foreign domination, civil strife and civil war, general breakdown of public order, gross and systematic violations of fundamental human rights—people so compelled to leave their home countries could (and can) not be recognized as refugees as long as this concept of individualized persecution prevails.

Refugee Definitions in Regional Law

The limitations of the current refugee definition have resulted in efforts to expand it. Because, at least in the 1960s, most mass exoduses of refugees occurred in Africa where the newly independent states were simply not in a position to establish the administrative structures necessary to conduct individualized recognition procedures, African leaders soon understood the need to expand the traditional definition. Thus the 1969 OAU Convention, while incorporating the 1951/1967 Convention definition in its Article 1 (1), added—in Article 1 (2)—a new category of refugees, namely, victims of external aggression, occupation, foreign domination, or events seriously disturbing public order in (and this is quite important) either part or the whole of the country of origin (Oloka-Onyango 1991, 453 ff.; Hofmann 1992, 318 ff.).

Although the civil wars fought in Central America since the early 1970s resulted in phenomena similar to those in Africa, it was almost a decade before ten Latin American states adopted the 1984 Cartagena Declaration which in 1985 was approved by the OAS General Assembly (Cuéllar 1991, 482 ff.). The declaration includes a refugee definition resembling that contained in the 1969 OAU Convention: in addition to convention refugees, protection was extended to "persons who have fled their country because their lives, safety or freedom have been threatened by generalized violence, foreign aggression, internal conflicts, massive violations of human rights or other circumstances which have seriously disturbed public order."[1] This definition shares most of the innovative concepts of the OAU Convention. A major difference seems to be that the Cartagena definition does not contain the formula "in either part or the whole of the country of origin," which might be interpreted as excluding individuals who might find refuge in another region of their home countries (the so-called concept of alternative refuge considered to be inherent to the 1951 Convention system). Moreover, by referring to "the lives, safety, or freedom" of the people concerned who "have been threatened," the declaration requires an objectively demonstrable risk of such harm, whereas the 1969 OAU Convention seems to emphasize the refugee's subjective perception. All other textual differences do not seem to entail any practical differences (Hathaway 1991, 20).

A final point to be mentioned concerns the legal status of the Cartagena Declaration: Unlike the 1969 OAU Convention, it does not have the standing of binding treaty law; nevertheless, it seems justified to state that it reflects regional customary international law. Thus in two of the most refugee-stricken regions of the world, the universally applicable refugee law as enshrined in the 1951/1967 Convention is supplemented by far-ther-reaching regional law specifically drafted to cope ade-quately with existing refugee situations.

The Absence of Regional Refugee Law in Asia, Europe, and Oceania

The absence of any regional refugee law in Asia (Muntarbhorn 1992, passim), the third continent characterized by large-scale transboundary movements of people who do not qualify as con-vention refugees, might be explained by the lack of any regional organization capable of drafting the necessary legal instrument, a phenomenon also to be found in the area of general human rights protection.

As regards Europe and Oceania, there seem to be several reasons for the absence of regionally applicable instruments. Although the Council of Europe provides the necessary forum for elaborating such a document, there was—and still is—a lack of sufficient political will to embark on the endeavor. One reason might be that, until very recently, Europe did not experience refugee situations—with the possible exception of those involv-ing persons of Turkish citizenship—that necessitated expanding the 1951/1967 refugee definition in order to assist and protect persons originating from European countries, and notwith-standing the wars in the former Yugoslavia and the prospects of further deterioration of the situation in Russia and other suc-cessor states of the former Soviet Union, it remains most doubt-ful whether these factors will result in a change in the existing political climate. Another reason might be that European states have been unwilling to accept an expanded refugee definition for fear of attracting even larger numbers of asylum seekers from non-European countries. When European countries have been at all prepared to accord some legal status to such people, they have preferred to do so on the basis of (more easily amendable) national legislation that to a large extent seems to reflect a (par-tial) implementation of policies influenced by the concept of temporary refuge. As regards Oceania (Hyndman 1991, 19 ff.), there exists neither the appropriate institutional framework to draft such a regional instrument nor does there seem to be suf-ficient practical need to do so: so far, this region has been spared both large-scale refugee-generating situations and, because of geographical reasons, massive refugee movements from outside the region.

Major Problems in Interpreting the 1951/1967 Definition

Vagueness

As noted in the preceding section, the refugee definition of the 1951/1967 Convention as such has gained quasi-universal applicability, as a norm of both international (treaty or customary) law and national asylum law. Even so, there is a widespread and sharply increasing dissatisfaction with this definition, in particular, over whether it provides sufficiently clear and unambiguous criteria to guarantee its uniform application and interpretation (Arboleda and Hoy 1993, 66 ff.), a normative quality that is—rightly—considered to be essential to any legal norm of universal applicability.

It must be stressed, however, that this vagueness is by no means a phenomenon to be found only in international refugee law. The same observation (or criticism) applies to many (if not most) areas of international law; consider, for example, the enormous possibilities for debate over the correct interpretation of international human rights norms. Moreover, vagueness is also a very common feature of vast areas of national legislation. This has to do with the very purpose of law making, which is not intended to provide detailed regulations covering every foreseeable (and possibly also unforeseeable) situations but rather to furnish general rules, a normative framework within which legally correct decisions may be taken. Legal norms must be worded in such a way as to allow flexibility in their interpretation and application in order to enable decision makers to take into account the (dynamic) developments of social structures and the particularities of every case at hand. On the other hand, one of the most important (if not the most essential) aspects of the *Rechtsstaatsprinzip* (the rule of law) as a very fundamental principle of modern (at least Western) societies is the predictability—and thus nonarbitrariness—of administrative and judicial decisions.

On the domestic level, such foreseeability is guaranteed by the existence of institutions vested with the power to determine, with binding force *erga omnes,* the correct interpretation of a given norm: the courts and other judicial bodies. This leads to one of the most obvious and unfortunate drawbacks of the present international legal order: namely, the absence of judicial institutions vested with such powers. Because no institution is authorized to hand down binding decisions as to the exact interpretation of the various components of the 1951/1967 refugee definition and there is, moreover, very little hope that states will be willing to change this situation in the foreseeable future, international refugee law will have to cope with the fact that national authorities interpret and apply the definition in differing ways.

In reality, however, it seems that the pertinent practices of those states that have to deal with the largest numbers of refugees (or forced migrants, to put it in other terms) do not show such a large degree of variety, and, considering the basically similar fundamental structures of such states, this observation is by no means surprising. In other words, notwithstanding the vagueness of the international norm—i.e., the 1951/1967 refugee definition—national authorities generally apply and interpret it in a rather uniform way. This does not mean, however, that there is no need for an international body authorized to render legally binding decisions on such application and interpretation. If our aim is still to establish a world order truly based on the rule of law, the existence of such an institution is a conditio sine qua non given that there is no guarantee whatsoever that the present quasi-uniform practice of the national authorities will last forever.

In sum, the very fundamental critique with regard to the so-called vagueness of the 1951/1967 refugee definition (which, by the way, also applies to all other existing international refugee definitions) is profoundly unjustified; on the contrary, its flexibility (to put it in a positive way) is necessary in that only such flexibility allows for its adaptability to changing situations and can ensure just decisions in every given case *(Einzelfallgerechtigkeit).*

Given this, what accounts for the widespread dissatisfaction with the refugee definition? It seems to stem from an increasingly felt uneasiness among refugee lawyers that the spirit of generosity in which the definition ought to be applied according to the (perhaps only assumed) intentions of its drafters is decreasing, a development that is perceived as jeopardizing the capacity of the definition to provide sufficient protection to forced migrants in general and refugees in particular. Putting it more simply, it might be said that international refugee advocates criticize the national authorities that apply the refugee definition for violating not its letter but its spirit; this view seems to imply that if international institutions were authorized to render legally binding interpretations of the refugee definition, the development leading away from the original intent of its drafters would not be taking place. Such a conclusion does not seem to be very convincing, however, given the heterogeneity of the international community. As can be seen in the field of human rights, the establishment of international institutions— i.e., international courts—is accepted only among states sharing a common understanding of fundamental values. Thus what might and should be achieved is the establishment of regional bodies authorized to render legally binding decisions as to the application and interpretation of a regional refugee definition; this seems to be the only realistic approach.

Other Problems

From the inherent flexibility of the 1951/1967 refugee definition flow several other interpretation problems.

First, there is the question of whether the condition of being persecuted is fulfilled not only in cases of individualized persecution but also when persecution is directed against a distinct national, political, religious, or social group as a whole. Whereas relevant practice in the early 1980s seemed to indicate that states were increasingly prepared to recognize as refugees members of persecuted groups, this trend seems to have shifted in recent years toward a growing reluctance to admit people as refugees merely on the basis of their membership in such a group (Hofmann 1987, 2051).

Second, there is the fundamental question relating to the conditions under which a fear of persecution is considered to be well founded. Obviously, people who have suffered from individual persecution will as a rule be recognized as refugees. The real problem, however, concerns people alleging that they will be persecuted on their eventual return to their home countries. Again, comparative research of relevant state practice seems to indicate a strongly evolving tendency to recognize such people as refugees in cases where there is clear evidence or objective credibility/ probability that persecution will take place in the immediate future. In these circumstances, the evaluation of the relevant facts is usually based on the allegations put forward by the applicants themselves and a corroborating analysis by the diplomatic missions and/or information provided by international bodies such as UNHCR and nongovernmental organizations such as Amnesty International. It seems therefore justified to state that establishing whether an individual's fear of being persecuted is well founded comprises both subjective and objective elements (Hofmann 1987, 2051; Hathaway 1991, 65 ff.). Whether the increasing tendency to attach more importance to the objective element is compatible with the notion of well-founded fear, remains an open question. Obviously, fear is a most subjective state, yet by the refugee definition, it must pass the objectivity test inherent in the notion of well-foundedness.

The third problematic issue concerns whether persecution committed by private individuals or groups is to be considered as persecution in the sense of the 1951/1967 refugee definition. It seems that, although government persecution still constitutes the focus of refugee protection, private persecution may be attributed to the government if it actually endorses such persecution or is unwilling to stop the persecution and/or protect the victims (Hofmann 1987, 2051; Hathaway 1991, 124 ff.).

Much more complex, however, is the correct legal answer in circumstances where the government is unable to prevent persecution; such scenarios are common features of situations ranging from a general breakdown of public order in part of a state's territory to cases of civil war. In this context, it must first be stressed that the traditional view, shared by most competent national administrative and judicial bodies, that persons escaping from such situations—often referred to as de facto refugees—do not qualify under the 1951/1967 refugee definition still seems to prevail. This applies in particular to situations characterized by a general breakdown of public order or involving persecution by forces whose activities cannot be controlled effectively by governmental forces notwithstanding their efforts to do so.

As regards civil war, however, it should be stressed that some national asylum law systems show a somewhat modified approach, still with regard to government persecution. The jurisprudence of the German Federal Constitutional Court,[2] for example, endeavors to draw a line between measures of state organs that may be considered normal in such situations and so do not require recognition as refugees of the persons concerned and those that are characterized by an intent to exterminate a group of the state's population or destroy its ethnic, cultural, or religious identity, which, as a rule, do result in such recognition.

This jurisprudence is closely connected, however, with the issue of alternative refuge within the country of origin. Under this concept, which is applied in almost all national legal systems and is—rightly—considered as being compatible with the 1951/1967 Convention, persons are not recognized as refugees if there is a clear probability that a change of residence within the country of origin would offer full protection from persecution, in particular that pursued by private individuals not subject to government control.

In practical terms, the legal response may be summarized as follows: People originating from a specific region of a state in which that state is unable to protect them from persecution committed by individuals not subject to governmental control despite bona fide efforts to prevent such acts will be denied recognition as refugees, unless it can be shown that they cannot find alternative refuge in another region of that state. Likewise, people fleeing from civil war who are victims of governmental measures characterized by an intent to exterminate the group to which they belong or destroy that group's ethnic, cultural, or religious identity will be denied recognition as refugees unless it can be shown that they cannot find alternative refuge in another region of that state. Finally, persons originating from a country suffering from a total collapse of public order or fleeing from a civil war in which they are victims of persecutory measures by nongovernmental forces will, as a rule, be denied recognition as refugees. It should be mentioned, though, that such people will generally be permitted to enter and remain—for a limited period of time—in the territory of the prospective country of asylum under specific legal provisions or administrative practices; however, it must be emphasized that their legal status differs most considerably from that accorded to recognized refugees and is to a large extent similar to that of persons who are not recognized as refugees but may not be deported by virtue of Article 3 of the 1950 European Convention on Human Rights or similar provisions.

The fourth problem to be mentioned concerns the notion of *refugiés sur place* (Hathaway 1991, 33 ff.). Under this concept, people may be recognized as refugees even though there does not exist a causal link between persecution and flight. The principle covers cases in which people have a well-founded fear of persecution if returned to their country of origin, stemming either from a fundamental political change in that country while they were abroad or from political activities directed against the government of that state that they began while abroad. The second scenario raises the rather controversial issue of whether the 1951/1967 system need only admit as refugees those persons whose political activities clearly constitute a continuation of a political conviction that had already found its expression in previous activities in the country of origin. This would imply that all those who were not politically active in their home countries before moving to their present country of residence, would be excluded from being recognized as refugees, except in the context of a change of government. Yet such an interpretation of the 1951/1967 refugee definition is clearly incompatible with its wording, according to which the decisive factor is the concurrent existence of a well-founded fear of persecution and a stay outside the country of origin. To put it in even stricter terms: the 1951/1967 definition does not presuppose a causal link between previous persecution and subsequent flight.

It would be intolerably naive, however, not to admit that there are numerous cases where people who are not permitted to remain on the territory of a given state by virtue of that state's general aliens law engage in political activities with the sole purpose of establishing reasons for obtaining asylum. Provided that such an intention can be proved beyond any reasonable doubt, it does not constitute a violation of the 1951/1967 refugee definition to reject these people's claims to recognition as refugees. Obviously, this solution implies putting a heavy burden on the competent national authorities; it seems, however, that it is inevitable in order to respect the 1951/1967 Convention.

The fifth issue to be mentioned in this context relates to whether people may be excluded from recognition as refugees if they have previously obtained effective protection in another country (Hathaway 1991, 46 ff.). Already in the mid-1980s comparative research showed that most countries followed the en route principle, according to which refugee recognition could be denied in such situations, possibly with the additional prerequisite that the country of first asylum was a party to the 1951/1967 Convention and provided that the refugee's stay in that country had not been of only a very short duration and that the principle of nonrefoulement was scrupulously observed by that country (Hofmann 1987, 2052). The understanding underlying this approach—namely, that people who seek recognition as refugees do not have the right to choose their preferred country of asylum—has become part of almost all European national asylum laws and practices. As a rule, this approach appears to be fully compatible with the 1951/1967 refugee definition; only under exceptional circumstances, e.g., in cases where the denial of admission would result in a family being separated, might states be under a human rights obligation to refrain from applying this principle.

Finally, it should be mentioned that the criteria in the 1969 OAU Convention and the 1984 Cartagena Declaration that expand the 1951/1967 refugee definition apparently entailed neither thorough scholarly discussion or considerable practical problems. This, however, is due less to their wording than to the fact that those countries where such expanded refugee definitions apply either are not in positions to conduct proper recognition proceedings but instead usually rely on statements by UNHCR that such persons are "of concern" to UNHCR, which, with other international organizations, seeks to secure the survival of such persons by extending assistance and offering protection, or are, for whatever reasons, not faced with large numbers of forced migrants who do not qualify as convention refugees.

New Developments Relevant to the Refugee Definition

Safe Countries of Origin and of First Asylum

Two concepts that have emerged recently in many national asylum law systems have been criticized as breaches of the 1951/1967

Convention: the concept of safe countries of origin and the concept of safe countries of first asylum. Although neither concept is directly related with the refugee definition as such, it makes sense to examine each briefly here.

The concept of safe countries of origin (Hailbronner 1993, 31 ff.; Zimmermann 1993, 60 ff.), introduced into national asylum legislation first in Belgium and Switzerland and then Germany, seems to have become an almost common feature of current European asylum laws. It is characterized by the possibility, to be exercised either by an executive body such as the minister competent in asylum matters or the government as such or by the legislative organs, to determine those countries that are considered "safe" for the purposes, meaning that, in view of the general situation in those countries, well-founded fear of persecution does not exist.

One has to distinguish here between, on the one hand, lists that automatically preclude from admission as a refugee anyone arriving from such countries and, on the other hand, lists that only imply a rebuttable presumption of freedom from persecution in these countries. Several studies have demonstrated convincingly that the latter alternative is consistent with the 1951/1967 Convention whereas the first is equivalent to a territorial reservation, which is prohibited under the system. It is therefore most encouraging that the national systems into which this concept has been introduced all chose the second alternative.

The concept of safe countries of first asylum (Zimmermann 1993, 73 ff.), which could be considered a variation of the en route principle discussed above, means that countries of second subsequent asylum are entitled to return (forcibly) people who have entered from states in which they do not fear persecution irrespective of whether they can in fact claim to be refugees under the 1951/1967 refugee definition. In other words: people who claim to be refugees have to apply for recognition as refugees in the first "safe" country they actually reach. This concept is thus of a basically procedural nature in that it excludes such people from the right otherwise existing under national law to have their applications for asylum determined by the competent authorities of the country in which they apply. In contrast to the en route principle, the concept of safe countries of asylum is applied even when the stay in the country of so-called first asylum has been very short. As has been shown convincingly, this concept is compatible with the 1951/1967 Convention provided that the country of first asylum is a party to the convention; moreover, it must be established that the country to which the refugee will be returned is indeed safe and that the person will not be returned by this state to another state in which he or she will be persecuted. In particular, care must be taken to ensure that there is no risk of the person becoming a "refugee in orbit." In Europe the practical implementation of this concept is based on the obligation of readmittance contained in both Article 10 of the Dublin Convention and Article 31 of the second Schengen agreement and numerous bilateral refoulement agreements.

Changes in the Refugee Definition

Among the most important recent developments directly related to the interpretation of the 1951/1967 refugee definition is states' apparently ever-increasing willingness to consider severe forms of discrimination, in particular as a result of criminal law sanctions, against people on the grounds of sexual orientation as giving rise to a well-founded fear of persecution. Even more important, however, is the fact that a great many states seem prepared to consider acts of sexual violence, committed in particular against women and children, as grounds for persecution under the 1951/1967 refugee definition (Castel 1992, 39).[3] It must be emphasized, however, that this does not seem to mean that all acts of sexual violence are to be considered persecution; instead, only those committed because of the victims' membership in one of the groups mentioned in the 1951/1967 refugee definition are to be considered as "persecutory acts."

Another relevant issue to be addressed in this context concerns whether gender-related persecution is to be (or may be) considered a sufficient reason for according refugee status. At the outset, it should be mentioned that—at least so far—this issue (or, really, cluster of issues) seems to have assumed far greater prominence in Canada and the United States than in Europe. In fact, the competent authorities of both Canada (Immigration and Refugee Board 1993) and—most recently—the United States (U.S. Department of Justice 1995) have developed guidelines for the evaluation of gender-related persecution claims. It should be added, moreover, that the U.S. guidelines were preceded by a decision by the U.S. Board of Immigration Appeals finding that the gang rape of a Haitian woman by military attachés was a form of grievous harm that amounted to persecution; this decision was designed as a binding precedent. Although, for obvious reasons, it is still too early to comment on the possible impact of these guidelines on U.S. asylum practice,[4] their establishment raises the following general considerations.

The guidelines recognize that women may experience discrimination unique to their gender and that this can meet the standards of refugee status; they include "sexual abuse, rape, infanticide, genital mutilation, forced marriage, slavery, domestic violence, and forced abortion" as forms of gender discrimination (U.S. Department of Justice 1995, 9); they state that "severe sexual abuse" can be as much a form of persecution as the "beatings, torture, or other forms of physical violence" commonly recognized as grounds for granting asylum (9); they recognize that women who are beaten or tortured for refusing to renounce beliefs about the equal rights of women may be considered for asylum; and they encourage the use of female asylum officers and female interpreters to interview women with gender-based claims and urge that such women not be interviewed in front of male family members or children. Without going into details, it may be stated that these guidelines are moderate and sensible, avoiding extremes, and should, in general, satisfy the pertinent proposals of various pressure groups (Kelly 1993, 642 ff.) such as Cambridge and Somerville Legal Services and the Women Refugees Project of Harvard Law School's Immigration and Refugee Clinic, which, in fact, the U.S. Immigration and Naturalization Service credited as having been "instrumental in the development" of these guidelines. If applied as generously as is apparently envisaged, these guidelines should indeed constitute a sufficient legal basis for adequately dealing with the specific needs of female asylum seekers.

Doubts remain as to whether and to what extent similar adjustments will take place in international refugee law and other national legal systems, particularly Europe's. Moreover, although sexual abuse, in particular rape, as a deliberate means of persecuting women who are either politically active themselves or related to male activists or suffering such abuses because of their membership in a racially, ethnically, or socially defined group is increasingly recognized, on both the international and national levels, as sufficient grounds for recognition as refugees in the legal sense, this does not (yet) seem to apply to all the forms of gender-related persecution itemized in the guidelines quoted above, in particular the one concerning women refusing to renounce beliefs about the equal rights of women. Notwithstanding the fact that practically all governments orally support, in the relevant international fora, the struggle for the equal rights of women, there remains, in my opinion, a question as to whether such statements are more than mere lip service being paid to a political and legal movement considered to be presently en vogue. In this context, it must also be mentioned that current international developments seem to indicate quite far-reaching differences as to the precise substantive contents of such rights as well as the extent to which such rights may be subject to qualifications under domestic law. The formula used in this regard in the U.S. guidelines—namely, the recognition that "women who are beaten or tortured for refusing to renounce beliefs about the equal rights of women may be considered for asylum"—seems to reflect, to some extent, this situation. In my view, it constitutes a well-balanced compromise that could and should be adopted by other states given that being beaten or tortured for one's political beliefs clearly constitutes persecution even under a more traditional understanding of the refugee definition, provided that such action is attributable to the government.

This leads to the difficult issue of defining the circumstances in which acts of gender-related persecutory acts are in fact attributable to the government. It has been suggested that such acts are clearly attributable to the government if they are committed by government officials as part of an official governmental policy; the same conclusion would apply to such acts committed by government officials outside the context of any such policy if the respective domestic legislation does not provide for criminal sanctions against such acts or the governmental authorities refuse to prosecute their perpetrators. The situation is even more complex when acts such as infanticide, genital mutilation, forced marriage, forced abortion, or domestic violence, in particular with regard to women refusing to renounce beliefs about the equal rights of women, are committed by private citizens (parents, husbands, other family members, etc.). Some suggest that such acts may only result in refugee status for the women concerned if they are—explicitly or implicitly— backed by an official governmental policy, or if national legislation in the relevant state does not provide for criminal sanctions for such acts, or if the governmental authorities do not prosecute the perpetrators of such acts.

In sum, the approach reflected in the above-mentioned guidelines has a considerable political advantage: it could easily be implemented, both on the universal level by virtue of, e.g., a corresponding resolution of the UNHCR Executive Committee and on various national levels by administrative guidelines or instructions, without any need for prior amendment of the relevant legal texts, which, for political reasons, might be difficult to achieve. Bearing in mind the ultimate aim of refugee law—namely, to accord effective protection to people in need thereof as victims of persecution attributable to the government—such a pragmatic approach seems preferable to attempts aiming at specific amendments of the relevant legal texts to include gender-related persecution as a basis for a woman's recognition as refugee.

Finally, the following observation should be made: From the perspective of those women who are victims of such treatments referred to in the above-mentioned guidelines, it is somewhat irrelevant whether they are accorded protection as refugees on the grounds of their political opinions or their membership in a particular social group (Fullerton 1993, 505 ff.). The important thing is that they are accorded such protection through recognition as refugees, which, in most of the cases addressed by the guidelines, is clearly possible by applying the traditional techniques of interpreting legal language. Thus, if one shares my opinion as to the politically motivated impossibility of achieving, at least for the time being and the imminent future, an express amendment of the relevant international and national legal texts specifically addressing the issue of gender-related persecution, the often-criticized vagueness of the refugee definition proves to have the rather welcome effect of being flexible enough to grant refugee status to women who are victims of gender-related forms of persecution.

Developments Aimed at Filling the Gaps in International Refugee Law

Probably the most important recent development with regard to the 1951/1967 refugee definition, however, is the fact that renewed attempts to address what are rightly perceived by many as gaps in the present international protection system for refugees have gained considerable momentum, as may be seen in the most recent *Note on International Protection* submitted by the High Commissioner to the Executive Committee on 7 September 1994 (UN Doc. A/AC.96/830).

The fundamental conceptual importance of this note stems from its emphasis on the need for protection as the key to identifying people as refugees and as persons of concern to UNHCR and the international community (7). Referring to the wording of the preamble to the 1951 Convention, it stresses that the overall objective of international protection is "to assure refugees the widest possible exercise of ... fundamental rights and freedoms." Thus international protection is premised on human rights principles (Coles 1992, 31 ff.; Hathaway 1992, 9 ff.) and to be provided by the international community as a whole because refugees do not enjoy the effective protection of their own governments; in other words, to some extent, international protection becomes a substitute for national protection.

In the context of this paper, particular attention must be focused on those parts of the note in where the High Commissioner deals, on the one hand, with identifying the gaps between the coverage of international instruments and the categories of people actually in need of international protection, and, on the other hand, with exploring ways and means to fill these gaps.

Leaving aside the problems connected with and arising from the geographical and temporal limitations of the applicability of the 1951 Convention, which could—and should—easily be solved by all states becoming parties to the 1967 Protocol, the fundamental problem of contemporary refugee law relates to those people who objectively need international protection but do not qualify as refugees under the 1951/1967 system or are denied recognition because of a narrow interpretation of the refugee definition. What should be underlined, however, is the doubtlessly correct conclusion that the lack of a complete correspondence between the categories of persons covered by the 1951 Convention and the 1967 Protocol and the broader class of persons in need of international protection is not simply a matter of a broad or narrow interpretation of the elements of the refugee definition, nor of the difficulty of applying the 1951 Convention in situations of large-scale influx. However liberally its terms are applied, some refugees fleeing the civil wars and other forms of armed conflict fall outside the letter of the Convention. Although many refugees from armed conflict do have reason to fear some form of persecution on ethnic, religious, social or political grounds at the hands of one or more of the parties to a conflict, others typically are fleeing the indiscriminate effects of armed conflict and the accompanying disorder, including the destruction of homes, harvests, food stocks and the means of subsistence, with no specific element of "persecution." (*Note on International Protection,* 15)

The note continues by describing the efforts to bridge this gap between the need for international protection and the inherent limitations of the 1951/1967 Convention; such efforts involved, in particular, a broadened UNHCR mandate combined with reliance on regional instruments such as the 1969 OAU Convention and the 1984 Cartagena Declaration, other international instruments, customary international law, and ad hoc arrangements relying on humanitarian policies (18 ff.). The discussion concludes by realistically stating that, although these efforts have in practice yielded considerable success (20), there remains the problem that, outside the reach of regional treaties or customary international law, such protection depends on governments' continuing goodwill. In this context, it is rightly observed that, despite the generosity shown by most countries, such goodwill is not necessarily permanent or stable and can be unduly swayed by the vagaries of public opinion; moreover, such generosity is often inconsistently applied because, as a result of political considerations, people fleeing from situations of disorder or civil war in one country may benefit from (temporary) asylum accorded ex gratia, while others fleeing from similar situations in another country may be denied such protection.

Ways need to be found to guarantee effective international protection for all those who require it, whether or not they are within the scope of the treaty obligations of individual governments. In this context, the note states quite realistically that "while regional legal instruments may appear to show the way, hopes of widening the scope of international instruments to cover refugees beyond those provided for in the 1951 Convention and the 1967 Protocol are confronted with the reluctance of many States to undertake internationally binding legal obligations towards refugees beyond those that they have already assumed" (21). Given this, the High Commissioner, while insisting on the preferability of establishing global or regional conventions for the protection of refugees in the broader sense, proposes a more pragmatic approach based on the experiences with the 1984 Cartagena Declaration, i.e., the drafting of a declaration of guiding principles for international protection on a global and/or regional level, complemented by regional (or global) harmonization processes recommending and leading to the adoption of parallel national legislation and coordinated ad hoc international responses to specific refugee situations. In this context, the key notion is the concept of temporary protection.

Keeping in mind the political and social realities currently existing in most of the countries of refuge that, in meeting the financial and other needs of people not covered by the 1951/1967 refugee definition, do not rely on international assistance, this approach appears to be the most—if not the only—realistic one. Whether one likes it or not, hoping that the legislative and executive organs of Western countries will incur further international legal obligations with respect to persons not qualifying as refugees under the 1951/1967 Convention is—and most probably will remain for some time to come—nothing but wishful thinking.

The Concept of Temporary Protection

The concept of temporary protection as identified in the UNHCR *Note on International Protection* is explicitly said to be based on experience gained in the context of providing assistance to the victims of the conflicts and systematic human rights abuses in the former Yugoslavia. From a legal point of view, it appears to constitute a further development of the concept of temporary refuge applied, under different denominations, in various countries since the mid-1970s to provide some kind of assistance and protection to people not eligible for refugee status under the definition in the 1951/1967 Convention. The major aspects of temporary protection include (1) "its use as a tool to meet protection needs in mass outflows"; (2) "the definition of beneficiaries on the basis of the need for international protection"; (3) "the description of the basic elements of protection"; (4) "the focus on return as the most appropriate solution"; and (5) "the provision of international protection as part of a comprehensive programme of concerted international action that includes prevention and solution" (22 ff.). Since it is conceived as an emergency measure of only short duration, temporary protection does not involve respect for basic human rights; rather, its beneficiaries will be offered a more limited range of rights than would customarily be accorded to refugees under the 1951/1967 Convention (22).

Temporary protection would be offered to all people who have fled from areas affected by conflict and violence, who had been or would be exposed to human rights abuses including ethnic cleansing, or who for other reasons specific to their personal situations are presumed to be in need of international protection. In practical terms, this definition encompasses all those covered by the expanded refugee definitions of the 1969 OAU Convention and the 1984 Cartagena Declaration, as well as all those who clearly qualify as refugees under the 1951/1967 Convention (23).

The basic elements of temporary protection include, in particular, admission to safety in the country of refuge; respect for basic human rights, with treatment in accordance with internationally recognized humanitarian standards; protection against refoulement; and repatriation when conditions in the country of origin allow (23). Given this description of its basic elements, temporary protection should not result in problems if voluntary repatriation can be implemented within a short period of time (23 ff.); experience shows, however, that this is often not the case.[5]

Assessing the Concept of Temporary Protection

For how long should the concept of temporary protection remain applicable, and what measures should be taken when it expires? In other words, what treatment is to be given and what legal status accorded to temporarily protected persons once it is clear that repatriation cannot be achieved at all or at least not in a foreseeable future? This question is closely linked with the inherent conflict created by two of the fundamental principles of refugee law: on the one hand, the law aims at the most efficient protection of refugees, which usually implies that measures have to be taken that will facilitate the integration of refugees into the societies of their respective countries of (temporary) residence; on the other hand, it is rightly emphasized that any refugee situation is per se unnatural and best solved by the voluntary return or repatriation of refugees to their respective countries of origin.

It is clear that all situations that force people to leave their countries of origin and result either in their qualification as refugees under the 1951/1967 Convention or in their being accorded temporary refuge are characterized by most serious violations of fundamental human rights. This again raises the question of whether and to what extent the international community, acting in particular through the Security Council, should take more frequent and more efficient action both to prevent such situations from developing and to restore circumstances conducive for the return of refugees. The recent, if still deplorably selective, practice of competent international organs, on both the universal and regional levels, of determining situations of massive flows of refugees as constituting a threat to international peace and security in a given region of the world may be seen as an interesting shift in the international community's general approach to addressing such situations.

Even if it is true—as spelled out in the UNHCR note—that the concept of temporary protection was developed in response to the forced expulsion of people from their homes in the former Yugoslavia, it must still be stressed that the experiences of the European countries that admitted such people under this concept will unlikely strengthen their readiness to do so more often in future. Suffice it to mention, in this context, the shocking lack of political will to implement effectively the provisions of the so-called Vance Agreement concerning the Croatian territories presently not controlled by the Croatian government. If that agreement's provisions, in particular those demanding the establishment of conditions necessary for the return of the non-Serbian populations of these areas and those aimed at preventing further acts of ethnic cleansing, had been implemented as envisaged, a very large number of people presently outside Croa-

tia benefiting from the concept of temporary protection could
have been expected to have returned to their homes. In other
words, how can the international community press governments
to admit people in need of temporary protection if it fails to show
that it is at least willing to adopt the measures necessary to
ensure that such temporary protection does not develop into a
durable solution?

In sum, it must be said that the concept of temporary protection as presented in the UNHCR *Note on Protection* in principle
offers a viable solution to the obvious protection needs of people
not qualifying as refugees under the 1951/1967 Convention outside of Africa and Latin America, in particular those fleeing in
large numbers from situations characterized by general and systematic human rights abuses and/or civil war. From a legal point
of view, however, this concept urgently needs clarification as to
the extent of the rights to be accorded and the standards of treatment to be applied to such temporarily protected persons. With a
view to convincing states to apply the concept—namely by making it the subject of a legally nonbinding declaration of guiding
principles as long as states do not seem prepared to accept additional legal obligations in the context of forced migration—what
is probably even more important is to strengthen the political will
to make—less selectively and much more efficiently—eventual
use of the possibilities offered by international law, in particular
by the UN Charter, to prevent refugee-generating situations and
implement programs of voluntary repatriation, both sponsored
and supervised by the competent international bodies.

Conclusion

Regarding the widespread critique of the 1951/1967 refugee definition as being too vague to allow sufficiently predictable decisions to be taken by the competent national authorities, it
should be reemphasized that this alleged vagueness must be
seen as necessary to the flexibility that is a conditio sine qua non
for just decisions taking into account the particularities of individual cases. This, however, does not mean that there is no need
for the establishment of an international body competent to
hand down legally binding decisions as to the interpretation and

application of the various elements of the 1951/1967 refugee definition. As can be seen from the relevant developments in the field of international human rights law, realistic prospects for the establishment of such an organ seem to exist—if at all—only in the context of regional arrangements of states sharing the same or very similar systems of basic values. In this respect, it remains to be seen whether the harmonization of European asylum procedures as effected by the Dublin and the Schengen II conventions and recent initiatives in the field of asylum law under Article K.1.1 of the Maastricht Treaty (Hailbronner 1992, 917 ff.) will eventually result in the creation of such an organ or at least in a far-reaching harmonization of national administrative practices, which seems indispensable.

As to the concept of temporary protection, it must be said that, if implemented by way of a legally nonbinding declaration formulating a set of guiding principles to be taken into account by national legislative and executive organs, it does seem to offer the most realistic possibility of providing, outside the reach of regional treaties or customary law, an international framework for more adequately addressing the protection needs of people not qualifying as refugees under the 1951/1967 definition. It seems vital, however, that governments be better assured that such protection, as a rule, will be temporary, which implies that the international community will implement programs of voluntary repatriation and, even more important, make much greater and, in particular, more efficient use of the mechanisms offered by present international law with a view to bringing about the conditions necessary for such voluntary repatriation. This, however, relates to the fundamental problem of international (refugee) law: on the one hand, the need to prevent situations characterized by massive human rights abuses, whatever their reasons, and, on the other hand, the duty to eliminate such situations. In both contexts, attention should focus on arguments pro and contra increased pertinent international actions, which might include, if only as a last resort, recourse to nonpeaceful actions subsequent to authorizing decisions taken by the Security Council. This conclusion seems inevitable given that the international community is faced with the necessity to find ways and means to solve a whole range of profoundly complex economic, ecological, and social problems; in such circumstances, it can no longer afford (to be forced) to expend an enormous amount of human, financial, and other resources on coping with severe problems predominantly arising from violations of the most basic human rights.

Notes

1. See Annual Report of the Inter-American Commission on Human Rights 1984–85, OEA/ser.1/II.66, Doc. 10, rev. 1, 190–93.
2. Judgment of 10 July 1989, *Entscheidungen des Bundesverfassungsgerichts* (Decisions of the Federal Constitutional Court) 80: 315 ff. On this, see, e.g., Hofmann 1996).
3. See, in particular, *Report of the Forty-fourth Session of the Executive Committee of the High Commissioner's Programme* (UN Doc. A/AC.96/821) of 12 October 1993, in which the EXCOM "supports the recognition as refugees of persons whose claim to refugee status is based upon a well-founded fear of persecution, through sexual violence, for reasons of race, religion, nationality, membership of a particular social group or political opinion" (15).
4. It has been reported, however, that in the two years since Canada adopted such specific guidelines, 195 gender-related claims have been accepted, accounting for about 2 percent of all Canadian asylum claims filed since the guidelines went into effect; see "INS Expands Asylum Protection for Women," *Washington Post,* 3 June 1995.
5. In this context, it must be stressed that the UNHCR note unfortunately does not spell out which human rights must be accorded and which standards of treatment applied to all people eligible for international protection and which may be reserved for people qualifying as refugees under the 1951/1967 system.

References

Arboleda, Eduardo, and Ian Hoy. 1993. "The Convention Refugee Definition in the West: Disharmony of Interpretation and Application." *International Journal of Refugee Law* 5: 66–90.

Castel, Jacqueline R. 1992. "Rape, Sexual Assault and the Meaning of Persecution." *International Journal of Refugee Law* 4:39–56.

Coles, Gervase J. L. 1992. "Changing Perspectives of Refugee Law and Policy." In *Problems and Prospects of Refugee Law,* ed. V. Gowlland and K. Samson, 31–45. Geneva: Graduate Institute of International Studies.

———. 1978/79. "Temporary Refuge and the Large Scale Influx of Refugees." *Australian Yearbook of International Law* 8: 189–212.

Cuéllar, Roberto, Diego García-Sayán, Jorge Montaño, Margarita Diegues, and Leo Valladores Lanza. 1991. "Refugee and Related Developments in Latin America: Challenges Ahead." *International Journal of Refugee Law* 3: 482–501.

Fullerton, Maryellen. 1993. "A Comparative Look at Refugee Status Based on Persecution Due to Membership in a Particular Social Group." *Cornell International Law Journal* 26: 505–63.

Goodwin-Gill, Guy S. 1986. "Non-Refoulement and the New Asylum Seekers." *Virginia Journal of International Law* 26: 897–918.

———. 1983. *The Refugee in International Law*. Oxford: Clarendon.

Grahl-Madsen, Atle. 1966. *The Status of Refugees in International Law*. Vol. 1. Leiden, The Netherlands: Sijthoff.

Hailbronner, Kay. 1993. "The Concept of 'Safe Country' and Expeditious Asylum Procedures: A Western European Perspective." *International Journal of Refugee Law* 5: 31–65.

———. 1992. "Perspectives of a Harmonization of the Law of Asylum after the Maastricht Summit." *Common Market Law Review* 29: 917–39.

———. 1986. "Non-Refoulement and 'Humanitarian' Refugees: Customary International Law or Wishful Legal Thinking?" *Virginia Journal of International Law* 26: 857–96.

Hathaway, James. 1992. "Reconceiving Refugee Law as Human Rights Protection." In *Problems and Prospects of Refugee Law,* ed. V. Gowlland and K. Samson, 9–30. Geneva: Graduate Institute of International Studies.

———. 1991. *The Law of Refugee Status*. Toronto: Butterworths.

Hofmann, Rainer. 1996. "Recent Jurisprudence of the Federal Constitutional Court on Asylum." In *The Living Law of Nations: Essays on Refugees, Minorities, Indigenous Peoples and the Human Rights of Other Vulnerable Groups. In Memory of Atle Grahl-Madsen,* ed. G. Alfredsson and P. MacAlister-Smith, 97–112. Kehl am Rhein: Engel.

_____. 1992. "Refugee Law in the African Context." *Zeitschrift für ausländisches öffentliches Recht und Völkerrecht* 52: 318–33.

_____. 1987. "Asylum and Refugee Law." In *The Legal Position of Aliens in National and International Law,* ed. J. A. Frowein and T. Stein, 2045–65. Berlin: Springer.

Hyndman, Patricia. 1991. "Developing International Refugee Law in the Asian-Pacific Region." *Asian Yearbook of International Law* 1: 19–44.

Immigration and Refugee Board. 1993. "Guidelines Issued by the Chairperson Pursuant to Section 65 (3) of the Immigration Act: Women Refugee Claimants Fearing Gender-Related Persecution." Ottawa: Immigration and Refugee Board, 9 Mar.

Kelly, Nancy. 1993. "Gender-Related Persecution: Assessing the Asylum Claims of Women." *Cornell International Law Journal* 26: 625–74.

Kjaerum, Morten. 1994. "Temporary Protection in Europe in the 1990s." *International Journal of Refugee Law* 6: 444–56.

Muntarbhorn, Vitit. 1992. *The Status of Refugees in Asia.* Oxford: Oxford University Press, Clarendon.

Oloka-Onyango, Joe. 1991. "Human Rights, the OAU Convention and the Refugee Crisis." *International Journal of Refugee Law* 3: 453–60.

U.S. Department of Justice, Immigration and Naturalization Service. 1995. "Considerations for Asylum Officers Adjudicating Asylum Claims from Women." Washington, D.C.: U.S. Government Printing Office. 26 May.

Zimmermann, Andreas. 1993. "Asylum Law in the Federal Republic of Germany in the Context of International Law." *Zeitschrift für ausländisches öffentliches Recht und Völkerrecht* 53: 49–87.

Chapter 8

Conclusion
Immigration Admissions and Immigration Controls

Kay Hailbronner, David A. Martin,* and

Hiroshi Motomura

Introduction

Germans and Americans approach the issues of admission and migration control from divergent conceptual structures and within sharply different institutional settings. The differences are deeply important and subtle. Even experts in the field in both countries can talk past one another unknowingly, because the same terms often carry dissimilar connotations.

Some of the difference arises from traditional distinctions between "insular"-type systems, more common in Anglo-American practice, and the "continental" systems developed in Western Europe (though by the 1990s there are many points of convergence). Since the U.S. immigration system took its modern shape in the 1920s, it has placed emphasis on clearly establishing the terms and conditions of admission from the moment a foreigner arrives in the territory, or even before. Visas have been required of the vast majority of aliens coming to the United States, and these make distinctions between immigrants, who come with permission to establish permanent residence, and nonimmigrants, who come for clearly defined purposes and temporary stays (tourism, study, temporary labor, etc.).

Germany, by contrast, has not considered itself a country of immigration, and so it has not traditionally made explicit provision for aliens who assume permanent resident status on arrival. Instead, Germany has provided for control less through visa issuance than through a system of residence and work permits. Many levels of residence permit have been available, and an individual might move to a more favored level after a specified number of years in the country, after a grant of asylum, after marriage with a citizen, or in other ways.

The German system thus lends itself to the notion that stronger rights accrue gradually with the passage of time, whereas the U.S. system tends to function in more categorical terms. These different outlooks sometimes leave U.S. observers puzzled, for example, as to why so many supposedly temporary guest workers were allowed to remain in Germany after the immigration stop in 1973, whereas most Germans find it natural that such persons could not be uprooted after many years of de facto residence, whatever may have been the initial expectations about their stay. In the United States, some aliens acquire permanent residence through various types of relief from deportation that recognize de facto residence (or "equities"). But as a general rule aliens move from nonimmigrant (or more tenuous) status to permanent residence only through a formal, deliberate governmental decision to shift a given individual from one category to another (referred to as "adjusting status").

Although the United States is now moving more systematically to add labor market controls to its immigration enforcement tool kit, it lacks many advantages enjoyed by German enforcement officials. Germany's labor market is highly centralized. Virtually all job postings and placements are handled through the government employment service, and enforcement of all types of labor market controls, including prohibitions against work by unauthorized aliens, is coordinated and integrated under the labor ministry. Persons not citizens of a member country of the European Union (EU) must have work permits, documents that are ordinarily distinct from their residence permits. In the United States, in contrast, the employment market is quite diffuse; only a fraction of hirings are accomplished through state employment service offices. Enforcement of federal labor-related laws is divided among the Department of Labor, the Immigration and Naturalization Service (INS), the Equal Employment Opportunity Commission, and a host of other agencies or bureaus. Over twenty different documents may be presented to an employer to show employment authorization, although the INS is working now to reduce the number. Germany also has a highly developed system of residence monitoring and registration. Everyone, citizen and alien alike, who takes up a new residence must register with the appropriate office, providing comprehensive information regarding family status, former residences, the date of moving, and the like. Even hotels collect data—though far less comprehensive—on overnight guests. Residence information can be shared, within limits established by law, among different law enforcement offices, and a Central Aliens Register compiles information on foreigners living in Germany. Lacking such methods of locating individuals, the United States is far more dependent, for successful deportation enforcement, on detention of aliens believed to be present illegally. Few aliens in the United States who are not detained are successfully deported, although this may change as the INS receives substantial new resources to improve the overall capabilities of the enforcement system.

Residents of Germany possess identification documents and must often produce them in connection with acquiring jobs, licensing, accessing public services, opening bank accounts, and the like, albeit under statutory and constitutional limits. The requirement for the identity card is not controversial, nor is it regarded as an infringement on civil liberties, whereas in the United States the notion of a national ID card is often denounced as a potential threat to freedom. But other practices regarded as routine in the United States are considered questionable or controversial in Germany, such as fingerprinting (which is closely tied, in the public mind, with criminal offenses) or the taking of a national census. Indeed, the fingerprinting of asylum seekers now provided for in the asylum procedure law has stirred a human rights debate in Germany that would seem peculiar to most Americans.

Equipped with the labor and residence monitoring systems described above, Germany does not have an "illegal alien" or "undocumented alien" problem of the magnitude known in the United States; it is not possible for large numbers of foreigners to live and work underground in Germany. Instead, such "black work" as occurs is largely performed by people admitted for short stays (especially from Eastern Europe), who may work outside the confines of the normal system, especially in construction or janitorial services. Germany's issue is not undocumented migration but irregular migration, especially of people who have misused the asylum system or who remain under various forms of tolerated status after the rejection of their asylum requests.

The closer monitoring of jobs and residence in Germany comes hand in hand with a system that assures far more systematic public assistance than is the case in the United States. This system covers all residents, even those with (as yet) only the most tenuous ties to the society. For example, asylum seekers in Germany are given room and board at assigned residences at public expense for the first six weeks of the procedure, being forbidden to work in the meantime. Each *Land* (state) and district in Germany must receive its fair share of asylum seekers, allocated and distributed according to an elaborate formula worked out in advance. In the United States, no central arrangements exist for the housing and feeding of asylum seekers. They may live where they like, and indeed, as prima facie illegal migrants (unless and until their claims are successful), they are denied access to most public assistance programs. Until recently they were expected to work to support themselves pending a decision and were generally granted work authorization promptly after lodging their claims. Because this system seemed to stimulate the filing of mala fide claims by undocumented migrants seeking valid work permits, however, 1994 regulatory amendments delayed such work authorization for at least 180 days (unless the asylum claim is granted sooner). The resulting gap in support is apparently workable only because of the rather ready availability of false documents that enable unauthorized employment. Indeed, it is common in the United States for aliens to be present for many months or even years before filing for asylum, having simply lived and worked in undocumented status during this initial period. In Germany, such an existence is virtually impossible; asylum seekers there typically file their claims at or shortly after entry with visas or falsified documents. Many, however, try to sneak past the border before lodging their claims, in order to avoid the less favorable procedures that may apply in Germany to airport and border claims.

One final difference deserves mention. In the United States, immigration is clearly regarded as a virtually exclusive function of the federal government, both in setting admission policy and enforcing the laws. State and local law enforcement officers may cooperate with the INS in enforcement, but in times of deep controversy over immigration policy, this relationship may become strained. In the 1980s disagreement with federal policy toward Central America led some localities to adopt formal policies of noncooperation, declaring themselves "sanctuary cities" or otherwise refusing to notify the INS of apparent violations of the immigration laws. In the 1990s opposite complications have arisen: some states or localities that seek a crackdown against illegal migration have chosen, out of frustration at the federal government's perceived enforcement failures, to adopt their own measures using the relatively few levers of control within their competence, notably public schooling and state-managed public services. This has led to what, to European eyes (and those of many Americans), appears to be a perverse and disproportionate set of measures. Proposition 187, the initiative adopted by California's voters in 1994, is the best known of these efforts. It would bar undocumented children from schools, close off non-emergency assistance to undocumented aliens, and require service providers to inquire into the immigration status of their clients, notifying the INS of anyone believed to be present illegally. (These measures have been blocked from implementation pending court decisions as to their constitutionality.)

Germany's federal system assigns authority over immigration and aliens matters quite differently. General substantive policy may be set at the federal level, but much of the actual street-level implementation and enforcement is carried out by the aliens authorities of the *Länder*. Many discretionary enforcement policies are also set by a conference involving the federal interior minister and the interior ministers of the *Länder*. The division of competencies in Germany also has another dimension unparalleled in the United States. Germany is a member of the European Union, a common market that has moved progressively toward free movement of labor within and among its member states. Recent efforts to develop a Europe free of internal frontiers have necessarily entailed measures to bolster and harmonize controls at the outer borders of the EU territory (leading some to charge, a bit hyperbolically, that the EU is becoming a "fortress Europe"). Besides the growing role of EU institutions in setting migration policy, Germany is also subject to the European Convention for the Protection of Human Rights and Fundamental Freedoms. The European Court of Human Rights, established by that treaty, may hear challenges to migration policies alleged to violate the treaty. For Germany, therefore, some important policies governing migration are set at the transnational level, some at the federal level, and some at the *Land* level.

Policy Recommendations

Comprehensive migration policy embraces at least these elements: prevention of unwanted migration, border and interior controls, admission and residence provisions, and integration. All these elements are important and are best designed in combination, but this working group left detailed discussion of the first and last to the other working groups, instead concentrating on admissions and controls, as well as refugee and asylum policy, which involves both control and admission questions.

Admission and Residence Provisions

Admission and sojourn policy remains largely within the discretion of potential receiving states, save for certain refugee and related humanitarian questions regulated by international law. For nearly all countries, admission for permanent residence is granted on one or more of the following bases: family reunification; occupational and educational grounds; and/or humanitarian reasons. Some countries also provide admission opportunities for groups showing other special connections, such as Germany's *Aussiedler* provisions for admitting ethnic Germans from other countries, today almost exclusively from the former Soviet Union. The United States is unlikely to develop anything comparable, unless perhaps the "diversity" admission program, enacted in 1990 and now admitting annually some 55,000 persons chosen by lottery, could be thus described. (In any case, the working group recommends the elimination of that program and reallocation of those admission spaces to other categories.)

While acknowledging the wide margin of discretion permitted to individual states, the working group agreed that certain basic principles should govern admission for the purpose of family reunification or on occupational and educational grounds (humanitarian admission and comparable permission to stay are treated separately below).

1. The highest priority should continue to be reunification for the closest family members, those most likely actually to live together or nearby if given the opportunity. Admission on this basis is not nepotism, as some critics have charged, but instead responds to basic and valid human needs and desires. This principle necessarily entails a major focus on uniting spouses and minor children, and it applies with equal force to citizens and resident aliens. Other parts of the admission system should be adjusted as necessary to honor this priority.
2. Family reunification provisions should truly serve to reunite families; provisions that carry long delays do not meet this criterion.
3. Occupational admission criteria should not treat individuals only as factors of production but should respect, first and foremost, their rights as fellow human beings. This means providing adequate safeguards governing their living conditions and compensation, freedom from undue dependence on a single employer (who may use that dependence to abuse or cheat the employee), protection of family unity, and other measures to assure respect for basic human dignity.

Some specific recommendations flow from these principles.

Family Reunification

Both Germany and the United States should reconsider their admission and residence provisions to assure better observance of the principle of family reunification. Germany, in cooperation with its EU partners, should consider reducing certain waiting periods and refining measures meant (quite properly) to guard against sham marriages, so as to reduce the impact on bona fide relationships. The United States should revamp its second-preference admissions (for spouses and minor children of lawful permanent resident aliens) to eliminate the lengthy delays, of four years and more, that now apply. This change is likely to require the reduction or elimination of other categories, because an increase in total U.S. immigration is unrealistic in the present political climate. In particular, admission spaces now devoted to diversity admissions should be diverted to family members, as should those for the fourth preference defined in the law (for brothers and sisters of U.S. citizens, a category now backlogged nearly ten years and thus also failing to meet the second principle defined above).

Occupational Admissions

Admissions here should probably focus on those with advanced skills and training or with highly specialized knowledge. Temporary or geographically limited labor shortages should be met not through immigration but through the usual workings of the labor market: bidding up wages to attract workers already resident in the country into the field or the region experiencing the shortage, altering industry practices (for example, through mechanization), or finding other ways to meet the need for the product or service. Immigration is also an unpromising path for satisfying the so-called demographic deficit: an insufficient pool of younger workers to support the increasing expenses of social security for a growing population of retirees. Immigrants brought in as workers in order to bolster the revenues would, of course, also age. The constant levels of high influx required to satisfy the demographic deficit on a continuing basis are wholly unrealistic.

Some in both Germany and the United States have proposed a major revival or expansion of temporary worker programs, constructed this time so as to reflect the supposed lessons taught by failures or problems in previous such programs. For example, because in the past much temporary migration became permanent, it is variously proposed to limit admission periods strictly; to escrow a portion of the wage, with this to be paid only after return to the home country (to assure rotation of workers); and to forbid the migration of family members with the principal worker. These proposals should not be adopted. Experience offers no indication that such admissions can truly be kept temporary without unacceptable intrusions on personal liberty.

More important, programs of the sort envisioned fail the third principle (except perhaps for certain high-level, high-salary employees who can afford to return frequently to their home countries). As the novelist Max Frisch commented on earlier temporary worker programs, "We asked for workers, but human beings came." If people are worth admitting for inclusion in the economic life of the receiving state, they are equally worthy of inclusion in that state's social and cultural life, subject, of course, to their own decisions to make the stay temporary. (Obviously, such individual decisions are far more likely in those limited circumstances where an alien's home country is nearing economic takeoff, leading to employment prospects that might naturally attract the return of workers after brief periods of earning enhanced wages abroad.) And clearly workers cannot be expected simply to suspend their needs for family contact for the duration of their temporary admission. These realities imply a strong presumption for permanent admission of any workers deemed necessary, along with their immediate families.

Quota Systems

The United States has long made express provision for admission of aliens for permanent residence. Over many decades it has evolved a system of preference categories and quotas in order to impose a certain order on the process, adding quantitative limits to the qualitative requirements elaborated in the immigration laws.

In Germany today, the call is often heard to adopt express provisions for permanent admissions, including the use of quotas. Some make the claim that providing express avenues for the migration of those who wish to participate in the labor market—occupational categories of admission—would reduce abuse of the asylum system by people who are in reality economic migrants. The U.S. experience indicates that this hope is illusory; the United States has seen its greatest growth in asylum claims during a period that coincided with a major increase in occupational admissions. No conceivable set of occupational admission categories could satisfy the potential demand, which is itself elastic. Quota systems should not be adopted in the expectation that they will obviate the need for hard choices regarding who should be granted asylum.

But Germany might consider adopting a quota-type system for other reasons, primarily in order to recognize and limit a process of permanent immigration that has long been a reality there. Germany already admits several hundred thousand people each year, in effect as aliens coming for permanent residence, primarily for purposes of family reunification and as *Aussiedler*. The *Aussiedler* fall into a kind of shadow-citizen category as ethnic Germans, but the process by which they enter is comparable to how other countries regulate permanent admission of aliens. Beginning in 1993 the *Aussiedler* program gave Germany its first real experience with the use of quotas as an immigration management tool. In 1990 nearly 400,000 ethnic Germans took advantage of these provisions, a peak that taxed the country's reception capacity and also coincided with a period of great concern about high admission of asylum seekers. In consequence, the *Aussiedler* provisions were amended to impose a ceiling (225,000), starting in 1993, on the number of ethnic Germans who could enter in a given year. The amendments also require advance screening and processing in German embassies or consulates. These changes are generally regarded as having brought welcome order and the assurance of reasonable control. These advantages could be generalized by applying similar methods to other categories of admission, setting ceilings where justified (as a tool for management and predictability), and requiring advance screening through consulates empowered to issue permanent resident visas. It is, however, difficult to define what other categories might be appropriate for consideration under a predetermined admission system. For immigration in Germany, already quite high due to family reunion, the admission of asylum seekers, and *Aussiedler*, it is widely acknowledged that setting quotas must not lead to an increase in immigration beyond its present level but rather to a reduction. This may result in more restrictive admission policy relating to certain categories of aliens who have previously been admitted either on permanent or temporary bases (asylum seekers, civil war refugees, admission for humanitarian purposes). Since temporary admission frequently ends up as permanent immigration, admission would have to be reduced, but this may well raise legal problems.

Controls

Both Germany and the United States have fallen short in providing adequate controls on unwanted migration. During some periods in the United States, an unacknowledged policy of benign neglect, which served many political interests, tolerated high levels of undocumented migration. In Germany, irregular migration received a kind of ratification because of long delays in the asylum system coupled with the general inability or unwillingness of enforcement officials to remove those denied asylum after such delays. Both countries are now responding with measures that should improve enforcement. Germany, for example, has adopted more comprehensive visa requirements backed up by carrier sanctions, while the United States has enacted sanctions on employers who knowingly hire unauthorized workers. And both countries have adopted comprehensive reforms in their political asylum systems. Nevertheless, in the long run, the earlier failures have helped foster backlash when increased migration pressures, economic difficulties, or other factors have tempted political leaders to pander to, or even promote, antiforeigner or anti-illegal-migrant sentiments. A well-functioning and credible control system is not necessarily the servant of xenophobia; it can be part of the antidote.

Controls focus on two main areas: border enforcement and interior enforcement. The latter consists of traditional interior enforcement, labor market controls, controls through the social services system, and residential controls or alien registration.

Border Enforcement

Given modern systems for entry control, which uniformly prescribe designated ports of entry, all people apprehended sneaking across the frontier are prima facie in violation of migration laws (though some may ultimately establish a right to protection as refugees). Moreover, most people apprehended at the border typically have neither established the ties that often complicate interior enforcement nor yet obtained the hoped-for gains that may have induced the migration in the first place. For all these reasons, border enforcement deserves a high priority in any strategy of control, especially where, as in the United States, the relatively undeveloped state of information systems and pre-

vailing notions of civil liberties make interior enforcement difficult. At the same time, enhanced border enforcement demands
increased measures to assure against abuse of the broad powers
vested in border patrol officers.

Improving border controls is largely a matter of resources,
and both Germany and the United States are providing additional funding for these purposes. More ambitious, but costly,
strategies of control—such as Operation Hold the Line in El
Paso, which stations Border Patrol officers within sight of each
other along the frontier to deter entry—also hold promise and
have proven to be much more efficient than chasing aliens after
entry. Technical advances in border lighting, sensing equipment,
and information systems also deserve determined pursuit.

Germany has shown some success in working out arrangements with neighboring states, particularly the Czech Republic
and Poland, for the cooperative policing of the borders. These
and similar efforts should be strengthened, and the United
States might also work for similar agreements (although the
political sensitivity of these questions along its southern border
are not to be minimized). The working group encourages the
development of wider multilateral border control regimes that
can ultimately provide for replacing controls at the borders
between cooperating states (as is envisaged in the Schengen
agreements and for the European Union) with reliance on har-
monized standards and procedures for external controls. The
working group is acutely aware of the risk that such systems
may tend to harmonize at the least common denominator,
spreading the most restrictive or least humanitarian practices
among all cooperating states. But this outcome is not inevitable,
and such predictions are not a reason to reject the entire effort
to create cooperative regimes of this sort. All involved—governmental, nongovernmental, and intergovernmental players
alike—must be careful to use the opportunity presented by such
developing regimes to assure the wider adoption of the best
practices. NAFTA states should begin cautiously to move toward
such cooperation as well, recognizing the substantial obstacles
to achieving anything like what is being attempted in Europe
(although Canada and the United States could probably pioneer
certain modest arrangements along these lines). Full implementation, if it ever comes, will doubtless require first a dramatic

reduction in economic disparities. But this, too, was the European Community's experience, where progressive elimination of trade barriers starting in the 1950s reduced economic disparities to the point that very ambitious provisions for free movement became politically thinkable.

Interior Enforcement

No matter how successful a nation may be at improving border enforcement, both clandestine entries and visa overstays will persist. (Indeed, in the United States, visa abusers account for an estimated 50 percent of out-of-status aliens.) Credible interior enforcement is therefore indispensable. Weaknesses in this area, particularly the glaring inability of German and U.S. systems to deport many people whose illegal or irregular presence is conceded (and who do not qualify for asylum or related protections), have fed both cynicism and backlash, demoralized the agencies and officials assigned to these functions, and doubtless attracted additional illegal migrants. Recent attempts in Germany to overcome this situation by a considerably stronger enforcement policy have met with sharp criticism by churches and other organizations.

Traditional Enforcement

Traditional enforcement involves detection and apprehension, possible detention, adjudication of deportability and any defenses (including refugee claims), and actual removal. Improvements here are largely dependent on increased resources, especially in the U.S. context, and greater detention capacity, which would also enable a more effective use of bonds to guarantee appearance for both proceedings and ultimate departure if deportation is ordered.

It is also important, in both countries, that all levels of government work together to enforce the immigration laws adopted at the national level. In the United States, as noted, some local or state authorities, usually owing to disagreement with national policies on aliens, have selectively refused such cooperation or tried to supplement national enforcement with haphazardly draconian local enforcement. Such disagreements over national policy should, of course, find full expression and be debated in appropriate arenas, but this kind of local action against national policy can be especially debilitating for a credible and integrated enforcement strategy. If policy is unwise or unjust, it should be amended directly, not undermined in piecemeal fashion. (At the same time, local officials should not be asked to engage in enforcement for which they are inadequately trained or funded.)

Other steps would also improve the credibility of interior enforcement. Particularly in the United States, the substantive and procedural provisions for relief from deportation should be reexamined, simplified, and rationalized. For example, people should still be able to cite special hardships as reasons for overcoming formal deportability, but this should be possible without either overly technical restrictions or overly elaborate and cumbersome procedures. More generally, the incredible complexity of the provisions governing the status of aliens should be reduced.

Both administrative and judicial review systems should be comprehensively reconsidered. Dual objectives for a review system, inevitably in tension, must be balanced, to assure a reasonable check against error or abuse by the primary decision makers but at the same time to reach conclusions efficiently and without undue delay. Expeditious conclusion of proceedings and appeals is especially important in this realm of administrative practice. Delay increases uncertainty for the alien and potentially raises detention costs for the government or, in nondetained cases, may unfairly extend employment and residence for the alien. Delay may also permit the alien to develop greater "equities"—ties with the host society—that may require further reconsideration of the case.

Those initiating deportation proceedings in the United States should pay greater heed to prioritizing the use of scarce adjudication resources. Aliens with serious criminal convictions or criminal involvement should receive top priority, of course, and efficiencies such as those achieved by the U.S. Institutional Hearing Program—completing deportation proceedings while individuals are still incarcerated on criminal charges—are to be encouraged. But the interior control system, to be credible, cannot focus only on criminal alien cases. Among noncriminal aliens, prosecutorial discretion should be used to initiate proceedings only against those aliens the agency really intends (and reasonably expects) to remove. This may mean placing priority on more recent arrivals, individuals without families, and similar more easily removable cases, rather than indiscriminately processing whoever is first detected in ostensibly illegal status. Mechanisms to foster voluntary cooperation from aliens in enforcement proceedings, such as improved bonding arrangements or more effective procedures to penalize those who abscond after the issuance of a deportation order, should be applied wherever possible. Finally, the entire adjudication system—not just the aliens involved—would benefit from enhanced legal representation for deportation respondents early in the process. In the United States, direct provision of appointed counsel is probably unrealistic, but experiments with various alternative mechanisms for enhanced pro bono representation should be encouraged.

Once a deportation order has been entered, noncooperation by individuals (such as concealing or destroying passports) has often combined with resistance or delays from their home-state governments to defeat actual removal. These problems are shared by all industrialized democracies, and those countries should act more fully on this common interest. Germany has pioneered in negotiating bilateral return agreements with major source states in order to minimize formalities and speed returns. The United States should seek to emulate this model. But major opportunities for wider-scale multilateral cooperation exist here, particularly with regard to especially resistant home countries that have not been willing to execute bilateral return agreements. All major receiving states should cooperate (not solely within regional groupings) to find better carrots and sticks that might pressure resistant home states to accept return of their nationals. Possible strategies could include coordinated moves to alter aid packages or restrict legal migration from such states.

Labor Market Controls and Information Systems

Traditional interior enforcement is cumbersome and expensive. Controls applied in the labor market hold promise for greater efficiency, because in principle they can reduce the very attraction that draws most undocumented migration. Employment restrictions are more easily imposed in a tightly regulated and centralized labor market like Germany's than in the diffuse and largely private U.S. labor market. Changing U.S. employment practices to the German model is not practicable, but improvements in the employer sanctions scheme adopted in 1986 can profitably draw on German experience in other respects. For example, the current U.S. system has been hampered greatly by the availability of fraudulent documents. Development of a single, counterfeit-resistant employment identifier would ameliorate that problem, but, as noted in the introduction to this section, movement in that direction has often been stymied by civil-liberties concerns about a national identity card. Germany's practice, however, suggests that these fears are exaggerated. A unified system for employment identifiers, if carefully designed, can provide fully adequate protection for human rights. In fact, a unified and comprehensive system of that sort, requiring the same employment identifier for both aliens and citizens, might better protect against discrimination than less systematic approaches do. Further progress toward an improved employment identification system for the United States should be resolutely pursued.

In a related area, the working group encourages efforts to standardize U.S. systems for the issuance of birth certificates (traditionally, a local government function), in order to avoid misuse of counterfeit or fraudulently obtained certificates as "breeder documents" for obtaining other improper documentation. These efforts can draw inspiration from the model of German framework statutes and other provisions of German law that provide similar standardization of registration procedures handled by local and state authorities within Germany.

In connection with improved information systems, either for use with employer sanctions or more generally in traditional enforcement (in either country), ongoing vigilance is necessary to assure that human rights and constitutional requirements and, more broadly, the freedom of informational self-determination are honored. The laws establishing these systems should define clearly what kind of information may be gathered, where and by whom it is to be collected, which public authorities are to have access to the information and under what conditions, the purposes for which the information may be used, and the conditions under which data are to be expunged from the files. To prevent abuse and harm from incorrect data, the law should guarantee that the people concerned can have access to the information collected on them (subject to strictly drawn exceptions for national security or law enforcement purposes) and that false or outdated information is speedily erased or replaced with correct information.

Controls through Social Service Systems

The working group strongly recommends that enforcement strategies focus on restricting employment opportunities—the major factor attracting illegal migration in the United States— rather than denying medical care or elementary and secondary education, as was done in California's Proposition 187, adopted in 1994. The control strategies contained in that measure are both off target and inhumane, at least in the context of a system whose other controls on illegal migration are so weak. In the United States, state-level enforcement using the social service system may undermine relationships of trust that are essential to accomplishing the purposes of the service programs or educational programs themselves. Moreover, they carry potential long-term risks to public health and to the sound development of children who may yet wind up as long-term residents.

Residence Controls and Registration

Germany has fewer problems than the United States does in locating out-of-status aliens because of its comprehensive requirements for reporting residences (imposed on all individuals, citizens and aliens alike) and its Central Aliens Register. A similar residence reporting system would not work in the United States, given its different constitutional and governmental traditions, but lessons might be learned for possible improvement in the far more limited alien registration system the United States employs.

Refugee Claims and Political Asylum

Any measures that indiscriminately restrict access to the primary system for determining refugee claims or political asylum are undesirable in principle, because they would affect both bona fide and abusive potential claimants. Nevertheless, as a practical matter, some restrictions may be necessary. States considering such measures, however, should choose carefully from among the available models, because some carry far more potential for harming genuinely endangered individuals than do others.

Most common and perhaps least objectionable are visa regimes, policed through a system of sanctions on carriers who bring to the country individuals lacking proper visas or visa substitutes. Visa regimes at least allow for a measure of self-help by threatened individuals because they do not foreclose other ways of reaching the borders and escaping the country of persecution. Carrier sanctions are a necessary element in the effective enforcement of visa regulations at airports, and they are also essential tools for inducing carriers to comply with their obligations under the Chicago Convention not to transport passengers without the requisite travel documents. Part of U.S. practice since the 1920s, carrier sanctions were made obligatory in the Schengen Implementation Agreement of 1990 as well as the Draft EU Convention on external border control.

Most objectionable and problematic are across-the-board interdiction arrangements that intercept all who flee, returning them to their countries of origin without first inquiring into possible refugee claims (as was practiced by the United States off the shores of Haiti from May 1992 to May 1994). For such a scheme ever to be acceptable, it would at least have to assure a fully functioning in-country refugee system whereby consular officials of potential haven states would receive and consider refugee claims within the country of origin. Such a system would also have to include firm safeguards to guarantee that people found to be at risk could leave in safety.

Between visa regimes and the strongest forms of interdiction lie various other access-restriction methods that still incorporate some form of genuine consideration of refugee claims. These include shipboard screening outside the country of origin, but before arrival in the territory of the haven state, and expedited adjudication procedures at the border or in airports. If used, they should be carefully crafted to assure that bona fide claims may be fully aired. In their best form, they provide only preliminary screenings and do not attempt to reach full final judgments. Those claimants whose applications pass a certain threshold (variously described as showing that the applicant has a "credible fear" or that the claim is not "manifestly unfounded") should have access to the normal procedure for full development of their asylum claims.

It is desirable to harmonize asylum regulations between and among receiving countries that are closely linked economically and politically. Under the Maastricht Treaty member states determine whose nationals require visas to enter the territory of the European Union. Clearly, the community needs to set common visa requirements. With the introduction of common visas, alien and police authorities should be given the right to enforce common rules and administrative decisions originating in other member states of the community. The rules relating to the entry and residence of third-country nationals, including rules with respect to asylum claims, should be drawn up with the full participation of democratically elected representatives of member states as well as of the European Parliament.

It is vitally important to develop and sustain effective asylum adjudication systems that deter unfounded recourse to asylum claims. Only if government officials feel some confidence in this capacity of the regular adjudication system will they be willing to reduce reliance on policies restricting or interdicting access to the national territory.

Temporary Protection

Persons fleeing from conditions of violence and civil war may, for a limited time, need shelter during the period of disorder and danger. Temporary protection may be used as a more flexible instrument to accommodate the needs of certain groups of refugees who do not meet the specific requirements of the Geneva Convention. The inherent risk of the concept of temporary protection, however, is that "temporary" may easily become permanent. Temporary protection should not be used to remedy political and economic crises by resettling large refugee groups in the more industrialized regions of the world. Effective measures have to be taken to prevent temporary protection from becoming yct another instrument for permanent immigration.

In order to sustain political support for temporary protection decisions, protection must remain demonstrably temporary whenever possible. When the emergency that initially led to the call for protection has ceased, return proceedings may be in order. They should not preclude the opportunity for individuals to claim asylum or refugee status, but if conditions have genuinely improved, any such claims may well be appropriate for expedited consideration under "safe country of origin" clauses. That is, claimants may have to overcome a rebuttable presumption that return is generally safe for all, and those who do not overcome the presumption may be treated as manifestly unfounded claimants, with the attendant restrictions on administrative and/or judicial appeal rights.

Temporary protection is not necessarily to be provided in the major target states for asylum. Alternatively, protection can be provided in internationally monitored safe zones and internationally administered refugee settlements in neighboring states. Despite the problems with UN-guaranteed safe zones in former Yugoslavia, new forms of international protection on a temporary basis have to be considered. A new concept of temporary protection can be realized in the long run only within a larger framework of international administrative arrangements including return agreements and burden-sharing treaties.

First Host Country and Safe Third Countries

Under the Dublin Convention, EU member states are obligated to take exclusive responsibility for those who first seek asylum within their borders. This concept of first host country is a reasonable instrument to prevent uncontrolled immigration, successive and multiple asylum applications, and the abuse of asylum procedures by claimants in search of better economic conditions. Member states may moreover reject asylum seekers at their borders or within their own territories, provided that the asylum seekers have traveled through a safe third country that offers a fair opportunity to file an asylum claim. It is acceptable to deny protection to those who have found protection elsewhere or who can be sent to a country that is willing to provide protection against persecution. Neither the 1951 Convention Relating to the Status of Refugees nor public international law specifies that refugees have the right to choose their countries of residence.

In order to establish whether a nation can be considered a safe third country, certain fundamental requirements must be fulfilled: it must be established that the life or freedom of the asylum applicant is not threatened, that the asylum applicant is not exposed to torture or inhumane or degrading treatment, and that adequate procedures are in place to review the asylum claim. Moreover, the host third country must offer the asylum applicant effective protection against refoulement. It is important that Germany and the United States adhere to these requirements before rejecting asylum seekers and returning them to host third countries. It is also appropriate that both countries actively work to improve asylum review procedures in host third countries.

Safe Countries of Origin

Recently, Germany and several other European countries have declared that some countries should be declared "safe," that is, there exists a presumption that individuals from such countries are not at risk of persecution. A fast-track procedure for asylum seekers originating from such countries can be a useful instrument to accelerate proceedings and discourage individuals who are not in need of protection from seeking asylum. However, individuals from so-called safe countries should not automatically be denied the right to seek asylum; the classification is merely intended to channel cases into accelerated procedures. EU member states have therefore declared that they will consider individual claims of all applicants from such countries and any specific evidence presented by applicants that might outweigh the general presumption.

The reasonableness of a safe country of origin classification depends essentially on the standards used to determine whether a country should be classified as safe. The following criteria should be used as elements in the assessment: the observance of human rights in law and in practice, the existence of democratic institutions and in particular the availability and effectiveness of legal means of protection and redress, the stability of the political system, and, judged in light of these criteria, previous numbers of refugees and recognition rates in the country in question.

Return Agreements and International Mechanisms for Repatriation

The effective implementation of asylum claims depends in large measure on the willingness of the country of origin to accept without punishment individuals whose claims have been rejected and to permit individuals to return when the reasons for granting protection have ceased to exist. Too often states have prevented repatriation by imposing unduly high requirements for establishing nationality and possessing valid travel documents. Governments have sometimes made return dependent on financial assistance or have failed to provide travel documents, practices that are in violation of customary public international law relating to a state's duty to permit the return of its nationals.

Both bilateral and multilateral agreements regulating return and repatriation are needed. A promising step in this direction may be the intergovernmental agreement between Germany and Turkey on the treatment of rejected Turkish asylum seekers on their return to Turkey. A link between economic development assistance and return and repatriation may also be appropriate.

Exclusively domestic answers to the asylum issue are doomed to failure. The management of asylum requires coordinated international action ranging from international monitoring for return and repatriation, through coordinated international human rights initiatives against refugee-producing countries, and all the way to international peacekeeping and peace enforcement.

---

*Professor Martin left the project in August 1995, when he took leave from the University of Virginia to become general counsel of the U.S. Immigration and Naturalization Service (INS). He was therefore not involved in the final editing and shaping of this volume or the policy recommendations it contains. In any case, the views expressed herein do not necessarily reflect the views of the INS, the Department of Justice, or the U.S. government.

Notes on Contributors

Joseph H. Carens is professor of political science at the University of Toronto. Author of *Equality, Moral Incentives and the Markets* and numerous articles on political theory and editor of *Democracy and Possessive Individuation* and *Is Quebec Nationalism Just?* he is currently writing a book on the ethics of immigration.

Joan Fitzpatrick is professor of law and foundation scholar at the University of Washington School of Law. She received a B.A. from Rice University, a J.D. from Harvard Law School, and a Diploma in Law from Oxford University. She is author of *Human Rights in Crisis: The International System for Protecting Rights during States of Emergency* (1994) and numerous articles concerning refugee and asylum law, international human rights, and the death penalty. She is chair of the Standing Committee on Mandate of Amnesty International.

Kay Hailbronner is professor of international law, European law, and constitutional law at the University of Konstanz and director of the Research Center of European and International Law of Immigration and Asylum at that institution. He is the author of numerous books and articles on immigration and asylum matters, among them *Current Asylum in Germany* (University of California, Berkeley, 1995).

Rainer Hofmann, formerly a senior research fellow at the Max Planck Institute for Comparative Public Law and International Law, in Heidelberg, is now professor of German Public Law and International at the University of Cologne. He is the author of numerous publications in the field of German and comparative constitutional law, international human rights, and refugee and minority rights law.

David A. Martin is Henry L. & Grace Doherty Professor of Law at the University of Virginia. From 1978 to 1980 he served in the Human Rights Bureau of the U.S. Department of State, and in August 1995 he took leave from the university to become general counsel of the Immigration and Naturalization Service (INS). Work on his chapter in this volume was virtually complete before he assumed that office, and he was not involved in the final shaping of the project's policy recommendations or the conclusions printed in this volume. In any case, the opinions expressed therein do not necessarily represent the views of the INS, the Department of Justice, or the U.S. government.

Jörg Monar is a professor of politics and director of the Centre for European Politics and Institutions at the University of Leicester (U.K.), where he specializes in the institutional development of the European Union, EU cooperation in the areas of justice and home affairs, EU external economic relations, and the EU's common foreign and security policy. His recent publications include "The Maastricht Treat on European Union, Legal Complexity and Political Dynamic" (with W. Ungerer and W. Wessels; Brussels, 1993), "The Third Pillar of the European Union" (with R. Morgan; Brussels, 1994); "Justice and Home Affairs inthe European Union (with R. Bieber; Brussels, 1995); annuals reviews of EU external economic relations in the *Jahrbuch der Europäischen Integration* (since 1993); and articles in the *Common Market Law Review, European Brief,* and *Integration.*

Hiroshi Motomura has been a professor of law at the University of Colorado School of Law in Boulder since 1982. Before that, he was an attorney in Washington, D.C., with a practice that included immigration law matters. He writes and lectures extensively on immigration law and policy topics, with an emphasis on constitutional issues. Publications include the law school casebook *Immigration: Policy and Process* (with T. Alexander Aleinikoff and David A. Martin; 3d ed. 1995) and the articles "The Curious Evolution of Immigration Law: Procedural Surrogates for Substantive Constitutional Rights" (*Columbia Law Review* 1992) and "Immigration Law after a Century of Plenary Power: Phantom Constitutional Norms and Statutory Interpretation" (*The Yale Law Journal* 1990).

Olaf F. Reermann began working at the Germany's Federal Ministry of the Interior in 1965. Since 1992, he has been the director general of the department dealing with legislation pertaining to foreigners, asylum, and migration since 1992. His writings on matters relating to asylum law and migration have appeared in a variety of regional law journals.

Rosemarie Rogers is professor of international politics at The Fletcher School of Law and Diplomacy at Tufts University. Her current research focuses on issues in international refugee policy, on the integration of foreign populations in West European countries, and on patterns and policies of return imigration of labor migrants and asylum seekers from Western Europe. In 1988 she initiated at the Fletcher School a program devoted to the critical analysis of major issues in global and U.S. refugee policy in the 1990s. Professor Rogers's most recent publications include (with Emily Copeland) *Forced Migration: Policy Issues in the Post-Cold War World* (Medford, Mass., 1993); "Les Migrations forcées aujourd'hui" (*Agenda Culturel* 1995); "Asylum," in *Encyclopedia Americana* (Danbury, Conn., 1996); and the forthcoming coedited volume *Toward a New Global Refugee System*.

Index

in Germany, 152, 154–56,
160–62
in Middle East, 150–51
in Netherlands, 157–58,
159
in South Africa, 150
in Sweden, 158
in Switzerland, 151, 152,
158
in Western Europe, 151–52
incentive programs for,
148–49, 162–65, 190

Uberseidler, 75n 3
United Nations Convention
against Illicit Traffic in
Narcotic Drugs and
Psychotropic Substances, 210
United Nations Convention
against Torture and Other
Cruel, Inhuman and
Degrading Treatment or
Punishment, 210
United Nations Development
Program (UNDP), 170, 171
United Nations Disaster Relief
Coordinator (UNDRO), 151
United Nations High Comissioner
for Refugees (UNHCR),
167–68, 169, 170, 171, 174,
177–78, 181–82, 191, 206, 217,
218
Note on International
Protection, 245–46, 249,
250, 252n 5
United Nations Security Council,
218, 228
United States
as country of immigration, vii,
58, 255
border controls in, vii
citizenship laws in, 83, 112
immigration control in, vii,
255
immigration policy in, 71–72
"diversity" admissions, 72,
104, 105, 262
family-based admissions,
80–81, 84–85, 88, 89–90,

91–92, 94–96, 96, 97–99,
99–101, 104–106,
107–109, 110, 261–62
quota systems, 57, 72, 109,
110, 263
*United States ex rel. Kanuff v.
Shaughnessy,* 101, 114n 10
Universal Declaration of Human
Rights (1948), 87, 215, 216

Vance Agreement, 249
Vienna conference (Council of
Europe, 1991), 124, 130
Vietnam, 166, 176–77, 178–83,
192
Vlaams Block, 63–64
Voluntary Return and
Reinsertion Programme for
Chilean Refugees, 195n 14

Working Group on Immigration,
London, 123, 124
World Bank, 171
World Vision, 180

Yepes-Prado v. INS, 114n 10
Yugoslavia, former, 172–73, 194n
8, 195n 11, 214, 218, 228, 249